Role P

Role Play

Theory and Practice

Krysia M. Yardley-Matwiejczuk

SAGE Publications
London • Thousand Oaks • New Delhi

SAGE Publications Ltd
6 Bonhill Street
London EC2A 4PU

SAGE Publications Inc.
2455 Teller Road
Thousand Oaks, California 91320

SAGE Publications India Pvt Ltd
32, M-Block Market
Greater Kailash – I
New Delhi 110 048

British Library Cataloguing in Publication data

A catalogue record for this book is available from the British Library

ISBN 0 8039 8450-2
ISBN 0 8039 8451-0 (pbk)

Library of Congress catalog card number 97-065037

Typeset by Mayhew Typesetting, Rhayader, Powys
Printed in Great Britain by The Cromwell Press Ltd,
Broughton Gifford, Melksham, Wiltshire

To my daughters Andréa and Keira, with love.
To all our futures, individuated and shared.

Contents

Acknowledgements

To my colleagues in the Department of Clinical Psychology in the Merthyr and Cynon Valleys (North Glamorgan NHS Trust), especially Ruth Bagshaw, Juan Delport and Mike Oldridge for stimulating conversations, support, and kindness; and in particular to my personal secretary Sharon Richards for sharing the load so willingly and well (not forgetting Karen Yates and Kath Toy). Thanks are due also to the North Glamorgan NHS Trust for supporting my work. To Jeremy Hazell, psychoanalytic psychotherapist for providing a good space in which to professionally and personally 'grow'. To the Lashbrookes, Lynne, David, Kirsty, Ben, Barnaby and Sam, for being there during the good times and not so good times and to T.H. for the value of past times. Last, but not least, acknowledgement and heartfelt thanks to my parents Babs (née Merchant) and Marian Yardley (Matwiejczyk). Sto Lat!

1

Introduction

Role play as a term describes a range of activities characterized by involving participants in 'as-if' or 'simulated' actions and circumstances. For example, someone may be asked to 'imagine' being in a dentist's waiting room anxiously awaiting a painful procedure, or to be a victim following a mugging. Role plays may range from very minimalist settings of short duration, to highly complex extended situations such as the Grindstone experiment, where a whole island was taken over and participants role played the aftermath of a nuclear disaster for several weeks (Olsen and Christiansen, 1966). In brief, role play or simulation techniques are a way of deliberately constructing an approximation of aspects of a 'real life' episode or experience, but under 'controlled' conditions where much of the episode is initiated and/or defined by the experimenter or therapist.

Role plays have been widely used within research and applied psychology. In social psychology research the use of role play was particularly popular in the 1960s and early 1970s in the highly focused areas of group dynamics, attitude change studies and risky shift experiments (see Alexander and Scriven, 1977), but also in larger attempts to simulate social institutions such as prisons (Haney et al., 1973). However, partly because of an unresolved debate centring on validity issues, the use of role play in experiments and empirical research has declined within social psychology since the 1970s. Somewhat distinct from the above has been the extensive use of clinical role play in therapies, particularly within the social skills/assertion therapy areas, and also within psychodramatic activities, where there has been continued steady, indeed increased, use of role play (within the period 1982–92 there were at least four hundred articles published involving role play). None the less, both arenas produce rather few and sparse technical guidelines. This probably accounts for the lack of development of these techniques within research, despite the demand for radical alternative methodologies in research. It also accounts for the under-exploitation of role play techniques in current therapies. Parallel use has been made of role play within training settings, for example with clinicians, doctors, social workers and managers. Here again the full potential of role play techniques is almost never realized, and descriptions of them are skimpy and, generally, uninformative.

However, role play, used well, offers considerable potential, largely because of its flexibility with respect to range and depth of focus. Role play may involve one 'actor' or many, may involve overt activity on the part of subjects or covert imaginative activity on the part of subjects, it may involve a 'snapshot' of reality or a longitudinal experience of an 'as-if' event. Instigators can focus on overt behaviour via observation of a role play event, or they can focus on attitudes, experience or emotions by gathering accounts and recordings in relation to the role play events. Whatever the focus, role play allows, above all, the infinite manipulation of time and space, restricted only by pragmatic considerations. If the instigator wants to place a party of neo-Nazis on the moon he or she can do so. What is more he or she can construct the moon exactly as he or she pleases. Such is this flexibility that the instigator can move participants from the moon to shopping at Safeway's within moments. Anything can be asked of participants in terms of characterization – although this does not mean that anything can be delivered, as we shall later consider.

Beyond such obvious advantages, for example, as not having really to 'beat up a victim' for the purposes of training a police officer to deal with a victim who has been mugged, in using role play one can replay action, stop and start it at any juncture, and gather accounts at any point in a sequence. One can also change either incidental or highly significant details, and replay a role play event to explore the impact of such changes. Indeed role play is only limited by pragmatic and methodological considerations.

Research and therapy are often beset with the difficulties of having to generalize from over-constrained or over-controlled fields of observation. (In formal research this tends to be in the form of relying upon the experiment; in therapy and training techniques this reliance tends to be upon discursive, reflective interaction between therapist and client.) Equally, at the other end of the research spectrum, field studies or participant observation events are multi-layered and move with such speed that much is lost to observation, and certainly it is not possible to gather concurrent accounts. The latter have to be collected *post hoc*, and, depending on the nature of the action being observed, the time lag between 'action' and the collection of accounts can be quite long and is indeed customarily too long for subjects or clients to recall accurately or in much detail. Role plays lie somewhere between the polarities of field observation and conventional controlled laboratory experiment. It cannot and will not be claimed here that role plays reproduce 'total reality', but they do provide us with possibilities for considerable external and internal 'manipulation and control'. Role plays also potentially provide us with the engaged awareness of subjects-in-action, who have the opportunity for an 'experience' *and* for accounting. As we shall also see later, there are opportunities for various levels of subject/client versus experimenter/therapist control, which provide an entrée in relation to a choice of any methodological and epistemological stance.

Children explore their worlds with play, they posit 'as-if' conditions: they exercise and practise powers and aspects of their identities, in both bizarre and banal make-believe settings. They 'research' each other's reactions, powers, knowledge and identities when joining in make-believe play with other children. Researchers, therapists and educators are in a similar position but most frequently use little freedom with respect to the selection of tools and media of exploration. Some time ago Illich, in *Tools for Conviviality* (1973), pleaded for researchers to become anarchic in their use of language and research tools, to open up the sterile epistemological grounding that characterized most research methodology. This plea has been little heard and even less acted upon. Role play could facilitate a less hampered approach, indeed could provide fun and real interest in a research or therapy collaboration with subjects and clients – experiences unimaginable within conventional paradigms.

Most of us involved in working with people within a psychological framework, whether in clinical, educational or organizational practice or research, will probably have engaged in some form of role play activity. This experience, for some, will have proved desultory and uninspiring, even aversive, leading to a firm intention not to participate again. For others, the experience will have proved facilitatory and highly rewarding, even inspiring. Many will have a foot in both camps, having attended – and even conducted – the most appalling and unsustainable role plays but also having participated in, and conducted, stimulating and valid ones. What makes the difference? Is role play an art, a science or a serendipitous happening? Are there 'rules of engagement' or only good 'actors'? Can anyone set up a good role play? Can one do anything in a role play and for any purpose? Here, we try and explore these questions via a systematic description and definition of role play technique. This is grounded in a conceptual approach based on an humanistic/phenomenological position, but does not exclude its use within a positivistic framework. Furthermore, it gives rise to precise induction procedures, which have been tested against objective and subjective criteria. Earlier conceptual descriptions of role play will be considered, as well as the use of existing role play technique within research, clinical and training practice. Above all, we will concentrate upon precise technical issues, drawing not only on theory but also on case studies, empirical studies, the experiential accounts of role play participants, and extensive personal experience.

Anyone reading this book, whether clinician, researcher or educator, should acquire a clear strategy for inducting ecologically valid role plays. They also should have a comprehensive idea of the questions that a role play inductor should ask him or herself, and an understanding of the technical and methodological issues which must be considered before even embarking on a role play. This book, however, does not pretend to a 'cookbook' approach. It is hoped that the reader who wishes to consider, or reconsider, using role play techniques will be facilitated to make a new, and more thorough and searching examination of any act or decision made. This book is also for those who will never use role play but who may hopefully approach a psychological task with more questions than answers.

Before proceeding with a particular and exclusive focus upon role play it is important to lay out the epistemological basis from which the author is working. Broadly, the book first takes a critical view of the major traditions within psychology which have tended to dehumanize or undervalue individual experience, and, second, is sympathetic to a range of radical and innovative perspectives that are trying to relocate the subject at the centre of the research and theory. These views are considered in greater detail in Chapter 2.

2

An Epistemological Context
for the Use of Role Play

Researchers and applied practitioners alike are faced with a common quest: how to approach the attempt to understand human action and experience. No longer is there complete confidence in the procedures, methods and theoretical systems that appeared to be the bedrock of the disciplines of psychology. Psychology research and applied practice, especially within social and clinical psychology, have been bedevilled since the 1970s with growing concerns over epistemological values (for example, Woolgar, 1988; Elliott, 1983a; Goldfried and Padawar, 1982; Omer and London, 1988; Denzin and Lincoln, 1994; Nicholson, 1991; Edwards and Potter, 1992; and Smith J.A. 1995). That is to say, researchers and practitioners are increasingly concerned with understanding the ways in which we derive knowledge, and the extent to which the status of the knowledge gathered must be moderated by the inevitable limitations of our methods of gaining it. Thus, we are currently much more aware that the kind of knowledge we seek is, to a great extent, dependent upon the kind of generative models and theories of knowledge to which we subscribe (which commonly consist of unarticulated a priori assumptions on the part of researchers and practitioners, rather than formal expositions). So in carrying out psychological enquiry, whether in the course of 'pure' research or applied practice such as therapy, we have expected, and unfortunately still generally expect, as a matter of faith, that certain procedures of gathering information or of generating events will provide us with knowledge about, for example, mechanisms, structures, social cognitions and representations, social constructions or important dynamics. These assumptions must be scrutinized, and we are still very slow to do this. A major tenet of this book will be that such scutiny is intrinsic to good role play practice and that indeed role play, as technique in itself, can offer tools with which to facilitate such reflexive scrutiny.

These more reflexive concerns we see currently emerging over epistemological values are grounded in earlier major criticisms that have substantially shifted significant parts of the research culture. These criticisms first voiced powerfully and most influentially in the 1970s, with the onslaught of criticisms by social psychologists such as Sherif, 1977; Bowers, 1973; Levine, 1974; Harré and Secord, 1972; Thines, 1977; Gergen, 1978; McGuire, 1973; Menzel, 1978; Bakan, 1967; Feyeraband, 1975; Rychlak, 1977; Thorngate, 1976 (and also by clinicians, particularly within the domain of humanistically oriented psychotherapy research and practice, such as Romanyshyn, 1987; Mair, 1970; Elliott, 1983a; and Horowitz, 1982).

With respect to psychology research in general, as early as 1959 Orne (and subsequently Rosenthal and Rosnow, 1969) alerted us to demand characteristics within experiments: that subjects guessed the intentions of experimenters and, wishing to be helpful, provided the wished for behaviours (to the extent that only where subjects could verbalize hypotheses were experimental results in accordance with prediction). Later Bowers (1973) criticized experimenters as situationist and as entirely neglecting subject variables; similarly Levine (1974) commented that subjects were treated inappropriately as interchangeable units (see also Kiesler's 1981 uniformity myth concerning patients as subjects in psychotherapy studies, where he argued that, even in such research, patients are fallaciously treated as no more than interchangeable units). Moreover, Bowers pointed out in 1973 that, within research in social psychology, there was (and arguably still is) among experimenters an almost total ignorance of the population of environments from which treatments are sampled. Rychlak (1977) and Gergen (1978) argued that experimenters had concentrated on constructing such powerful variables that individual differences would necessarily be overcome, leading to a contrivance of experimental situation, entirely demonstrative rather than truly investigative, with little relevance to the mundane social world and, therefore, having little or no ecological validity.

The criticisms then (and still) revolved most profoundly around the ideas that research in psychology, and resultant applied practice, most commonly reduce and control out the 'natural' complexity and contextuality of the social world – the very social world that practitioners such as educators and clinicians routinely have to confront. Gergen (1978) argued that, from a methodological point of view, it is impossible to manipulate any variable in isolation from any other because variables have a complex interrelationship. Harré and Secord (1972) accused traditional experimentalists and theorists of distorting the social world by selecting only that which was likely to lead to the endorsement of their academic theories. Thus the experimental worlds created by experimenters are argued to lack verisimilitude.

Underpinning all these criticisms was, and continues to be, the assumption or belief that the social world is much more complex and subtle than that construed and constructed by experimenters. Feyeraband (1975) explicitly stated that history is too complex for the best methodologist to imagine; and Thorngate (1976), reflecting on the problematic status of the discipline of social psychology at that time, suggested that this disorder may actually reflect the complexity of social phenomena.

As has been already stated, most frequently experimental variables/ stimuli and 'objects' of observation were and are disembedded from the cultural circumstances in which they mundanely occur, these variables then artificially being placed in a laboratory context. By isolating these variables/objects, and giving them an artificial context, not only is their mundane interrelatedness (to other parts of the social world) denied, but their meaning is drastically changed (see, for example, Romanyshyn, 1978; Mischler, 1979; and Schultz, 1968), and then a new configuration of meaning emerges which may have no equivalent in the mundane world.

Major philosophical arguments also underpin such criticisms. Harré and Secord (1972), Kuhn (1962), Feyeraband (1975), and Thines (1977), among others, attacked the framework of philosophical assumptions which underlined traditional paradigm psychological research and application, such as behavioural interventions. It was argued that adherents of the paradigm first make the error of seeing positivism as the only possible scientific method; which leads them to the second error of adopting the Humean metaphysical view, in which stimulus–response connections are equated with causality. Hence, that which is observed is totally divorced from the process of observation. Not only is such a positivistic view philosophically naive but, as Koch argued in 1964, the emerging definitions of human knowledge in science, begun thirty years earlier, rendered obsolete the Humean view of science still regulative of psychological research and, indeed, practice. Of course, clinicians in applied psychological settings have long wrestled with the ever-present difficulty of differentiating 'observer' self from that which is observed as 'belonging' to the client, but, even here, it is only relatively recently that this difficulty has been widely formulated in a sufficiently acceptable way to be communicated publicly within academic circles, allowing more radical mainstream researchers and clinicians to feel able to distance themselves, with more authority, from conventional positivistic wisdom (see Goldfried and Padawar, 1982; Stolorow et al., 1987; Romanyshyn, 1982; and Elliott, 1983a).

From the 1970s onwards, and increasingly today, there has been a growing realization that scientific and theoretical activity cannot be divorced from the culture in which it occurs; for example, the dominance of certain assumptions, within a scientific activity or therapeutic theory and practice, may be more a function of socio-political forces than a function of the quality of knowledge achieved, or the appropriateness of these assumptions to the objects of enquiry (see Pilgrim, 1984). Hence, radical behaviourism can be seen as a logical rhetorical extension of the socio-political emblem of the self-made man of American immigrant mythology; and conventional psychoanalytic theories of female sexuality can be seen as an extension of the voice of a massively repressed Victorian society that could not stomach the realities of child sexual abuse, and from which societal blindness Freud himself could not, in this instance, distance himself. There is, relatedly, the realization that all laws and theoretical models are constructions. The idea of the pure fact is no longer tenable. Facts are already subject to the view of the observer, and, all observations contain theoretical assumptions. Hence, the object of observation can never be separated from the process of observation.

This line of reasoning clearly has profound implications for all of psychology, both pure and applied, and is entirely consistent with the position taken in this book. The science and practice of psychology has been overwhelmingly concerned with human subjects as 'objects' of enquiry; in this respect both traditional analytic and behaviourist/cognitive perspectives have been unwitting and unrelated bedfellows. Despite different epistemological roots, both espouse science as objectivistic. More recently there is a growing acceptance of the phenomenological perspective: both the observer and the observed may be seen as having the same essential epistemological status, co-constituting each other, and only arbitrarily or pragmatically distinguished as observer or observed. Any separation of observer from observed must either be accepted as a pragmatic necessity (see Thines, 1977; Cantril, 1960; Stolorow et al., 1987) or as a separation that needs to be continuously negotiated and accounted for (Brodbeck, 1995; Romanyshyn, 1982). This and other methodological themes will be discussed specifically with respect to role play in Chapter 3.

The other central denial of 'objectivism' and reductionism, in addition to the interrelatedness of observer and observed, has been the status of the individual subject as an individual agent. There is again acceptance and awareness that the human subject does not respond passively to stimuli but makes sense of stimuli, responds selectively, constructs the world and acts upon the world, thereby changing the status of the environment while being part of it – just as the experimenter does. In the traditional experiment or therapy (whether psychodynamic or behaviourist), reality, and the significance of acts, has only generally been defined by the experimenter or therapist; alternative realities let alone co-constituted realities have not been considered (see Chapter 6).

Clinicians within psychology have been somewhat slower to become critically involved, explicitly and publicly, in these methodological concerns. Yet, informally communicated evidence has been growing that the individual clinician's privately experienced gaps between theories of psychological therapies and actual practice stood up to objective scrutiny, and were also increasingly experienced as pervasive within the therapeutic community of practitioners. Clinicians, on an everyday basis, know that there is a much heavier reliance upon methods and understandings tailored to individual clients, and that clinicians unreflectively employ a variety of often quite disparate models to understand their clients, and, indeed, use their own subjectivity and intuition, tempered by experience. Yet, as already stated above, despite such everyday experience, it was not until quite recently that formal analysis and research made such views publicly explicit and acceptable (for example, Morrow-Bradley and Elliott, 1986; Kanfer, 1990; Simionato, 1991). Furthermore, echoes of this debate are increasingly to be found, particularly with respect to psychotherapy research, and there is a growing confluence of concerns shared by social psychologists and psychotherapy researchers alike (for example; Elliott, 1983a; Horowitz, 1982; Butler and Strupp, 1986; Fajardo, 1993).

Emerging alternative strategies in psychological enquiry

Increasingly, despite the continued dominance of methodology rooted in logical-positivism and Humean causality on one hand (behavioural/ cognitive approaches), and a priori theorizing on the other (analytic theories), a range of alternative approaches to knowledge and understanding have become available, resulting in quite different research strategies in social and clinical psychology. Such different approaches have increased over the past twenty years and concern themselves predominantly with research and understanding. The foci of these various strategies are discussed below.

The agency of the individual is placed at the centre of causal explanations

Within social psychology, Harré and Secord's 1972 ethogenics has been seminal in this regard. Since that time, the ethogenic agentic view of the individual has been highly influential, and has laid the foundations for deconstructionist and feminist research (see below). Within both social and clinical psychology Kelly's 1955 construct theory (1955a, 1955b) was an early precursor of the attempts to place the agentic individual at the heart of explanation, and Kelly has had a huge impact on modern practice and research. To this day Kelly's grid methodology (op.cit.) is used within a wide variety of idiographic approaches to research (see Smith, 1990; Gillett, 1995). Many clinical psychologists continue, directly or indirectly, to use derived Kellyian methodology within clinical assessment and therapy. It could be argued that to some extent modern cognitive approaches in clinical psychology place the agentic individual at the centre of concern, but such approaches tend to be heavily circumscribed by assumptions about the need for corrective changes in the direction of normative 'reality based' thinking and are not particularly concerned with experience, which Kelly was. Of course, existential and humanistic approaches have long placed the individual as agent at the heart of therapeutic endeavour and explanation, and mainstream psychotherapy researchers have become increasingly strongly influenced by such values (for example, Strupp, 1978). (Strupp was an early proponent of the need both to take into account and to preserve the phenomenological experience of the patient in research.) Increasingly, moreover, psychodynamic thinkers are taking on board this more agentic view of the person and in such approaches the latter is deeply interwoven with the subjective and indeed the intersubjective (for example, Kohut, 1971 and 1977; Stolorow et al., 1987).

The focus upon the resubjectivization of explanation

Bakan's classic text (1967) on research in the social sciences and that of Schutz (1971, 1973) are central to this even more radical strategy.

The safeguarding of the subjective view is the only, but sufficient guarantee that
the world of social reality will not be replaced by a fictional non-existent world
constructed by the scientific observer. (Schutz, 1971: 8)

Such powerfully expressed views have influenced generations of social
scientists, along with the equally powerful thesis of Bakan (1967), who
propounded the paramount need for the subjective to become relegitima-
tized within the domains of human research and understanding. More
recently Denzin (1987a and b), a phenomenological sociologist who has
taken a particular interest in mental disorder, has written of the need for
subjective approaches in psychology. Of even more direct relevance to
clinical work is the writing of Hollway (1989) who combines a subjectivist
– phenomenological rationale and method, to the understanding of individuals' gender experience, within a constructivist and psychodynamic
framework of analyses. Romanyshyn (1987), a noted American clinician
and theoretician, also propounds a phenomenological – subjectivist
approach. Lastly here, and of recent great impact among psychoanalytic
thinkers, is the work of Stolorow et al. (1987), whose writings within the
domain of psychoanalytic theory powerfully promulgate the need for a
phenomenological and intersubjectivistic approach to understanding the
psychoanalytic process, as against the more traditional objectivistic
methods (see also Brodbeck, 1995).

Feminist research also typically combines a dedication to subjectively
sensitive method, personal experience and reflexivity in critical analysis,
(Duelli Klein, 1983; Henwood and Pidgeon, 1992, 1995; Hollway, 1989, see
above). Erins (1992) delineates the manner in which feminism impacts upon
therapeutic practices and the need for reflexive awareness in this arena.
Although feminist research is wary of false comparisons with deconstruc-
tionism (see below), there are degrees of commonality concerning method.
The feminist interest in subjectivity and experience is distinctive, however,
the concern with exposing unseen or suppressed assumptions upon which
knowledge is premised, and an especial interest in discourse, are common.

The use of idiographic, biographical and case study methods

This strategy utilizes the accounts of fully informed subjects as the prime
procedure for gaining knowledge (see Bromley, 1986, 1991; Honess and
Edwards, 1987; Smith, J.A., 1994; Smith, 1995; Plummer, 1983, 1995). A
recent example of such research is that of Smith, J.A. (1995) who uses
idiographic (including Kelly's grid methodology) and phenomenological
methods to understand transitions to motherhood. Evidently case study
methods have predominated within psychoanalytic research. However, until
recently and distinct from the approaches cited above, such methods have
been heavily circumscribed by an almost total reliance on understanding
through closed theoretical analytic systems of thought, almost without
exception already pre-espoused by the researcher. Mahrer et al. (1986),
Yardley (1990), and Horowitz (1979, 1982) have strongly argued for a

much more open-ended and case study approach to researching psychotherapies so that, for example, a plethora of commentaries and perspectives are actively sought. Moreover, the recent common factors approach (see Goldfried, 1991; Marmar, 1990; Shapiro, 1995 and Wachtel, 1977), together with more radical approaches, are leading the research community away from such theoretical blinkeredness.

The focus is upon the the recontextualization of the social act

This seeks to unpack the considerable depth of texture of social and/or personal significations underlying and surrounding any utterance or social action.

Of interest here is a burgeoning clinical literature on psychotherapy process research, with Elliott (1983b) probably being the most important researcher. He has used a research method that purposefully recontextualizes significant moments of therapy that have been initially isolated as a focus of enquiry (see also Heatherington, 1989; Shoham and Salomon, 1990 and Greenberg, 1986 on the importance of context). Naturalistic research (Lincoln and Guba, 1985) has insisted on this need for local contextual understandings of human action and experience, a concern that is foremost in the deconstructionist and dialogic approaches below.

Deconstructionist research with its emphasis upon discourse and text   (For example, Much 1992; and Potter and Wetherell, 1995.) According to Henriques et al., 1984 p.106 a deconstructionist position asserts 'that any given body of statements, whether in everyday conversation or a scientific paper, depends on a number of other bodies of statements, some of which carry deeply entrenched convictions and explanatory schemes fundamental to the dominant form of making sense of the world at any particular period in a culture. Deconstructionism retraces the system of dependence of a discourse', and accounts for the emergence of this discourse. The use of discourse analysis, within a deconstructionist position, is centrally concerned with content, modern semiotics and accounts related to the production of knowledge. Every discourse is viewed as embedded in a complex of other practices, material and discursive. The status of knowledge is approached with radical scepticism and through textual analysis covert assumptions and social constructions are exposed. It is these socially constructed systems that are seen as creating meanings and relationships of power and authority.

In addition to its profound influence on latter day social psychological research (for evidence of this see British Psychological Society, 1995, where discourse analysis within a deconstructionist approach appears to have become the dominant methodology), there is a growing clinical literature also espousing constructivism (see Neimeyer, 1993 and Swartz, 1986 for an overview). Family and systemic therapy approaches, in particular, have been increasingly aware of epistemological and constructivist concerns in relativizing notions of truth and normality within family contexts (Wamboldt et al., 1985; Wassenaar, 1987).

Relatedly, an increasing number of clinical theorists and researchers are using more traditional discourse approaches as analytic tools in a variety of very different settings, although not necessarily within a deconstructionist context. For example, Zimmerman and Dickerson (1993) have used discourse analysis in relation to couples therapy, Musiol (1992) has explored schizophrenic thought processes, Lewis (1995), Blanchet et al. (1991) and Esseg and Russell (1990) have explored therapist–patient interactions using discourse analytic methods; finally, Osiejuk (1993) has among others used discourse methods to research brain dysfunction.

Other relevant language based contextualist approaches are discussed below.

Dialogism, the study of interaction in its social and cultural context   (See Markova and Foppa, 1990; Shotter, 1994.) Dialogism, with its strong ethnomethodological and symbolic interactionist roots and its close relationship with conversational analysis, has been defined by Heritage (1984) as having as its central goal: 'the description and explication of the competencies that ordinary speakers use and rely on in participating in intelligible socially organized interaction. At its most basic, this objective is one of describing the procedures by which conversationalists produce their own behaviour and understand and deal with the behaviour of others' (1984: 95)

In this work there is a close reliance upon material collected from naturally occurring everyday occasions of interaction which are recorded, transcribed and analysed. Clearly, the emphasis is upon what language performs as action, and upon a particular sensitivity to local contexts (see Bergmann, 1990, for discussion of the significance of local contexts on topic and content and Hedberg and Stoel-Gammon, 1986 on topic analysis in language disorders).

Narrative analysis   This focuses on thematic and/or story like constructions which emerge in text/dialogue. Such an approach is becoming increasingly commonly used in research upon the experience of schizophrenia or the construction of schizophrenic language, (for example, Alvis and Rosenberg, 1990; Parry, 1991; Davidson, 1993 and also in psychotherapy research, e.g. Nye, 1994 and on research on illness see Riessman, 1990).

Hermeneutical approaches   (See Reason and Heron, 1995; Van Langenhove, 1995.) These researchers place emphasis upon interpretation and understanding with close attention to detailed scholarship, Reason and Heron (1995) place particular emphasis upon the co-operative nature of such research with subjects. The hermeneutic method has strongly influenced discourse analysis, but is a seemingly more open approach and less closely associated with a priori positioning, indeed is somewhat intolerant of it. Recently Vandendriessche (1991) has described hermeneutic approaches towards research in psychoanalysis. Horowitz (1982) and Bouchard & Guerette (1991) have suggested using a hermeneutic method drawing upon Literary Reader Response theory, where the 'text' of psychoanalytic sessions is 'interrogated' from a number of theoretical perspectives (see also Yardley, 1990), opening up diversity and richness of interpretation.

Although there has not been the same extent and degree of epistemological awareness among clinicians and clinician/researchers, there is a shift in this direction which lags a little behind social psychology. Yet above all, within clinical arenas, there has frequently been an informal attitude emphasizing the actuality of clinical work, and the need for more subject-centred and open-ended creative conceptualizations of human experience and action. Such ideas have been set against the constrictions of reasoning produced by the mainly positivistic formal psychological systems, that initially underwrote therapeutic applications. Clinicians, especially psychotherapists, have particular concern with the detailed observation and understanding of behaviour based overwhelmingly on the detailed attention to discourse. This is shaped by a motivation to respond helpfully to individually experienced and mediated suffering which, in practice, leads most often to flexible construing and theorizing on the part of the clinician.

Implications for role play

It is against such a methodological background of criticism and emerging diversity of methodology that role play methodology is here promoted. It is not suggested that role play is in any sense a panacea, or necessarily a radical methodology or set of techniques; as we shall see, role play equally embraces conventional and non-conventional paradigms and applications. None the less, it will be argued that role plays do offer unique potential with respect to the enhancement of subjectivist, deconstructionist and contextualized approaches to the gathering of knowledge, and to the 'generation' of action, whether in research or therapy. The key to this potential lies entirely in relation to the choice and quality of techniques used for inducting role plays, and the amenability of role play methods to a high degree of reflexive methodological interrogation. Indeed, it will be argued that a prerequisite of good use of role play techniques is thorough methodological reflexiveness. The major thrust of this book will thus concern the hitherto almost entirely neglected area of role play technique within a variety of metholodological contexts. This will be informed, but hopefully not constrained, by an interest in more radical psychological approaches.

There is, in practice, no common epistemological or methodological grounding for the variety of uses of role play. There have, however, been central debates concerning the validity of role play procedures which are grounded in epistemological issues. In Chapter 3 we will start to consider these in addition to presenting a picture of the current use of role play together with history of its use. Epistemological issues will be returned to throughout the book as they are deeply significant to the development of good role play practices.

3
An Overview of Current Role Play Practice

This chapter will overview the variety of uses to which role play is generally put, and consider the history and origins of such uses. Epistemological and methodological concerns will be addressed, especially those focusing around validity. (Validity refers to the concept of the adequacy of the measurement tool or procedures to undertake the stated measurement. There are several types of measure of validity: *external, ecological, content, predictive and construct*. These will also be defined as and when they are used in the text.)

The use of role play as a practical technique in psychology and allied disciplines is of relatively recent origin, although idiosyncratic uses can be discovered earlier, such as that of Reil in the 1800s, cited by Zilboorg and Henry (1941). There are, of course, clearly identifiable, centuries-old antecedents within both the theatrical and pedagogical traditions (Way, 1967; Courtney, 1972). However, for present purposes, we will confine our interests to tracing the specific origins of role play in relation to social and clinical research, and in relation to clinical and closely associated, applied, psychological practice.

Role play in social psychology research

The earliest notable, and still much quoted, use of role play within experimentation, within social psychology, was by Janis and King (1954). Here, the impact of improvised versus non-improvised (scripted) role play was evaluated in relation to the impact upon attitude change to smoking behaviour. Improvisational role play technique, in particular, was seen as containing the active ingredients of a change mechanism, with respect to the active engagement of attitudinal processes. (Janis and King's methods were loosely cited as deriving from Moreno's psychodrama [1946/72, 1959 and 1969] but bear no direct evidence of his technique.) The very process of *actively* generating ideas, while enacting a role which involved taking an attitudinal stance quite contrary to that normally held by the 'actor', was seen, and indeed was demonstrated, to lead to attitude change. By contrast, such attitude change was demonstrated not to be effectively achieved via the 'passive' absorption of counter-attitudinal persuasive information, but gained only through reading the expression of the contrary attitudinal stance.

At about the same time another social psychologist, Borgatta (1951 [with Bales] and 1955), was directly comparing role play behaviour, actual behaviour and expected behaviour, principally on the basis of measuring interpersonal behaviours in groups, using the Bales category system (a system for classifying individual styles of behaviour in group contexts). Interestingly, Borgatta found good evidence for the *external* validity of role play procedures on the basis of these comparisions. (External validity refers to the extent to which that which is being purported to be measured within an experiment truly relates to the 'external' reality of which the experiment is supposed to be an equivalent. In contrast, ecological validity refers to the individual's experience of validity. The distinction between these two latter concepts will be key to our understanding of the necessary requirements of good role play induction.)

By the 1960s, role play procedures were being used ever more widely, though they were not always clearly identified as such; for example, in risky shift person perception, leadership, attribution theory, and decision-making research (see Alexander and Scriven, 1977, for discussion of these). Here, role plays were used as a *medium for providing an 'imaginary' context within which independent variables could be manipulated.* For example, *actual* fear-inducing stimuli (independent variable) could be manipulated to assess their impact upon behaviour within an otherwise role played ('as-if') event. Generally speaking, in such circumstances no attention was given either to the validity of role play techniques as such, or to precise aspects of technique. More considered utilization of role play technique only occurred in the realm of *replication* studies, where role plays were used to substitute for the more usual experimental designs, which most frequently involved deception paradigms and which were increasingly being viewed as ethically problematic. It was in relation to these early replication studies that controversy and contention arose (see below).

Bem's 1967 study appeared to mark a watershed for social psychology. Bem used role play to replicate the forced-compliance experiments of cognitive dissonance theory (these concern explanations of studies in which individuals are 'forced' to act in a manner inconsistent with usual behaviour or standards and where individuals then seem to seek to make their own action consistent or justifiable by actively reinterpreting the initial stimulus and its value. Such reinterpretations allow them to reduce any discomfort experienced by their carrying out the inconsistent behaviour), in order to support his own model of attitude change through self-observation. Stimulated by the controversy around this replication experiment, a vigorous debate commenced in the late 1960s and raged throughout the 1970s, around the **validity** of role play as an experimental technique – a debate which still remains unresolved. (Validity is the bedrock of arguments about the usefulness of role play approaches within social and clinical psychology. As we shall see below, validity and reality status are highly interdependent concepts. Reality is differently construed from differing theoretical and methodological perspectives, but, broadly speaking, ranges between ideas grounded in external observers' judgements of reality status and those grounded in more subjective, participant-based judgements. From this author's perspective, I will be arguing throughout this text, that greater weight must be given to participants' subjective judgement of reality – that is ecological validity – for role plays to have real value and usefulness.)

Much of this validity debate focused around the replication of conventionally carried out empirical experiments. Hence, Darroch, and Steiner (1970), Simmons and Piliavin (1972) and Holmes and Bennet (1974) failed to replicate experimental studies using role play (although such inadequacies of technique exist that the results are hardly surprising). However, O'Leary et al. (1987) and Mixon (1972) did successfully replicate the infamous Milgram studies on conformity, in which subjects were tricked into believing that they were giving near lethal electric shocks to other subjects as punishment for failing to learn given material in role play experiments. Stricker (1967) and Manstead (1979) successfully replicated aspects of Schachter and Singer's 1962 studies, on the cognitive determinants of emotional state. Horowitz and Rothschild (1970) and Willis and Willis (1970) also carried out relatively successful replication role play studies. However, several of the above studies produced some ambiguous results. For example, Willis and Willis (1970) replicated the main effect of a conformity study but failed to replicate more subtle effects.

Two sets of arguments drawn from opposing camps sought either to explain or invalidate these results. To summarize briefly, proponents of role play technique generally grounded their arguments in a humanistic and person-centred approach. And they argued that the experiment, as target of replication, was in any case an inappropriate criterion for *ecological validity*. (The criteria for ecological validity are individuals' subjective sense of appropriateness. The concept was coined by Bronfenbrenner (1977), a developmental psychologist, in a seminal and influential paper.) In particular, Forward et al. (1976), Hamilton (1976) and Baron (1977) argued that role plays – unlike their conventional counterparts, positivistic experiments – allowed subjects a greater latitude of response and more complex behaviour to be explored by introducing a greater number of variables. Mixon (1971), Hamilton (1976) and Geller (1978) argued that role plays approximated reality more closely, and involve participants more directly and profoundly. Geller (1978), among others, clearly attributed replication failures to the technical inadequacy of such role play experiments, particularly with respect to subject involvement. (The Stanford Prison experiment [Haney et al., 1973] was often cited as the example *par excellence* of subject involvement and ecological validity, and to this we shall return in Chapter 4.)

Quite distinct from such humanistic arguments, and grounded in a more conventional positivistic approach, Bem (1968) himself argued that role plays were not an adequate substitution for experiments but offered a *valid replication methodology*, provided that the experimenter met the demands of *functional equivalence* with respect to the experiment replicated. That is, that the behaviours of the simulation need not necessarily be identical to those of the target experiment or situation, but must provide an analogue that produces the same results or output. Darroch and Steiner (1970), who had ambiguous but mainly negative replication results, argued along somewhat similar lines. They maintained that role play success will depend on the experimenter's skill in deciding which circumstances (variables) are critical and how each is likely to affect its subject. They further argued, in relatively unusual, insightful and sophisticated terms:

> It seems obvious that role-playing subjects will sometimes fail to replicate the results obtained from laboratory subjects. This should be most likely to occur when subjects are asked to role play someone other than themselves whose implicit theory differs from their own, when the experiment involves highly novel circumstances which have not been assimilated into subjects' implicit theories, or when the laboratory situation is so complex that its important features cannot readily be discerned and communicated to role-playing subjects. (1970: 310)

From the opposing side, critics such as Cooper (1976), Freedman (1969) and Miller (1972), basing their claims on a conventional positivistic view of reality and the nature of scientific method, argued that role plays were less scientific because less controllable, less realistic and less involving of participants. We will now consider this very particular debate in more depth, given its continuing conceptual importance and above all its technical implications.

Preliminary discussion of technique, involvement and engagement in role play

The question of technique in role plays has seldom been addressed directly and in depth by researchers or therapists. The closest approximation to a focused concern with technique has been that held within the 1970s' social psychology debate (see above) on the issue of subject involvement within experiments, often the corner-stone of arguments and counter-arguments on the general efficacy of 'as-if' methods. Greenberg (1967) appears to have been the first social psychologist to have suggested that subject involvement might be a crucial variable in role play simulations of experiments. Since then Geller (1978), Baron (1977) and Alexander and Scriven (1977), among other role play proponents, have stressed the importance of such involvement for 'realism'. Mixon (1977) has queried whether involvement is necessary for simulations although on balance he appears to favour it. On the other hand Miller (1972), Aronson and Carlsmith (1968) and Cooper (1976) have asserted that role plays lack involvement in comparison with traditional methods.

The concept of involvement is, however, variously comprehended and hinges on a prior and invariably implicit understanding of reality. Thus the arguments concerning involvement are generally founded on those concerning 'reality status'. To summarize briefly, reality may be viewed at one extreme as the phenomenal experience of the participant (humanistic), and, at the other, as something that is expressed in the independent–dependent variable relationship, which can be said to be contaminated by subjective experience, and which can only be inferred through consensual validation provided by 'objective' observers (logical–positive/empiricist). From the extreme phenomenalist/humanistic perspective there follows a very close relationship between reality and the experience of involvement. Conversely from the extreme empiricist position, there follows only an indirect and tenuous link between the two.

Nevertheless, whatever the researcher's assumptions about reality or indeed about the nature of the source of action (independent controlling variables, subject plans, unconscious forces, role–rule models, etc.), *all experimenters share an interest in the subjects' being phenomenally involved in the overt task, although for different reasons.* Hence, a methodological behaviourist may be interested in ensuring subject involvement in specific actions, so that features of the environment can be manipulated without the subjects' conscious awareness, or at least without awareness of the significance of these. A humanist might be expected to attach greater importance to the process of involvement itself; to the objects of involvement; and to exploration of the significance of the objects of involvement.

Generally speaking critics of role play techniques, both those who have actually used role play and those who have not, espouse conventional empiricist methodology; whereas proponents of role play claim more humanistic intentions. Despite the latter's stated intentions and their particular claims about the superior involvement of subjects with respect to role plays, the experience of phenomenal involvement does not appear to be explored theoretically or, even more importantly, by talking directly with experimental subjects. Geller (1978), a role play proponent, makes some attempt to investigate the phenomenal involvement of his subjects, but does this by means of a simple rating scale and, indeed, appears to give more credence to indirect and 'objective' measures. Furthermore, Forward et al. (1976) and Geller (1978), for example, suggest that the achievement of involvement may be a matter of choosing skilled individuals or giving participants appropriate training. In particular, Geller suggests that training might proceed by exposing unskilled actors to training films of 'as-if' situations where the actors are skilled and their performance convincing, implying again that involvement is performatively evident and can be externally modelled or learned. This construction of involvement in terms of how convincing the individual's role play is according to external performance criteria, is quite contrary to a humanistic construction of involvement, which lays emphasis on an individual's phenomenal experience. It is also alien to concepts of ecological validity.

Most commonly, the technical problem of subject involvement is sidestepped by leading the reader to believe that involvement equals physical activity, an extremely naive belief in post James-Langian psychology. It is argued (Baron, 1977; Hamilton, 1976; Mixon, 1971) that the sheer activeness of role play methods leads to subject involvement and thus distinguishes active from passive role plays. Obviously, however, an act of pure imagination such as day-dreaming may be as involving and realistic, in the subjective and phenomenal sense, as any overt act. Hence, where passive imagining is being passed over in favour of overt activity, something different from subject 'involvement' is expected, which itself needs more precise exposition, for example an important component in an overt role play act is the presence of 'real others' – other participants, who place external demands on the subject by interacting with him or her and thus counter purely autistic involvement. In Chapter 9, this issue will be raised again in a discussion of some qualitative research I undertook on role play (Yardley, 1984b) where the participants' accounts of their participation is certainly more sophisticated with respect to the concept of 'involvement' than that of many role play proponents or opponents, and overwhelmingly favours mundaneness and familiarity rather than gross arousal *per se*.

Because the concept of involvement is problematic in the literature, the term **engagement** is preferred and introduced for present purposes here, to throw emphasis on the objects of engagement, rather than on internal and physiologically grounded states. Thus, one is not merely 'involved' in some free floating state, or whatever, but one is engaged with some *thing* some *body* or some *event*. Apart from representing a phenomenological approach, the above conceptualization provides a more objective basis for an assessment of 'involvement'. One may more easily enquire as to the 'objects' of an individual's engagement than one may elicit descriptions of the subjective state of involvement. For what matters, methodologically speaking, is not necessarily and foremost the *degree* of subjects' involvement, but the objects with which the subjects are involved or engaged (whether these be externally visible things, people or events or internal things, people or events). In an 'as-if' experiment, based on conventional methodology, it should not matter that person X is more or less 'involved' than another participant. However, it does matter that both participants are engaged with the *intended* objects of the experiment. In a deception paradigm, for example, the experimenter intends that these objects are different for him or herself than for the subject; in a humanistic enterprise, one would expect these objects, in principle, to be accessible to both.

If the experiment is intended to have ecological validity (role play proponents claim that role play facilitates such validity), other factors regarding these objects also need consideration. First, subjects must *feel* that the quality of their engagement with the objects of the experimental situation is roughly comparable and equivalent with that which they would experience in mundane reality. Secondly, and relatedly, subjects must *recognize the objects and their juxtaposition to be likely or at least possible objects of their mundane world*. This argument evidently finally develops into a strong humanistic/phenomenological position, where the engendering of objects absolutely appropriate to the individual would be paramount. Such research moves into the examination of these objects, as constructed and experienced by individuals, and to the search for the general grounded in the idiographic.

Role plays where role play is used as the medium for manipulation of independent variables

In addition to replication studies, and existing seemingly in ignorance of this critical debate, there have been studies where subjects are asked to role play various specific and highly focused conditions, in order to examine the effect of these conditions, as variables. Hence, for example, Adams-Webber and Rodney (1983) looked at the effects of role played, contrasted moods (independent variable) on self and 'other' constructs (dependent variables). Kopel and Arkowitz (1974) asked role play subjects to role play calmness or upsetness, to examine the effect upon perceived pain; and Sarup (1981) looked at attitude change related to role playing activity, following Janis and King (1954). Sarup's study showed that improvised role play around the expression of counter-attitudinal stance produced more attitude change in experimental subjects (particularly for high importance issues) than through passive exposure to discrepant information.

The most renowned and extensive study where role play was used to manipulate independent variables is the Stanford prison experiment of Haney et al. (1973) (which is critically reported in Chapter 4) where the brutality and de-individuating aspects of prison life were purportedly simulated to evaluate their effects on 'prisoner' behaviour.

Role plays used to generate a context of assessment

Here role plays are used to generate a context within which particular aspects of behaviour can be focused upon and measured. Such role play methodology has by far the greatest use in clinical psychology (see section below on clinical and therapeutic applications); however, it has been occasionally used within social psychology. Krueger and Smith (1982) for example, looked at marital communication styles by asking married couple subjects to role play their own behaviour. Here again, no details of induction technique are given, nor is attention given to validity – external or ecological.

The critical use of role play in social psychology research

Despite the conceptual debate of the 1970s, there have been very few studies in social psychology that have directly examined even the external validity of role play, with the exception of the early Borgatta studies (1955; with Bales, 1951). As we have seen, other more recent researchers have evaluated role play in relation to a criterion relating solely to the successful replication of traditional experiments. Moreover, there has been no research or conceptual analysis concerning technique. The situation is somewhat different within clinical psychology. There is a substantial amount of research concerning external validity, if not concerning ecological validity, and a much more varied use of technique, albeit with little evidence of much technical insight into the latter. However, as we shall see, despite the greater width of use and research into validity, the field continues to be overwhelmingly marked by a relative lack of sophistication and depth of exploration.

Clinical and therapeutic applications of role play: a general introduction

Within clinical and closely related applied fields of psychology, there are two major developmental lines, and several other significant contributions, with respect to role play. The first and certainly the most technically sophisticated is that of Psychodrama, as developed by the influential late Jacob Moreno (1946, 1959, 1969) and his many exponents (for example, Zerka Moreno, 1969; Greenberg, 1974; Corsini, 1966; Williams, 1989; Holmes and Karp, 1991). Moreno started developing his ideas in Vienna in the 1920s, and was publishing his major works through Beacon House in the 1930s and 40s. This rich and sophisticated role play tradition broadly informed the role play activities that pervasively occurred within the Encounter/Synanon/Gestalt/growth movements of the later 1960s and early 70s, as is evidenced in highly specific techniques, for example the 'empty chair' used in Gestalt work.

Other indirectly related role play techniques are to be found in the work of child psychotherapists, for example, Axline (1971), who uses, *inter alia*, *role play for the expression of impulses* – for the expression of anger that might otherwise be repressed, for instance. (There is also a strong tradition of play techniques within child psychoanalysis continuing to the present day, see Levinson and Herman, 1991.) We will return to psychodrama and similar activities later in this chapter and in Chapter 4. Suffice it to state at this juncture, there is negligible explicit concern with validity within this tradition. Indeed, external validity is a relatively meaningless concept here, as it is not in keeping with either the humanistic or the psychodynamic orientations associated with psychodramatic techniques. What is important here is not observers' judgements of approximation to reality, but the experience of the participants themselves. Ecological validity, although not addressed in such terms within this tradition, is nevertheless clearly a relevant construct given the emphasis here upon participants' experiences. There is, moreover, a concern in psychodrama with what we might term 'intrapsychic validity' hence: 'the aims of these sundry techniques is not to turn the patients into actors, but rather to stir them up to be on the stage what they are more deeply and more explicitly than they appear to be in life's reality.' (Moreno, 1972: 16). This would indicate that Moreno is not interested in producing 'slick' externally convincing portrayals of reality but in providing or facilitating experiences that express inner realities.

The second and distinctly important line of clinical development occurs within mainstream behavioural psychology in the early work of Wolpe (1969) on behaviour rehearsal; and contemporaneously in the work of others such as Lazarus (1966), Kanfer and Phillips (1969 – replication therapy) and Goldstein (1973 – structured learning therapy). Wolpe (1969) first used role play techniques within his general therapeutic strategy of the reciprocal inhibition of anxiety. He described role play thus:

> the therapist takes the role of a person towards whom the patient has a neurotic anxiety reaction and instructs him to express his ordinarily inhibited feelings towards that person . . . The patient is made to repeat each statement again and again, being constantly corrected until the utterance is in every way satisfactory. The aim of the rehearsal is, of course, to make it possible for him to express himself with his real 'adversary' so that the anxiety the latter evokes may be reciprocally inhibited, and the motor assertive habit established. (Wolpe, 1969: 68)

A variety of associated strategies have since been used in behavioural treatments, most particularly within the area of assertion and social skills training, but also within behavioural assessment. We will return to these in more detail below.

Rather less widespread, but none the less a significant and important contribution, is that of George Kelly, the highly influential originator of Construct Theory. In addition to the more general conversational practices of Construct Therapy, Kelly (1955a and b) developed a very specific technique called Fixed Role Therapy, to which we shall also return below.

An overview of the use of role play in clinical research

The existing literature here is substantially larger than that of social psychology. For the sake of convenience the material will again be organized into categories, broadly as above, with the exception of replication studies, of which there appears to be a dearth within this literature. The categories are:

1 Role play as a medium for independent variable manipulation;
2 Role play as an experimental context for an assessment and as an assessment tool;
3 Role play as assessment context in relation to measuring the effects of different treatment in interventions.

Role play as a medium for independent variable manipulation

This consists of setting up an imaginative context or scenario in which a putative significant feature is manipulated through role play and against which clients are asked to behave in order that some aspect of their behaviour may be measured. In parallel with use within social psychology, role play is frequently used in this manner (usually without any consideration of the validity of the technique). For example, Blumberg and Hokanson (1983) looked at the effect of different role played interpersonal confederate styles on the behaviour of depressed or non-depressed subjects. Despite evidence of good role play training for stooges here, issues of validity and technique are not directly addressed. Rhodewalt and Agustsdottir (1986) looked at the effects of role playing, in a high versus low choice condition, in a role played interview involving either self-deprecating or self-enhancing behaviour, in non-depressed and mildly depressed subjects. Klein (1982) examined the effects of different information on imagined distress in a role played dental treatment situation. (Again, in this latter study, there is evidence of relatively good induction technique, see Chapter 4, but this is not dealt with explicitly.) Finally here, Hovrath (1984) manipulated demand characteristics through role play to assess the differential effect on self-concept measures.

Role play as an experimental context for assessment and as an assessment tool

An example of this category of role play involves the setting up of an imagined scenario, such as a busy cafeteria, and against this context the social skills of participants are evaluated. Many studies have used role play in this way – again relatively uncritically – merely to establish a contextual background for behaviour that is to be measured or evaluated, without explicit discussion of validity or of role play's general appropriateness as a technique of choice. In particular, the 1970s saw a burgeoning of the use of role play in the assessment of social and heterosexual behaviour and skills, with little attention to validity with the exception of researchers such as Bellack, Hersen and Turner (1979) and Bellack, Hersen and Lamparski (1979), see below. It was most often viewed as a highly economical method in contrast to the difficulties of *in vivo* observation of 'naturalistic' behaviours. (For a useful review of many of these, see McNamara and Blumer, 1982.) A fairly early typical study which certainly provided a template for many later studies was that of Eisler, Hersen and Miller (1975). Eisler et al. used 32 *minimal* role play settings (inductions involved one or two lines of set-up instructions to role playing patients), varying one independent variable in order to assess the assertion skills of psychiatric patients.

The comparative social competencies of problem drinkers have been researched more recently in this manner by Abrams et al. (1991), Gammon and Sheldon (1991) and Monti et al. (1990), for example. Similarly Glueckhauf and Quittner (1992) used role play for the evaluation of the assertion skills of adults in wheelchairs. There also continues to be a very large literature on the assessment of social competencies in schizophrenics which relies on the use of minimalist role play techniques for the provision of contexts of assessment (Wirrshing et al., 1992; Bellack et al., 1989,

1990b; Meuser et al., 1990, 1991; Salto et al., 1990; Jackson et al., 1989). Role play is also commonly used as a context for assessing family systems and communication styles (for example, Mitrofan and Mitrofan, 1989) but again with almost no concern for validity, either external or ecological.

Moreover, the typical use of such minimalist technique (as alluded to above) involving only a one or two line contextualizing induction and a one line prompt (in expectation of a one line response) is still standard in the area of assertion and interpersonal skills assessment, training and research (see the review by Bellack et al., 1990b). (Such minimalist techniques and their inadequacies will be considered in detail in Chapter 4.) Hence, quite complex assessments of interpersonal skills are routinely made based on a simulated social episode of almost complete generality and banality. The standard types of instruction here are: 'You are at a party of a friend; please act as you normally would', or, 'You have been asked to take a book back to a library and you meet a girl you want to date'. These hardly provide the individualized and differentiated contexts that people mundanely find themselves in, and do not seem likely to produce ecologically valid behaviour. This is one of the most important areas of discussion in this book and we shall return to it in depth throughout this book.

Role play as assessment context in relation to measuring the effects of different treatment interventions

Role plays have been used, and continue to be used, as assessment contexts in relation to measuring the effects of different treatment interventions. For example, Moon and Eisler (1975) successfully evaluated the effects of three treatments for anger control, using role play to provide assessment contexts. Kadden et al. (1992) used role play to evaluate two types of alcoholism treatment programmes; Wirrshing et al. (1992) used role play to provide an assessment context for schizophrenic patients in relation to a comparison of symptom management and medication with psychotherapy group treatments. Several studies have used role play to assess the efficacy of single treatment and training interventions, but not within a comparative design; for example, there have been several studies on the effects of sexual abuse training programmes which have used role play to assess their success (Weist et al., 1993; Harbeck et al., 1992). Role play has been used in studies on the effects of social skills training in the learning disabled (Valenti-Hein et al., 1994; Foxx and Faw, 1992); studies with children to assess the effects of social-cognitive training for conduct disorder and attention deficit disorder (Kolko et al., 1990); and studies on the assessment of parenting skills following specific training packages, (Rickert et al., 1989; Gammon and Sheldon, 1991). Once more, minimalism predominates and there is little or no concern with validity or technique.

Somewhat distinctively, by including a new domain of observation, Bourque and Ladouceur (1979) investigated the relationship between self-report and behavioural measures. The latter might be termed a quasi-validity study, but is not presented as such. Finally, in a slightly different format from the minimal scenarios commonly employed above is that used by Thorley and Yule (1982). They use an extended, three-minute structured role play format with which to measure established parenting skills and acquired parenting skills following training. Although not principally a validity study, validity for their methods is claimed by virtue of a criterion of accuracy of measurement of established parenting skills – based on parental self-report. This moves us on to consider more specifically the vexed question of validity within clinical studies, which, as we have seen, is rarely addressed.

Clinical validity studies

Despite the general lack of concern over validity and allied methodological and technical issues, there has been some focused work on validity within the experimental clinical literature. McNamara and Blumer (1982) provide an excellent overview of much of this work, and consider whether or not the use of such early role plays demonstrated either ecological or external validity. They concluded that overall the evidence was at best indirect, in so far as it concerned only:

(a) the ability of role play to discriminate pre- to post-test treatments;
(b) the ability of role play assessment to differentiate 'known' groups of normal versus deviant populations; and that
(c) direct comparisons with behaviour in naturalistic situations were almost unknown.

They further argued, with respect to (a) above, 'that in a majority of instances involving treatment for heterosexual problems and assertiveness, role plays have effectively discriminated control and treatment groups.' (McNamara and Blumer, 1982; 525) and that this was similarly the case with respect to social skills treatment, but that, in both cases, effects that have been detected through role play, have tended to be less clear on follow-ups:

> However it is unclear whether lack of temporal generalization is more a function of the inadequacies of role play assessment, the specific follow-up procedures, or the strength of the treatment. Overall it appears that role plays are probably sensitive to behavioural change, and that this sensitivity is a contributory element, in understanding the procedure's ecological validity. (ibid: 552)

With respect to role play's ability to differentiate groups, McNamara and Blumer (1982) suggested that role plays do discriminate between groups known to be high or low on heterosexual competence, but these results tend to be even less clear than the results of treatment studies; in addition, global ratings appear to be more successful than highly specific ratings.

They also argued that social interaction is too complex for simple and highly specific indices, so that, for example, low eye contact is not a good predictor of dating frequency.

There are, notwithstanding the above, a few early external validity studies which are suggestive, indeed have implications, for ecological validity as well. For example, in the Bellack, Hersen and Lamparski study (1979) 'naturalistic' waiting room observations were compared with a role play test and with self-report measures. Although the correlations between the three were low, interestingly only 24 per cent of subjects reported that they acted like themselves in both the waiting room and role play situations, with more subjects acting as themselves in the former rather than the latter. Moreover, of those who reported that they did act like themselves in both, the correlations are much stronger, and only 17 out of 50 subjects felt able to role play at all. It is probably of relevance here to note the absence of any considered role play induction procedures here. Other interesting early studies are cited by McNamara and Blumer (1982), for example, that of Stanton and Litwak (1955), which demonstrated that subject behaviour correlated well between a role play test and a naturalistic situation *where the 'confederates' were people well known to the subjects.* This prior relationship seems likely to have called up more mundanely 'natural' subject behaviour.

It is also of some significance that there is a general finding in latter day studies of validity, that subjects are behaviourally more polarized (assertive) in role play situations than in similar contrived 'naturalistic' situations – see Higgins, Alonso and Pendleton (1979) and Wessberg et al. (1979). In both these studies role play behaviour was 'superior' to naturalistic behaviour (see also Gorecki et al., 1981; Higgins, Frisch and Smith, 1983). It is as if individuals feel more free to act strongly in situations of no real consequence, than when they believe their behaviour has consequences. (This point will be developed in the chapters that follow.) Another related finding is that the only significant positive relationship between role play and *in vivo* (contrived) situations occurs for assertive males (Rakos, Mayers and Schroeder, 1982) where behaviour is, arguably, both already more polarized and less shaped by external contingencies, in individuals of characterological independence. Hence, whether or not there are consequences for behaviour in a 'naturalistic' study rather than in a role play is of less significance to individuals with a more assertive independence.

Finally, to return to the comments of McNamara and Blumer (1982), they find that there are higher levels of correlation between role play and 'naturalistic' events when the criteria are at a very general impressionistic not at a more specific level:

> it appears that role play assessment is best used as a clinical screening device rather than as a method to accurately predict specific behaviours from the role play to its corresponding naturalistic situation. (1982: 539)

and, a

> potential explanation for the modest correlations yielded in validity studies of
> role plays is that rather than being only moderately valid, role plays are an
> accurate reflection of how a subject may behave relative to normal fluctuations
> occurring over time and in different situations. Just as the correlation between
> any two samples of behaviour has been modest, so is the correlation between role
> play and naturalistic behaviour. (1982: 542)

Of particular interest with respect to McNamara and Blumer's comments,
is their criticism that there are few attempts systematically to study how
differences in role play format affect the discriminative ability or ecological
validity of the many types of role play procedure.

Most recently, within this general tradition, Bellack et al. (1990b) have
critically looked at the reliability and validity of role play in the context
of assessing the social competence of psychiatric patients. Their study
examines the validity and usefulness of a role play test, with chronic
psychiatric patients, in discriminating different groups of patients from each
other and from non-patients. They compared other measures of social
functioning and instability. With respect to role play technique, they used
the usual highly limited and minimal induction prompts structure in each of
12 role plays. However, even with such a limited technical format, on this
occasion they do find strong support for the concurrent validity and
reliability of role play in a psychiatric population. Nevertheless, they
comment on three specific limitations of role play tests:

(a) that the areas of behaviour assessed using role play tests relate to very
     narrow areas of social functioning;
(b) very limited data exist on the extent to which these instruments relate
     to important aspects of social behaviour in the community; and
(c) the voluminous literature on role play validity provides mixed results.

None the less they conclude:

> Despite these limitations, role play tests continue to be among the most widely
> used approaches because their positive attributes (e.g. low cost, convenience and
> adaptability) compensate for their limitations. Moreover, it is also widely
> assumed that their validity and utility have been underestimated, because studies
> designed to evaluate their validity have generally addressed the wrong questions,
> used inappropriate criteria, or both. (1990: 248)

Other recent if isolated studies have also produced some modest evidence
of validity. Graham et al. (1989) have looked at the convergent and
discriminant validity of role play used as an assessment tool (that is, the
extent to which such produces results which converge with the results of
other assessment tools used to measure the same behaviour or which
produce results that discriminate) and found these satisfactory in relation to
the assessment of social skill in resisting an alcohol offer. Rohrback et al.
(1987) (the same research team as Graham et al., 1989) claim construct
validity (construct validity – a construct represents a hypothesis, expressed
as an abstract variable – that a variety of behaviour will correlate with

another) for role play assessment methods in relation to alcohol resistance in adolescence. Unusually, here again, is a more thoughtful though not explicated attempt to extend the ecological validity of the role play context by Personalizing (author's terms, see Chapter 7 for full exposition of this concept) the situation for subjects, albeit to a very modest degree, by asking them to imagine a party that they might go to, 'as-if' in real life. Similarly, a study by Chiauzzi et al. (1985) found that personalized role plays, as compared with standardized role plays, of social skills in depressed patients produced more valid indications of actual behaviour and more realistic feelings.

A particularly interesting validity study has been carried out in relation to counsellor training by Gallagher and Hargie (1989), with an even more extended format. These compared extended role played counselling sessions with their 'real' counselling counterparts. Moreover, a direct comparison was made between the same subjects in each condition. They found role play to be valid with respect to both molar (general skills: questioning, reflecting, self-disclosure) and molecular (head-nods, smiles, paralinguistics) aspects of counsellor behaviour. This study is significant and important *because of the closeness of the simulated to 'real' event and because of the extensive period of observation of each event.*

Finally, Ammerman and Hersen (1986) found that by manipulating role play subjects' expectations of confederate behaviour, significant differences in subject behaviour occurred. This result suggests that subjects read the total context of experimental enquiry intelligently and that part of this total context includes preliminary expectations, which, as in real life, structure and construct perception. This is not an explanation offered by the above authors and certainly is tangential in terms of technique. In the studies above, however, there is at least an attempt to come to grips with some elements of technique as they relate to validity, though it is detached from any conceptual grounding. Above all, in relation to the large and varied literature, issues of validity are inconclusively addressed. In Chapter 4 we will consider in more detail the range of techniques that does exist in the extant role play literature, especially where authors make a particular effort to suggest positive guidelines for good practice.

Deliberate manipulations of role play technique

Differences in role play format are rarely picked up by other commentators and, when they do, these take the form of general criticisms or deal with only highly limited aspects of technique; the above studies, with the notable exception of that of Gallagher and Hargie (1989), typically used role plays which consisted of one line verbal prompts, with a demand for single line responses. Moreover, the *in vivo* 'naturalistic' situations were, as frequently in such studies, the product of contrived situations with the subject interacting with a 'stooge'. These types of impoverished role play seem likely to have poor potential for tapping more enduring interactions in the 'real' world. Hence, the problems with clearly establishing validity are by no means surprising.

On a somewhat different but related tack, de Armas and Brigham (1986), in considering individual subjects' differential ability to role play in relationship to validity, argued that the current literature questions the overall validity of brief role play format for assessing social skills, yet such literature has both placed little emphasis on interparticipant variance and neglected the influence of the test taker upon the issue of validity.

> Validational research thus far has operated under the assumption that any discrepancy between natural responding and role-play responding must be due to a lack of role play test criterion validity. Perhaps a portion of the variance can be accounted for by the test takers themselves. It is quite possible that some people may be more amenable to role play testing than others. Although the behavioural literature has not directly addressed this issue, Bellack, Hersen and Turner, 1979 anecdotally report that not all their participants could role play equally well and that some could not 'get into' the roles described. (de Armas and Brigham, 1986: 341–2)

Interestingly, they cite psychodrama as an instance where particular induction procedures are used to involve participants, although they do not adopt or test out such procedures themselves. There are a couple of early studies, and a few more recent ones, that have minimally manipulated induction techniques. Galassi and Galassi (1976) hypothesized that technical differences in role play format would account for significantly different effects. In their own study they compared the response/s made to a *live* or *taped* prompt, and also compared the results of a demand for a *single* versus *multiple* response to the prompt. Differences were found chiefly relating to subject anxiety. Although this is an interesting if somewhat limited result, it must be stressed that the technical manipulations were themselves very limited, as indeed were the role play formats.

Bearing further on tentative explorations of such technical differences are two other validity studies: Kern et al. (1983) and Higgins et al. (1979). In the Higgins et al. study, three conditions were compared: an informed role play where subjects knew which behaviours were to be observed, that is, assertive behaviours; an uninformed role play; and a contrived naturalistic situation. Perhaps not surprisingly, the informed conditions produced the highest assertion levels in subjects, followed by the uninformed role play and lastly the 'naturalistic' situation (see also Chiauzzi et al., 1985). (It is of note that inductions here were uniformly poor, subjects being asked 'to pretend' they were in a particular situation of which they were given the most minimal description.) With respect to technical aspects the Kern study was markedly different in that the role plays 'ran' for an extended time – for three and a half minutes.

Clearly, the extent to which techniques have been manipulated is very limited but there is some evidence of differential effects in direct relation to differential techniques. (An empirical study, reported in Appendix 3, strongly supports this.)

Role play in therapy and treatment

There are two major traditions of psychological treatment that involve role play to a significant degree; the first is psychodrama and the second, broadly speaking, social skills training. Other therapies also use role play and we will touch upon these.

Psychodrama

We have already briefly mentioned Jacob Moreno's work with respect to technique. To attempt to summarize the clinical rationale behind psychodrama and the vast amount and range of psychodramatic clinical work still carried out is beyond the scope of this book. Interested readers are referred to the *Journal of Sociometry* and the journal of *Group Psychotherapy*, and to works by Moreno (1946, 1953, 1959, 1969), Corsini (1966) and Greenberg (1974). Validity *per se*, as has already been discussed, is not an important issue for psychodrama, unless one considers the importance of the reproduction and generation of intrapsychic reality for the protagonist.

The major concepts upon which Moreno's theory of personality and psychotherapy are based are:

1 spontaneity and creativity;
2 situation;
3 tele;
4 catharsis;
5 insight.

For Moreno, therapeutic growth occurs through the expression of repressed material, particularly as it relates to the past, with a strong emphasis upon re-education for the future, which involves the use of the individual's *creative* potential. *Tele* is defined as the non-objectifiable dynamic or relationship between individuals (the feeling that emerges between persons that is not measurable or overtly perceivable but nevertheless is somehow communicated); and *situation* relates to the importance of the experience of the 'here and now', for *awareness* and *cathartic* experience to occur. *Insight*, finally, is a successful restructuring of the perceptual field.

There is, despite tomes of clinical case material and descriptive proselytising, a paucity of empirical and comparative research on the efficacy of psychodrama in comparison to other therapy methods, although a paper by Greenberg and Rice (1981) on the split chair technique is of some research interest in as much as it focuses on a highly specific role play/psychodrama technique and links its utilization to a precise therapeutic process outcome. Comparatively recent papers by Jordan (1985) and Schramski and Harvey (1983), who have discussed the treatment of drug abusers within the correctional environment, indicate discursively the general scope of psychodrama but deal with neither empirical, conceptual nor methodological issues. Moreover, as specific aspects of technique are rarely if ever formally raised with respect to conceptual, methodological or ecological issues, further discussion of psychodrama is not relevant at this point. More general information on psychodrama induction will be covered in Chapter 4.

Rather similar in tone are the clinical works of Johnson (1980a, 1980b), a clinician and drama therapist, who used role play to measure aspects of self-functioning and self-boundary maintenance in schizophrenics. Wilson et al. (1982) also used a form of role play, with some similarities to psychodrama, within the context of regression therapy. Wilson's aim was to provide a re-parenting experience for young schizophrenics. (Regression therapies involve the therapeutic concept of providing an environment in which the patients purportedly return to an earlier developmental stage – usually one in which he or she had difficulties and, therefore, did not negotiate adequately. In such a context role play would involve role playing these earlier stages of the protagonist's history and providing 'new', more appropriate, parenting to renegotiate these problematic stages.) Johnson's work is of some clinical interest, but again there is little concern with broader aspects of using role play, although he does demonstrate a better understanding of some of the practical issues than most. Gestalt therapists also have used role play and/or psychodramatic-type techniques (see Perles, Hefferline and Goodman, 1973) but do not develop these separately as a technical form. Other uses of role play that have strong affinities to improvisational role play or psychodramatic forms are to be found within more general psychotherapeutic approaches and also within experiential professional training packages. The use of role play as a training tool is discussed in a separate section below.

Social skills training

Of greatest familiarity to mainstream clinical psychologists is the role play work within the social skills tradition, where role play is used to simulate interpersonal encounters for the purposes of teaching social skills, assertion and heterosexual skills (see British work emanating from the Oxford Social Skills research, Trower et al., 1977; Yardley, 1979) and an almost entirely independent American tradition involving principally, a focus on hetero-sexual skills and assertion skills. Neither tradition however, is particularly informative with respect to the use of role play itself. Moreover, within these studies, particularly the British social skills packages, there has been a tendency to use role play relatively uncritically, as part of a therapy package, with an assumption that role play has face validity (self-evident validity) as a technique. Although a similar state of affairs exists in relation to the American literature, it is certainly the case that there has been greater concern over issues such as validity, as evidenced by McNamara and Blumer (1982) above. The use of social skills training and assertion training continues to be widespread both in the UK and in North America, and as we shall see below it has widened its application. With respect to all these other applications, role play is used as an integral part of assessment and treatment but is rarely the focus of any technical consideration. The same minimalist techniques persist.

Interestingly of late, and closely tied to the social skills/assertion approaches, there has been an increasing amount of work with children in the area of sexual abuse prevention (both for victims and non-victims). Role play is used here for teaching and assessing the social skills of self-protection (Weist et al., 1993; Harbeck et al., 1992; O'Donohue and Elliott, 1991; Blumberg et al., 1991). At least two other studies in this area of sexual abuse have used role play within a more psychotherapeutic format (Wolf, 1993; Corder et al., 1990). Social skills, using role play, have been increasingly taught to adults with learning disabilities (Valenti-Hein et al., 1994; Foxx and Faw, 1992; Nezu et al., 1991; Muccigrosso, 1994; Sievert et al., 1988; Kelly and Christoff, 1985). Other recent applications of role play methods have included the treatment of trichotillomania (Rothbaum, 1992); the teaching of problem-solving strategies with chemically dependent women (Marr and Fairchild, 1993); and a variety of treatment interventions with children with special categories of difficulty: for example, Rasing (1993) uses role play to teach social behaviour to the hearing impaired. Social skills training is used increasingly within correctional environments (Jupp and Griffiths, 1990; Frederickson and Simms, 1990).

Other more idiosyncratic uses of role play have emerged, such as those found within Rational Emotive Therapy approaches (Smith, T.W., 1983), but these tend to be rather *ad hoc* and neither integral nor essential to the specific therapy approach. A variety of rather non-specific role play procedures which fall somewhere between social skills training, psychodrama and general drama therapy approaches, include: drama therapy with the learning disabled (Waite, 1993); job interview training with the learning disabled (Kelly and Christoff, 1985); role play to enhance expressive experience with the elderly (Sheikh et al., 1993; Huddleston, 1989), to explore perceived communication rules impeding communications between the elderly in an institution (Kaakinen, 1992) and to train to overcome nocturnal enuresis (Abe et al., 1988); in Gestalt therapy with abused children (Marr and Fairchild, 1993); training in social perspective training with socially maladjusted children (Chalmers and Townsend, 1990); to teach parenting skills (Knapp and Deluty, 1989); Cunningham (1985); as a pre-operative intervention to reduce anxiety in children (Demarest et al., 1984); counselling with family members of seropositive haemophiliacs (Greenblat et al., 1989); discrete communicating skills taught to head trauma patients (Ehrlich and Sipes, 1985); spouse aided therapy (Badenoch and Fisher, 1984) for persistent psychiatric disorders; exploration of family myths in family therapy (Bagarozzi and Anderson, 1982); and social anxiety training effects on erectile dysfunction (Reynolds et al., 1981). Again, these reported studies are not characterized by either evidence of methodological or technical sophistication.

The use of role play as a training tool

Role play is commonly used to train therapists, counsellors, social workers and teachers. A general picture here emerges of users having relatively greater sensitivity to the procedures of role play and the needs of role players. Thus there is a general but usually implicit concern with ecological validity; but there is no theoretical or systematic consideration, depth or thoroughness, and increased sensitivity is far from universal. In reports of such role play activities there is an overwhelming assumption that we all know what we are talking about when we mention role play. Occasionally hints emerge, about aspects of induction or technique, that suggest the authors might know a thing or two about good practice, but these are rarely articulated fully or made explicit. Moreover, there is no evidence of a critical stance towards the question of whether role play is being appropriately or inappropriately utilized.

Jessee and L'Abale (1981) describe using role play to teach clinical professionals how to increase their accuracy in understanding families. Trainees role play different family members, with the stated intention of countering the claims that professionals often tend to overpathologize families. Role play is used here within a long-term programme teaching clinical skills. Their aims suggest that the authors are unlikely to be satisfied with highly *stereotyped* role playing, but this can only be inferred as there is no explicit discussion of the technical requirements of facilitating role play. Fulmer (1983) has similarly used role play to create simulated families, working through a series of developmental, structured and systemic exercises – but again without specifics on technique. Le Unes (1984), in order to overcome any concerns about less able role players within training role plays, actually used trained drama students to enact the role of patients. These were charged explicitly with incorporating as many diagnostic signs and symptoms *as realistic*, in order that students learning about abnormal psychology could learn diagnostic interview skills. Similarly, Roman and Porter (1978) used scripted role plays to train group therapists with respect to theoretical and clinical issues. Clearly, here, the provision of a very definite script provided a demonstration of teaching points, in a highly structured and focused manner. This is suggestive of clearer technical concern and competence, but again the issue is not explicity dealt with. Holmes (1988) used role play to teach nurses and social workers about transference and countertransference, finding other traditional teaching methods unsuccessful, particularly because of the poor quality of recording of clinical events by such students. Klosinski, 1991 also used psychodramatic role play to train psychotherapists in sensitivity to the transference and countertransference issues involved in working with children and adolescents; and Cross and Gaffney (1984) used role play as a training technique for experienced therapists having difficulty with particular clients. Sterling and Bugental (1993) have used role play in psychotherapy supervision in order to overcome therapists' tendency to produce overly detached descriptions of clients. Moore (1984) has used relatively open-ended role plays to teach social workers to work with the terminally ill, specifically with a view to sensitizing individuals. Klingman (1983), again with a much more structured approach, used a rule-structured games model for teachers involved in death education to use with pupils in schools.

Other uses of role play have included the following. Keane et al., 1982 (training) and Schaffer and Hasegawa (1984) used role plays both as *part* of a training package and in order *to assess the effects* of a training package. McIntyre et al. (1983) used the typical minimal form of role play vignette – of one sentence responses required to minimal prompts – to assess the effectiveness of assertion training in nurses; and Eders and Smit (1992) have used role play to assess the effectiveness of a skills training programme for residential child care workers. Increasingly medical training programmes have utilized role play for consultation training (Kaaya et al., 1992; Smith and Hasnip, 1991; Mansfield, 1991; Gask et al., 1989; Baluk and O'Neill, 1990). Swink (1984) used role play with police officers to teach them interviewing skills and increased problem-solving skills. Rosnow (1990) used role plays to teach research ethics. Glenn et al. (1982) have used role play to teach problem-solving skills to children. Wehrenberg (1986), within ergonomics, describes utilizing role play for training pilots in simulation exercises; Armstrong (1982), an organizational psychologist, describes using role play to implement change in organizations – to illustrate problems to be dealt with and to evaluate individuals' successs in effecting organizational change (via participation in 14 structured situational role plays). None of the above studies is characterized by any interest in validity or in techniques of achieving it.

Although the sources cited above are drawn from the more accessible and available literature on the use of role play, it is evident that role play is commonly and widely used. Many individuals in professional training situations or involved in alternative education programmes for re-learning skills have come into contact with some form of role play, albeit of varying degrees of structure and formality. A huge variety of uses and types of role play are evidenced by the above, however, notwithstanding the obvious versatility and potential of role play, all that seems to bind the plethora and variety of such activities is the umbrella term 'role play'. The term is carelessly used by most, assuming the reader understands its implications, and agrees its usefulness and validity, without any attempt being made formally to define its meaning and the techniques involved. The lack of technical and methodological focus is clearly almost universal. However, some explicit technical guidelines have occasionally been provided, or tentatively offered, and it is to these we now turn.

4

Role Play Practice Today: Focusing Specifically on Technique

As indicated in Chapter 3, an exhaustive review of research utilizing role play, within social and clinical research, together with a substantial review of role play in clinical assessment and therapies, reveals very little detail about techniques used. Indeed, given the overwhelming lack of comment upon technique, one might reasonably infer that the vast utilization of role play is highly unsophisticated and unreflective. In this chapter, we will focus upon the small amount of direct information that does exist on technique, considering the type and range of techniques used over the past twenty years. Any technical guidelines that explicitly or incidentally may emerge, or which may be inferred, will be highlighted and their limitations considered.

Role play techniques in social psychology

Within social psychology, techniques have usually been very roughly differentiated. Hence role plays have been distinguished simply as follows:

(a) performed or imagined (passive or active) (Hamilton, 1976)
(b) scripted or improvised (Hamilton, 1976)
(c) involving one individual or many
(d) participants being required to 'play' themselves or somebody else
(e) participants being required to play themselves under a familiar or unfamiliar set of circumstances
(f) stooges may or may not be used in role plays – and sometimes are used as *agent provocateurs*
(g) subjects may be prebriefed and deceived, or prebriefed and not deceived, or not prebriefed at all
(h) scenario inductions can involve one line prompts or several
(i) participants may be constrained into a highly structured-response format or, alternatively, be given a free response format.

Although such a schema is useful, further detail on precise aspects of technique is generally lacking, and critical reflection is entirely absent. A few more detailed comments are found within the social psychology debate of the 1970s, however, such comments relate to rather isolated, *ad hoc* theoretical factors and are on such a general level as to give no sound methodological guidelines for setting up role plays. Thus, typically, Hamilton (1976) could generalize that both the *form and content* of role plays may affect experimental realism, and Alexander and Scriven (1977) could comment upon the general existence of poor induction techniques, but both studies then totally failed to address the matter of technique in any further detail. Somewhat more detailed, albeit limited comments, were provided by the following few social psychologist proponents of role play – although again these lack development. Baron (1977) suggested that some level of *temporal build up* might be useful for role playing some social behaviours, in order to allow *complexity* to develop; Geller (1978) suggested enhancing role players' involvement through *modelling* procedures, by observing 'good' role plays on videotape (which was also an earlier 'performance-concept' based solution proposed by Goldstein, 1973). (It is argued that this latter strategy is particularly problematic as the distinct views of observers and performers/participants are not reconciled within such a strategy – see Chapters 2 and 8 on the radically different views of these two groups with respect to the perception of reality and involvement.)

Mixon (1977), a major authority on the use of role play, has very little to say on the subject of technique, despite providing a schema for the description of different kinds of role play (where he also distinguishes between active and passive role plays, and between role plays where the individual plays a particular character or plays 'Everyman'). He did, however, propose avoiding artificiality by *specifying openly to participants the beliefs necessary* for the role play context, although further detail is not provided. Darroch and Steiner (1970) considered role plays would be more successful if *role players only played themselves*, hence avoiding the difficulty of taking on another 'character'; and Forward et al. (1976), after Sarbin, suggested that the *construction of roles must be in sufficient detail that common meanings might be inferred.*

From these skeleton guidelines one can infer the concerns of the authors, and in many cases these concerns are made quite explicit. They are, above all, trying to deal with issues of how to get subjects involved or engaged in the imaginary action and/or how to generate a 'realistic' role play. However, these suggested outline techniques have no conceptual linkages, nor are they developed in any detail.

Hendrick (1977) also drew attention to the '*stage setting*', to the importance of appropriately setting the scene to facilitate a sense of reality. Słoma (1983) explicitly refers to theatre practice with respect to induction technique, and focuses upon the lack of *attention to theatrical elements* in role plays; he advocates attention to 'props', clothing and physical surroundings. Lastly, Forward et al. (1976) direct attention to the need to assess the *role play skills of individual subjects* with a view to selection of only those who have good skills.

Almost all other technical considerations revolved exclusively around issues of whether or not to deceive *role players* with respect to the intentions of the role play instigator (for a review, see Ginsberg, 1979). This will be argued later to be a futile and misplaced task. However, most *role play* proponents are absolutely clear that deception is not a useful aid to involving role play participants, and is a breach of the trust necessary for full commitment to role playing. Baron (1977) also speaks of the importance of a *collaborative relationship with the subject.* Yet *deception paradigms continue.* Despite the contentious debates about the use of deception in role plays begun in the 1970s and still continuing – with the major role play proponents arguing vehemently against deception for both methodological and ethical reasons – recent role play experimental studies still employ deception as part of their methodologies. For example, Rhodewalt and Agustsdottir (1986) misled subjects in role play interviews into believing that stooge-interviewers believed the interviews to be real; Gallagher and Hargie (1989) deceived interviewers so that they were unaware that 'interviewees' were role playing; Blumberg and Hokanson (1983) also employed deception with subjects in an experiment on the effects of different interpersonal behaviour on depressed and non-depressed individuals. As will be argued elsewhere (see Chapter 6), the question of deception is not necessarily central to role play technique, but it is important in relation to more general methodological concerns.

Of those social psychologists who have specifically used role plays for *replications* of 'classic' experiments, technique is, as far as one can gather from their written accounts, poorly developed and extremely various. Glimpses of aspects of useful technique albeit used unreflectively do, however, occasionally arise. For example, Manstead (1979; see also Chapter 3), in replicating the Schachter and Singer experiments, albeit within a 'passive' role play format, used an induction procedure which involved *a second person form of address to the subject.* This unwitting strategy (which will later be considered and amplified see Chapter 7) seems likely to have helped the 'subjects' in the task of engaging with the objects of the role play in an apparently successful manner. Both O'Leary et al. (1987) and Mixon (1972) replicated Milgram's, 1963 now infamous experiments on conformity and obedience. In the O'Leary et al. experiment (1987) subjects enacted the whole experiment, with the exception that they were 'informed subjects' asked to act 'as-if' they were uninformed subjects. Unfortunately, working counter to an unusually full and detailed induction here is a form of words that underlines the conditionality of the event – *'imagine* that', 'what you think you *would* have if', *'if you had'* in fact taken part – which appears to run throughout the role play process. (The problems of employing 'conditionality' versus 'actuality' within induction strategies are dealt with fully in Chapter 7.)

A very few psychologists have been explicitly concerned, albeit to a limited extent, with the *epistemology of role plays* and have provided thoughtful views. Bem (1968), a well regarded and influential experimental social psychologist writing earlier on the epistemological status of inter-personal simulations, was concerned that role play replications should not be viewed as requiring identicalness with target experiments, but that the validity of a role play replication procedure lay in its achieving the same functions as the target experiment in terms of the *process* replicated. This goes a good deal further than the criterion of outcome equivalence that Mixon puts forward. Bem stated:

> 'a successful simulation thus implies the same thing that a successful computer simulation implies; namely, that the process model embodied in the 'program' is functionally equivalent to the process being simulated'. (1968: 273)

Others concerned directly with epistemological considerations have been Ginsberg (1979), Słoma (1983) and McNamara and Blumer (1982). Ginsberg, in an excellent article concerning broad methodological issues and role play, and grounded in a radical critique, stated that 'the effective use of role play technique requires a recognition of various questions in order to adopt a technique on a rational basis.' (1979: 127). He advocated consideration of the purpose of the simulation with respect to the distinction between verification and exploration tasks. He specifically drew particular attention to that which is being precluded in the simulation/verification model of social processes – attention to *detail, possible sources of ambiguity, time available, and to the enacted 'speed' of the episode.* He is also critical of the deception versus non-deception confusion surrounding role play controversies. Słoma (1983), a Polish social psychologist, also takes a more radical social psychological stance and in an interesting article advocates fully informing participants as collaborators, in keeping with his criticisms of traditional methodology in the social psychology experiment.

The Stanford Prison Study – a case study critique

Of all the replication studies carried out to date this one by Haney et al. (1973) remains the most frequently cited example of a simulation *par excellence.* Yet it is the study which most clearly demonstrates problematic methodological practice, leading to unwarranted conclusions. Because of both these factors, and because an extensive amount of detail about role play procedures has been put forward by Haney et al. (1973), this is a particularly useful study to consider in detail.

In this study an attempt was made to simulate an American penal establishment to test the general hypothesis that brutality lies in, and is engendered by, the nature of the institution rather than in the natures of the guards and prisoners who people the institution. Volunteer subjects, who had agreed to take part in a prison simulation for up to two weeks, were screened and selected for their 'normality' in terms of their personality traits and social history and were randomly assigned to be prisoners or guards. The basement of the Stanford psychology department was temporarily converted into a 'prison' for this experiment, with prefabricated walls and real prison doors but volunteers were '[N]either group received any specific training in these roles' (Zimbardo, 1974: 244).

Guards were introduced to their task on the day preceding the commencement of the role play. They were provided with uniforms, including mirror sunglasses which prevented eye contact. Their task was summarily presented, by the researchers, as the running of the prison and the containment of the prisoners; no further details were given. With regard to the experiment, they were told that it was the prisoners who were under observation and not themselves. It is to be emphasized that no personal information was given or elicited with regard to the 'parts' they were to 'play'. Further, all the guards, as indeed all the participants were 'initially . . . strangers to each other, a selection procedure taken to avoid the disruption of any pre-existing friendship patterns and to mitigate against any transfer into the experimental situation of previously established relationships or patterns of behaviour' (Haney et al., 1973: 73). Unlike the guards, who had some overt if minimal warm-up to the 'as-if' event, the prisoners were covertly inducted without their conscious co-operation. For the sake of 'realism', they were arrested in the early hours of the morning, on false burglary charges, by members of the city police who were co-operating with the experimenters. The prisoners were then subjected to police interrogation and taken, blindfolded, to the simulated prison. Prisoner subjects' queries to police concerning the relationship of the arrest to the experiment were frustrated and ignored by the police. Prisoners were then stripped, body searched, deloused, given numbers for identification purposes and issued with a smock (no trousers, no underwear). In this simulated prison were supposedly established

> functional equivalents [compare Bem, 1968] for the activities and experiences of actual prison life which were then expected to produce qualitatively similar psychological reactions in our subjects' feelings of power and powerlessness, of control and oppression, of satisfaction and frustration, of arbitrary rule and resistance to authority, of status and anonymity, of machismo and emasculation. (Haney et al., 1973: 72)

The experiment continued in this manner for a week until it was deemed necessary to prematurely terminate it due to the ensuing emotional disturbances among the participants, particularly among the prisoners. The data collected came from pre-test and post-test interviews and questionnaires, and – most importantly – from video and audio recordings of the events themselves. The researchers' findings referred to the loss of identity experienced by prisoners, their passivity, depression, and psychopathological and psychosomatic symptoms. The guards were reported to have become brutal, aggressive, arbitrary authoritarians with a strong group identity. Overall, the hypotheses were deemed to be strongly supported and the resulting US national interest was considerable – even resulting in some changes to prison induction procedures (Haney et al., 1973).

Despite its laudable intent and indeed its partial success in getting the penal system critically to evaluate its procedures in prisons, the study is seriously flawed in terms of its role play methodology. Considered in general methodological terms, the Haney study can be viewed as an example of what both Rychlak (1977) and Gergen (1978) have called 'demonstrative science': that is, a hypothesis is not truly tested but an appropriate context is chosen that will inevitably demonstrate the hypothesis to be true. Thus the experimenters in this study decided on the characteristics *they felt* to be most significant in the penal setting, and then designed events (see quote above from Haney et al., 1973: 72) *to create* these characteristics. They further denied to the simulation information such as individual biographies – which might have had a bearing on hypotheses counter to their own, for example the importance of dispositional traits in prisoners or guards. The demand characteristics of such a study are evident. The only pieces of information that the participants have to go on are those set up by the experimenters, who pay a great deal of attention to creating stereotypogenic cues by means of uniforms, humiliating body searches and so on but do not provide or facilitate any counters-stereotypical information such as personal biographies. If they argue, as they do at the beginning of the study, that a lay person would generally account for brutality in prisons by attributing it to the kinds of people imprisoned and working there, it does not take a great stretch of the imagination to question whether their 'role players' – provided with minimal yet stereotypical cues and with no specific 'role' information – might not make the similar inference (at whatever level of awareness) that their expected roles must necessarily be stereotypical and brutal. The further interaction of one complementary 'role' with another, guard on inmate, would obviously heighten this tendency.

The lack of induction detail (see Chapter 7 on particularization) that is addressed below as a technical problem is also related to the lack of mundane reality in the Stanford experiment; in turn, this is related to the demand characteristics described above. For example, failure to give participants particular information about their 'part' says a great deal about the experimenters' construction of a 'real' prison. Are we to suppose – and indeed were the experimental subjects to suppose – that prisoners normally enter prison devoid of personal identities, histories, etc., and that they enter a prison in which there is no subculture and where every prisoner or guard has the same historical status, that is, on their first day in a prison environment? Real prisons have well-established subcultures within them. Whatever the designed anonymity of the prison culture, in actuality it is full of prisoners with identities within a system that is the sociological result of certain antecedent events – events that the prisoners are generally aware of and have evidently contributed to. A great deal of a prison day is filled with trivia rather than epic emotional displays and experiences. Are we also to suppose that the Big Brother tactics of early morning surprise arrests on false charges, refusal of the arresting authorities to assert the reality or unreality of the situation, blindfolded transportation to an unknown destination and all while merely on remand, are normal practices?

It might be argued that the serious emotional disturbance of the prisoners cannot be accounted for merely by demand characteristics. Yet there are other features of the experiment that do account for this. These suggest that the behaviour exhibited was a very particular kind of acting out caused by the dynamics of the experimental situation and heightened by the framing, albeit ambiguous, of the event as an experiment of short duration with the concomitant expectation that there are no consequences for the participants in the mundane world. Real confusion must have been engendered since the normally impervious experimental frame was violated. The intrusion of the city police into the private lives of the 'prisoners' was mundanely real and yet, because they knew they were possibly about to take place in a simulation, ambiguous. Their attempts to clarify the status of this arrest were frustrated, adding to their real confusion and anxiety. In short, participants were neither entirely within the 'known' frame of mundane reality nor in role play ('as-if') reality. By the time they fully realized that they were indeed in an experiment, their feelings towards the experimenters must have been complicated and probably antagonistic. Further, it is likely that 'inmates' would have identified the guards with the experimenters (as indeed the guards themselves probably did), and that their expectations of the further behaviour of the experimenters would have made them insecure and anxious. So within the frame of the prisoner-participant's mundane experience, severe anxieties had been raised which, in all likelihood, did not relate to the features of the simulated prison but to the mundane characteristics of the total experimental situation. Further, given the constraints on behaviour established by demand characteristics, it is not surprising that these prisoner-participants acted out in an emotional, immature and polarized fashion if only to establish identities for themselves in this highly stereotypical yet ambiguous situation.

An analogy will perhaps serve to make this process clearer. Imagine a grown-up playing monsters with a child. The child pretends fear. The game continues. The child doubts the benevolence of the adult and the identity of the adult/monster and requests the game to stop. The adult persists. The child, torn between play excitement and growing fear concerning which is the 'real' situation, becomes hysterical. The adult stops and comforts the child: 'It was only a game'. Here it can be clearly seen that part of the child's fear emerges from a 'real' lack of control of the situation. There is a double bind because it is only supposed to be a game, the adult is known to be good, and yet the consequences of the game are unpleasant. There are multiple non-game dilemmas which can be read into this situation as there are in the Stanford Prison situation.

In Chapter 7 we consider technical changes that might have provided a more ecologically valid setting and avoided some of the difficulties that arose from this challenging but sometimes dubious methodology.

In contradistinction, another social psychologist, Smith, J.L. (1975), in a much less ambitious and less well known but more manageable study, provided an unusual degree of synthesis of techniques and research purposes, in an excellent and coherent set of role play games constructed for the expressed and limited purpose of exploring interpersonal strategies used in situations where one person tries to change the attitude of another. The techniques described are a good example of cautiously *tailoring techniques to highly circumscribed aims and foci.* Smith's methods are clearly and explicitly orientated towards *discovery rather than verification.* Moreover, he limited his enquiry to a highly specific area of behaviour, yet allowed complex behaviours to emerge between subjects; and indeed then paid close attention to the technique needed here. He started with a clear model of social cognition against which to explore and discover the socio-cognitive strategies used by individuals in attempts to persuade others to change their attitudes.

By having such a clear focus Smith, J.L. (1975) seems to have been able to engender appropriate role play techniques, having shown a thoughtful and logical concern for induction procedures that were congruent with his research intentions. Thus, he provided *background information to subjects, that focused upon the research problem and was not opaque to those subjects* – that is, they were given the explicit task of changing another character's attitude. Each set of background information was provided to subjects by the experimenter, based on his clear stated intentions, for the precise purpose of eliciting beliefs, attitudes and strategies related to attempts to change 'the other'. The information did not preclude stereotypical assumptions but attempted to avoid evident stereotypicality by a *deliberate use of a certain degree of ambiguity,* hence: 'the characters or roles were specified extremely vaguely so as to encourage the actors to fall back upon their own experience for character details' (Smith, J.L., 1975: 72). This was coupled with an *induction 'demand' that the subjects fill out the details of their characters themselves* (see Chapter 7 on Personalization). Indeed, before the enactment subjects were required to describe their own characters to the experimenter. Smith, unusually, reflected clearly and explicitly upon his *need to specify detail,* and made a judged choice. The enactment was then left to be improvised by subjects, with them having been given a specific task. Interestingly Smith, aware of the importance of actor involvement, remarked that evidence for such involvement was to be found in the fact that some subjects said they personally would have changed their attitude, but could not because their character would not have.

An opportunity seems to have emerged here which was not taken up by Smith (but then it did not fall within his stated remit): the interesting epistemological question of the extent to which the strategies used, and the content of decisions made, 'belonged' to the subject or to their character. It also raises the question of the degree to which each subject can successfully take on another 'character' and, indeed, what such 'success' means.

No claims are made by Smith that this is a 'naturalistic' task, or that it is a highly generalizable one, however, it may be felt that it has a good deal more validity than either a minimalist conventional experiment or an overly-ambitious replication, such as the Haney et al. (1973) study above. But Smith (1975) did demonstrate that various identifiable strategies of persuasion etc. are used, which are consistent with differing psychological theories. This study is clearly a rare example of a worthwhile exploratory endeavour, with good attention to technique, on which future research might build – within either further exploratory or verification modes.

Role play techniques in clinical psychology

The earliest common use of role play technique within clinical work (apart from psychodrama and fixed role therapy, which we will go on to consider) acrose within a behavioural paradigm. Wolpe, 1969 recommended the use of role play techniques with respect to the extinction of anxiety-conditioned responses, although he gave almost no detail of technique and offered no awareness of any potential difficulties of application. Most commonly, behavioural role play techniques were taken up in the areas of social skills and assertion training. Goldstein (1973), a clinician reviewing this use of role play, commented upon the general paucity of technique used within the assertion training skills area; particularly where role play was not *integrated with modelling the target behaviour, or where information was insufficient to compensate for clients' deficit skills.* In such cases, Goldstein (1973) observed that role plays typically intended to last for ten minutes lasted for only one minute. He concluded that role play was useful for behaviour rehearsal, but only where there was '*sufficient information and modelling material of a vivid, detailed, repetitive and rewarded nature*' (1973). He cited the following as examples of similar successful integrated approaches: Lazarus (1966), Higgins, Ivey and Uhleman (cited in Goldstein, 1973), and McFall and Marston (1970).

This sort of combination of role playing, instruction, modelling and behavioural rehearsal was also typical of the Oxford, Littlemore Social Skills training programme (Trower et al., 1977) in which the author was closely involved, and which has been profoundly influential in British mainstream clinical practice. Here, role plays of considerable length used for diagnostic and rehearsal purposes, were integrated with didactic teaching and modelling procedures, providing the cognitive and behavioural information which other clinical and research role play procedures appeared to neglect. However, even here, almost no explicit systematic account was given of role play technique *per se*; despite the fact that Yardley-Matwiejczuk introduced highly detailed warm-up procedures, as part of standard practice, to Littlemore social skills training. These techniques were not documented, not reflected upon at that time (see Trower et al., 1977) and are not part of derivative social skills training procedures, as they are generally used.

For the vast majority of researchers using role play – whether within social or clinical psychology, and whether using role play for assessment, for treatment, or for the manipulation of variables – all the techniques used tend to fall within a category that one might term *minimalist*. That is, a minimal scenario is devised which is thought most appropriate to the demonstration of a discrete behaviour, most commonly assertion behaviours. (The largest coherent group of researchers here have investigated assertion behaviours, see below.) Hence, the scenario is described in two or three short sentences to the patient to be assessed, or to the subject being observed, through a variety of presentational forms, for example, written, audio- or video-taped, via an intercom system, or a face-to-face briefing. Having set the scene, a confederate will typically offer a one-line prompt, and the subject is expected to provided a one-line response.

Researchers of note who have used minimalist role play techniques, particularly within clinical research include: Bellack et al. (1979a); Eisler et al. (1975); Bellack et al. (1979a); de Armas and Brigham (1986), Fielder and Beach (1978); McFall and Lillesand (1971); Bordewick and Bornstein (1980); Bourque and Ladouceur (1979); McIntyre et al. (1983); Rice and Josefowitz (1983); Rakos et al. (1982); Rohrback et al. (1987); Hersen et al. (1980); Ammerman and Hersen (1986).

Within such minimalist approaches, there is an attempt to standardize context, and to seek to reduce an interaction to a crystallized, supposedly normative, moment of measurable assertive behaviour. The complexity of a given interactional context is reduced; and no attempt is made to create ecological validity, within which might be found a complex interplay of social and personal factors. What is sought by such researchers is merely a lead into a specific, controllable, and supposedly consensually identifiable, act of behaviour the level of assertion in which may be determined by external judges. Induction, in the sense of engaging the subject in a meaningful way, is not a consideration here. The meaning of the induction narrative is believed to be self-evident, and to have a uniform set of connotations for participants, observers, researchers and clinicians alike.

However, using the same basic techniques, the following researchers have made some minor adjustments to minimalist strategy. Bellack et al. (1990b) used three prompts and demanded three responses, having allowed a 30-second period for the subject to imagine the scene, following a short narrative induction. Gorecki et al. (1981) and Hovrath (1984) also allowed a longer period of time for subjects to imagine the situation. Galassi and Galassi (1976) deliberately manipulated two aspects of technique with respect to whether the prompt was live or audio-taped, and whether a single or multiple response was demanded of subjects. Results here are somewhat ambiguous, but it is of note that within this design the confederates were not allowed to interrupt a subject responding, which of course is somewhat restrictive of and distinct from mundane interaction and discourse, and seems likely to have a stultifying effect.

Even more distinctively, Kern (1982) used an *extended* three and a half minute improvised role play, comparing it with the minimal response role play types discussed above. Kern (1982) found that the extended role-play tests were superior to brief role plays but also that more naturalistic replications of situations specifically previously encountered by subjects were superior to extended non-personal role plays. McReynolds et al.

(1981), assessing interpersonal styles, used a technique which followed on from the minimalist format but provided a brief, scripted induction dialogue for both subject and confederate. An improvisational period was then allowed which was only terminated when the experimenter felt that the response patterns of the subject had become fully evident or when the role play ran dry – typically within 10–20 interchanges. Even more unusual and considered was the approach adopted by Klein (1982) in exploring the role of briefing information in relation to dental distress. Although using a 'passive imagination' format, Klein provided a good example of attention to detail (see also Chapter 7 on Particularization) via an *enrichment* technique, in which great attention was paid to context setting, by getting each subject *to focus on imaginary contextual details, including highly specific detail about impacts upon the senses.*

Quite distinct from the above developments and returning to the therapy situation *per se*, George Kelly (1955a, 1955b) the creator and proponent of Construct Theory Psychology has provided a highly specific form of role play technique – **Fixed Role Therapy** (FRT) – which has continued to be used by clinicians influenced by construct theory. Here, given an emphasis on the individual client as existing in a world of his or her own cognitive elaboration and construction, the therapeutic emphasis has been on loosening up constructs and construct systems to allow new cognitive experiences, and thus new behaviours, to emerge. The therapist, with the client's co-operation, aims to change an important aspect of interpersonal functioning, by positing a set of new and challenging constructs through which the client is to view both self and the world. This is formally constructed by the therapist or by a team of therapists. A new characterological description, based on new or shifted constructs, is detailed and presented to the client. The client is then enjoined to act according to this role on a continuous basis in his or her everyday dealings with the world for a prescribed period of time. Preliminary rehearsals are undertaken with the therapist; Kelly is careful to assert that where the client does not have enough information to comfortably enact the fixed role, rehearsals of a highly specific nature are needed.

Interestingly and uniquely here, the usual 'safe' boundaries of a separate space for role play – removing the 'experiment' from real consequences in the social world – are broken down, as the individual is required to bring their own 'imaginary projections' into the mundane participant world. (The latter is a strategy employed as a literary device in Rheinhart's novel, *The Diceman*, 1972, taking this idea to its extreme with rather sensational and horrifying consequences.) Such a use would seem to force a definition of the purpose of role play outside the definition used in this text (see also Chapter 6), which states that role play almost always involves an abrogation of real-life consequences. However, as will later be argued, real consequences are always a possibility whatever the intention of the role play inductors. And within FRT some ambiguity is evident in the extent to which 'real' consequences are expected, although there is no doubt that the individual client here is encouraged to still believe that there is a boundary to such behaviour and limited consequences, in that the behaviour can easily be disowned after the event by clients, as a prescribed part of their therapy – particularly as the therapist takes responsibility for the overall 'script' or 'plot'. Needless to say, disowning the consequences of Fixed Role enactment may not be sufficient for those who are on the receiving end of such 'fixed-role' behaviour.

Apart from the stipulation that detailed rehearsal may be needed, together with the provision of clear guidelines for therapists on how to formulate the new character, based on construct theory, Kelly (1955a, 1955b) provides no further details about ensuing efficacious role playing More recently, McNamara and Blumer (1982), addressing role playing in clinical psychology research, especially social skills training, have much to say of general technical relevance to other practitioners and researchers. Their major explicit concern is that of ecological validity; that is, that role plays should be experienced by participants as having subjective or personal validity. Their proposition was that all such research exists ecologically within an interaction effect, based on the type of setting of the role play and on the procedural aspects of role plays. Unfortunately, they do not provide detailed argument or detailed guidelines for action, but their criticisms do have action implications. Moreover, it is suggested that participants need to mentally prepare, as might actors, and that participants might monitor their own behaviour in the 'natural' environment, so that they might model this 'natural' behaviour more naturally.

Explicit guidelines for good practice within the applied field

A variety of writers who have used role plays in more applied settings have provided *ad hoc* guidelines for role plays, although, as has been stated, none of these emerge from any theoretical framework. For example, Jessee and L'Abale (1981), training professionals in family therapy, warn against *overpathologizing clients* when role playing them. They note the tendency for professionals in role playing clients to characterize them by emphasizing their pathology rather than their ordinariness; they therefore deliberately introduce specific counters to this tendency into their inductions, but do not detail these methods. Gabriel (1982), in the training of child welfare professionals, offers the following guidelines in an attempt to steer well clear of psychotherapeutic intent, and to focus on more practical core professional skills with relatively unsophisticated workers:

- Not to use real names
- Involve participants in the development of role descriptions
- Indicate time limits to participants and allow no longer than 15 minutes
- Use volunteers for role plays

- Introduce role plays
- Ensure a follow-up discussion

Although clearly rather superficial and undetailed guidelines, these indicate the author's concern with overinvolvement of participants, and the clear need for structure and feedback as a safety mechanism.

Swink et al. (1984) describing the sensitivity training of police officers in relation to crises situations, clearly and purposefully sets up role plays which involve giving the officers *only the amount of information they would be likely to have in the mundane situation itself*. This is followed by a much more didactic and detailed analysis of these situations and their typical antecedent conditions (in order to enrich the officers' understanding of social psychological phenomena).

Simulation and games techniques

Distinct from all the above, however, by dint of their thoughtful and practical sophistication, are the simulation and games literature contributions by Benson et al. (1972), de Leon (1975) and de Weerd (1974). These contributions reflect a realistic, practical understanding of many of the technical issues that need to be addressed if one is to produce a quality role play. There is also a rare recognition that techniques have epistemological implications; for example, 'game culture will always reflect some complex interaction between the prior beliefs brought to the game by the participants and the scenario postulated by the simulator' (Benson et al., 1972) and 'the scenario is a statement of assumptions about the operating environment of the particular system' (de Leon, 1975, quoting Brown, 1968).

Benson et al. (1972), who dealt mostly with diplomacy and war games, itemizes and details basic considerations for the design of simulations. These comprise: the degree of control to be exercised by the simulator; the number of issues or problems to be addressed; the question of whether an instigator induces a crisis or leaves a simulation to run its own course; the purpose of the simulation; the time available; and the choice of participants.

De Weerd (1974), in similar vein, focuses upon: the skills of the player; the credibility of the scenario; the level of focus of the data; the data source; decisions concerning who controls the design; questions of what scenario information to omit; and a recommendation that events played are neither too close nor too far from the participants' own experience. He is emphatic that it is important to establish boundaries and to establish a rich context with due regard to the selection of information.

Finally, of this group, de Leon reiterates much of de Weerd's design elements and additionally focuses upon: the level of knowledge and gaming experience of the participants; the need to guard against overloading with detail; and the guarding against using simulations as mere demonstrative vehicles for the simulators' prejudices. The purpose of a simulation, for de Leon, is not perfect prediction but the generation of alternative options by participants, a view which commands a good deal of sympathy here. Lauffer (1973), who is also markedly concerned with context setting, states that these should reflect historical and social realities. In considering the level of information to be given to players, he suggests that the question must be asked as to what information the 'real' person in the 'real' situation would have. Lauffer is also of the view that a given scenario reflects the designer's view of the world and thus, to that extent, is limited.

Common to the above simulation and games views are the following:

(a) the importance of functional equivalence in simulation;
(b) the importance of knowing/defining the purpose of a role play;
(c) the question of the amount of appropriate detail and knowledge to be made available to participants;
(d) the importance of contextualizing;
(e) the importance of temporality;
(f) the degree of control enjoyed by the instigator;
(g) the number of issues to be addressed through the role play;
(h) the setting of boundaries;
(i) the suitability and type of participant;
(j) the external/physical setting and environment.

Although not addressing these issues systematically, comprehensively or in great detail, it will be seen that there is a substantial degree of compatability with the methdological concerns raised in the formal description of role play activity put forward in this book (see Chapters 6, 7 and 8).

Other related studies

Snippets of useful ideas are scattered throughout the plethora of published studies within various areas of education, therapist training, and occupational and organizational training. Some of these ideas echo across this varied literature.

Oppelaar et al. (1983), provided a commendable emphasis on *training confederates* in highly specific, distinct and detailed 'roles' for the purpose of teaching doctors clinical examination interview skills. Similarly, Blumberg and Hokanson (1983) trained confederates for 16 hours each; Bourque and Ladouceur (1979) trained confederates for five hours each; Schramski and Harvey (1983) trained confederates for 10 hours each. Clearly such a level of training reduces the variability of the behaviours of the confederates and allows for the emergence of targeted teaching points. Such specific training is likely to be useful only where highly specific circumscribed skills are to be elicited from and taught to trainees within a relatively didactic and non-negotiable teaching context. Gallagher and Hargie (1989) used trainee counsellors to present themselves as counsellors using aspects of their own lives (see Personalization, Chapters 6 and 7), with an *emphasis on spontaneity and mundane 'self' behaviour*. Rhodewalt and Agustsdottir (1986) similarly ask subjects to *think of themselves* on a good or a bad day, as the basis for the manipulated variable in the role play. Bourque and Ladouceur (1979), despite 'demanding' a *single response only*, did ask subjects to respond in their *usual* manner, as did Rohrback et al. (1987) in their study on teaching adolescents to resist alcohol offers. The replication experiments of Stricker (1967) also *required subjects to respond as they really would or might have done*. Of particular interest is a replication of Klein's (1982) where subjects, having been exposed to a waiting room situation within an experimental framework, were subsequently asked to replicate their own behaviour in that waiting room. Finally here, Klein (1982), experimenting on the effect of emotional state on subjects' reactions to electric shock, asked subjects prior to the application of shock *to imagine themselves*, as calm or upset. An interesting subtlety, which may actually vitiate the hypotheses of the experiment, was that participants were not so much asked to *role play* these emotional states but asked to allow either set of these feelings *to emerge*, given that both sets of feelings were argued to be available to each subject at any one time.

More in-depth role playing activities for teaching purposes are documented by Moore (1984), training social workers to deal with death and bereavement issues, and also by Fulmer (1983), teaching systemic therapy to therapists, where the focus is on using the individual's *own experience* within role plays that are designed to facilitate a *direct use of self*, albeit in contexts created to stimulate new learning. These role plays tend to use a format of structured exercises which provide a stimulus to action. They exist in, or already have created, a context of personal disclosure and personal growth that sets implicit and explicit demands on the level of depth of expected experience and role plays. This is not always made explicit nor is it necessarily easy to disentangle discretely, however, it is evident from a reading of these authors' articles.

Thorley and Yule (1982) are absolutely clear that, in their parental skills assessment role play, they demanded from the parent a personally valid response, in the context of strongly legitimizing the parents' own view of their own optimal behaviour. Several researchers use the *second person form of address to participants* in the induction, without seeming to be aware of the significance and power of such language usage (see Chapter 7 on the subject's experience). Examples of such researchers are: Armstrong (1982), Manstead (1979) and Adams-Webber and Rodney (1983) (although unfortunately these then return to the conditional form of address); Ammerman and Hersen (1986), in line with many of the social/assertion skills assessment studies, and Klein (1982) also use a second person form of induction address – again apparently without awareness of its significance.

Sustained over time

Clearly the vast majority of assessment *role plays* have a particularly short time span, arguably invalidating any serious attempt at generalizing outside the laboratory, with the exception of a very few isolated studies. Quite distinct in this respect are some of the replication role plays, such as Mixon (1972) and, most notably, the role play studies of Haney et al. (1973) and Olsen and Christiansen (1966) – the Grindstone experiment. The latter two extremely atypical studies extended *role play* over weeks, attempting to simulate total environments and 'real' time. There are a few other isolated examples of time extensive role plays, for example within training programmes which are sometimes extended episodically over sessions. For example, Bilaniuk (1988), in training housewives to enter the workforce, involved trainees in the same role play situation over several weeks. A particularly interesting initiative by Roman and Porter (1978) concerning the teaching of group therapy leader skills to therapists involved the role play creation of a group for therapy, with the trainees 'playing' client 'roles'; however, just as in real group therapy, the role play extended episodically over weeks. Between sessions the trainers would contact individual members of the group, giving them particular actions to undertake in the next 'therapy' session. These actions related to specific and explicit theoretical teaching points. The questions relating to Temporality had been initially neglected in relation to induction processes (see Chapter 6, 7 and 8 for more detail).

Role reversal

Very much a feature of psychodramatic activities (see below), and to some extent of behaviour rehearsal and modelling, is the use of *role reversal*. (This is, in its simplest form, the procedure of asking one person to exchange 'roles' with another role play participant, so that Mr Jones becomes Ms Elliot and vice versa.) The most fluid use of role reversal is undertaken in play therapy with children where the transition from child as self to child 'playing' the part of significant other, and from therapist as self to therapist as child seems particularly easily and unselfconsciously achieved (see Axline, 1971) and occurs without the need for elaborate warm-up inductions, which most untrained adults seemed to need in order actively to suspend disbelief. Levinson and Herman (1991) provide a very useful recent review of the use of role play with children in therapy.

Warm-ups

We have already touched briefly on the need for explicit warm-up techniques or inductions. Many authors, such as Fulmer (1983), mention the need for these but specify no details. Some role play users make a point of giving subjects time within which to try and imaginatively engage in the role play (see Bellack et al., 1990b; Bourque and Ladouceur, 1979) but usually give no guidance for subjects on how to achieve this engagement.

An impressive exception is Hovrath (1984) who explicitly, in an experiment on imagined dental discomfort, gave subjects very detailed instructions and eliciting frameworks on how to imagine, so as to create maximum involvement; this involved calling upon all the senses of the subject. McReynolds et al. (1981) set participants off with a scripted beginning and then allowed improvisation. Geller (1978) provided a training video of good role playing to be used as a model.

Distinctive role play contributions

Standing out from any of the above attempts to provide guidelines for role play practice are two renowned practitioners: one from the world of psychotherapy, the other from the world of theatre. Although neither would, in any sense, have seen themselves as contributing to a wide role play debate, each has contributed enormously to our understanding – and indeed to our potential further understanding – of the process of acting 'as-if'. First we will consider Moreno (the psychotherapist) and secondly, Stanislavski (the theatre practitioner).

Moreno

Moreno, who coined the term 'psychodrama', was by training a psychiatrist, who practised psychotherapy in Austria during the early 1900s and then moved to the USA where he continued to develop his practice and theorizing, and where he has been immensely influential. He is known for creating probably the most powerful role play therapy technique commonly used in psychotherapy, and for his writings on this subject and sociometry. The latter is a conceptual framework which gives rise to specific measurement techniques concerning social and interpersonal relationships. Much of his written work is grandiose and inaccessible; much of the best of his practice and teaching has been handed down and developed from practitioner to practitioner in training (although a large new literature continues to evolve, see for example, Williams, 1989; Holmes and Karp, 1991; the *Journal of Group Psychotherapy, Psychodrama and Sociometry*). Otherwise his technical wisdom often needs to be inferred from his writings rather than being overt and easily codifiable. We will concentrate on extracting those aspects of technique deemed to have particular relevance and power and which are compatible with the conceptual framework being put forward here.

Moreno's central concept was that of 'spontaneity'. He believed that it is the person's essential creativity and spontaneity that allow therapeutic change and personal growth. Psychodrama is seen as a method for releasing and facilitating spontaneity, most often with the purpose of using this to provoke catharsis – the purging of hindering and dark emotional states which stultify and impede good psychological functioning. This spontaneity at times has, for Moreno, almost mystical qualities, as has one of his other core concepts, 'tele', which he put forward as an intuitive communications process occurring between individuals. However, underneath the frequently used hyperbole are many highly practical and thoroughly well-structured techniques for evoking involved and spontaneous participation in psychodramatic role play, often with the specific aim of creating ecological validity – although Moreno would not have termed it thus – or with the aim of enabling individuals to express deeper levels of their personal reality: 'the aim of these sundry techniques is not to turn the patients into actors, but rather to stir them up to be on the stage what they *are* more deeply and more explicitly than they appear to be in life's reality' (Moreno, 1972).

Moreno did not explicitly articulate his induction principles as a cohesive set of induction processes, but, via a wide reading of his texts and more especially by the handing down of skills through practitioner training, these emerge clearly and can be categorized as:

(a) Relaxing the protagonist
(b) The director engages with the client (protagonist)
(c) The modes of address from director and co-director to protagonist (see concepts of Personalization, Chapter 7)
(d) The modes of address used in inducting alter egos (other players)
(e) The personal spatialization of the acting space (see Personalization, Chapter 7)
(f) The establishment of boundaries

The above is by no means an exhaustive list of all the techniques used in psychodrama; it is a selected list of those techniques which are here believed to be most salient with respect to getting participants able to suspend disbelief in the 'as-ifness' of the event, and which relate most closely to the principles of role play induction put forward in this book.

Relaxing the protagonist   Psychodramatists are, generally speaking, skilled psychotherapists, and value their ability to make a human and psycho-therapeutic relationship with their clients. Although psychotherapy cannot and should not be 'tension free', it is evident that a client paralysed with anxiety is not going to be able to work. Thus, the psychodramatist's first task, whether by using simple conversation, by focusing upon group dynamics or even through the use of 'gimmicks', is to engage the client in such a way that he or she feels comfortable to speak and to move. Hence, a *sine qua non* is the facilitation of a collaborative trusting relationship, where the client knows that he or she will not be deceived, bullied or any way made to feel foolish, self-conscious or a failure. The client has to know the director is *with* the client. Apart from the more subtle interpersonal aspects here, there is a quite precise psychodrama 'rule' that concretizes this intended relationship. The director or a co-director nearly always stays on the same spatial plane as the protagonist, especially in the warm up. While the director and protagonist are together setting the scene for the particular role play, the director either walks, sits, or whatever at exactly the same level as the protagonist. No one is left to 'set up' or start their role play on their feet while the director sits and looks on. The message is clearly 'I am here with you and I am explicitly demonstrating this and building this with you'. How many role players, poorly inducted, have stood un-nerved and self-conscious while all the others sat and watched?

The director engages with the client (protagonist)   Not only must the director relax the protagonist, but also indicate clearly and actively his or her interest in the client and their problems; an interest that is neither overly intrusive nor curious, but demonstrates a real concern with the client's view of the world, an undoubting belief in the 'trueness' of this view, and a wider concern of caring for that client. Nothing could be further away from the conventional experimental research model, where a subject is 'used' for the sake of the experiment/experimenter. The director helps the client elaborate that view and may even seek to widen or change it – but only from the position of first showing a deep respect for that view.

The modes of address from director and co-director to Protagonist   Language in the warm-up phase of psychodrama is used advisedly. The director, by the use of language, *shares* the world view of the client and *shares* the 'reality' of the 'as-if' situation (see Presencing, Chapter 7). Therefore no one ever says or should say, 'lets pretend this is your bedroom at home, now go and act as if you were just getting up'. The language used is immediate, actual and collaborative, hence: 'we are in your bedroom, you are in your bed, you are just getting up . . . etc.' Similarly, if asked to play a role other than self, unless there is a particular reason for 'distancing' the role, the director will address the protagonist directly: 'you are Mrs Thatcher, you are 63, etc. and today you have a cabinet meeting'. Language is used to stress the immediacy and the actuality of the event *and* the co-construction of the event. This will be emphasized when induction principles are discussed (see Chapters 7 and 8).

The modes of address used in inducting alter egos   Alter egos are co-participants, who facilitate the protagonist by playing out various complementary roles for the protagonist. Just as above with the protagonist, the director addresses the co-participants, and also instructs the protagonist to induct and address co-participants in a similar fashion – that is, directly and with collaborative actuality: 'you are my mother and you live over the shop in Grantham . . .'.

The personal spatialization of the acting space   When a scene is first set up the director pays a great deal of attention to ensuring that the protagonist knows his or her way around that space, both physically and psychologically. If there is a door the protagonist will know exactly where the door is, and so on for all salient observable items. Not only does this ensure that the protagonist can move freely but also the facilitation of the space and its objects, which bear a symbolic value, deepens the meaning of the enactment.

The establishment of boundaries   Not only is the physical space of the 'as-if' event given a boundary, between 'stage' or 'performance' area and 'audience' (Moreno's terms, 1972), but the director also makes sure that psychological boundaries are maintained by clear induction procedures. Most importantly, at the end of the 'as-if' event, the participants are told to come out of role, and their successful debriefing is checked out with the participants. Thus, all possible means are employed to give the players boundaries that will limit the possibility of the role play having immediate carry-over into (and potential consequences in) their mundane lives. Some psychodramatists (Corsini, 1966, for example) with a particular therapeutic intent do not create these 'coming out of role boundaries' but deliberately leave them to 'spill over' into real life for the purpose of moving things on. This is clearly a potentially dangerous procedure if not used by highly skilled psychotherapists.

Stanislavski

There are probably few serious film- or theatre-goers who have not heard of 'the Lee Strasbourg Method' or method acting, and many no doubt associate this with the Marlon Brando grunt. 'The Method' is essentially derived from the acting method of the late Constantin Stanislavksi, who has provided the most detailed, influential and systematic approach – and, indeed, philosophy – for the teaching of acting to actors.

His method remains the most influential acting technique, despite the influence of others such as Bertold Brecht (1964) with his dispassionate 'alienation effect' and well-observed demonstrative techniques, and, more recently, Grotowski (1975) and Peter Brook (1972) with their totalistic and ecstatic techniques. The Stanislavski Method is rooted in a so-called naturalistic approach which arose because Stanislavski strove to get away from the turgid and repetitive declamatory styles of acting of his theatrical predecessors, with their emphasis on reproducing the past performances of master actors, and to move towards a style where actors *generated* behaviour from their own genuine experience in the mundane world. Because of this shift in emphasis the derived Method moves easily into the current worlds of film and television that demand more naturalism.

Stanislavski's technique for acting combines: thought, intellectual analysis, emotional analysis of self, practical exercises conducive to creativity, and physical training. It is probably the balance of Stanislavski's inner versus outer attitude that is the source of the power of technique. His attitude towards observation and detail provided his actors with an epistemological orientation to the external world of events, and a way of decentring themselves from the potentially narcissistically focused style of some acting, a style more likely to be found within the poetic or expressionist theatre. However, observation that resulted in mere mimicry was eschewed by Stanislavski. He sought, in his actors, a spontaneity of expression that emerged from action generated by inner action, i.e. from motivation towards the world of 'external' objects. It is this relationship which results in a style of generating 'acting' that brings it close to ordinary mundane 'action'. Stanislavski was, in psychological terms, both a contextualist and a personalistic interpreter of the world. Above all, it was his attention to detail, to the particularity rather than to the general with respect to both the 'internal' and 'external' worlds, as well as the dynamic relationship between the two worlds, which drove and underpinned his technique. To 'warm up' his actors according to his method there are no violent techniques or powerful messages, there is only an orientation towards particularity and truthfulness, attention to context setting and on the search for inner motivation towards objects. Within context there is not only the present, but also the past and the future.

> There can be no present, however, without a past. The present flows naturally out of the past. The past is the roots from which the present grew . . . an actor must always feel that he has the *past* of his role behind him, like the train of a costume he carries along . . . Neither is there any present without a prospect of the future, dreams of it, guesses and hints about it. (Stanislavski 1968: 23)

The actor, states Stanislavski, must situate him or herself at the centre of the imaginative world, and actively engage in it by actively observing that world from that place.

> You can be the observer of your dream, but you can also take an active part in it – that is you find yourself mentally in the centre of the circumstances and conditions – which you never imagined. You no longer see yourself as an outside onlooker but you see what surrounds you. In time, when this feeling of 'being' is reinforced, you can become the main active personality in the surrounding circumstances of your dreams, you can begin, mentally, to act, have desires, make an effort, achieve a goal. (Stanislavski, 1968: 29)

Translated into specific directions for actors, Stanislavski insisted that actors map out the contextual details of their places of action. An object had to be placed precisely (even if an invisible ghost). Also all objects had to be imbued with meaning by establishing the playwright's intentions, the history of the object, its sensory qualities, and its personal meaning for the actor as person and actor as character. The actor must look outwards observationally at the object as well as inwardly, and must finally achieve the state of 'I am'. Any obligation to interest the audience, as prime mover of acting is defined as disastrous, producing a feeling for the sake of a feeling. This level of particularity, concentration and attention also leads to a highly tuned awareness of the other actor-character, with action generated from the interaction between the two. It was clearly Stanislavski's aim to induce actors into a relative state of fusion with their roles and situation, so that they believed the reality they were creating and expressing, albeit modified by the conventions of theatre and the demands of an audience.

What can we learn from the above and more broadly from Stanislavki's writings?

1 'Natural' behaviour emerges from prior concentration upon, and awareness of, history or preceding past moments (in order that these become a taken-for-granted part of background awareness) and consciousness of salient objects in one's field of awareness. This analysis is highly comparable with Polanyi's (1966) analysis of knowledge (see Chapter 7) and is compatible with the emphasis upon Particularization and Personalization expounded in Chapter 7.

2 'Natural' behaviour needs motivation, goals and a future prospect. This calls for role play participants to be included in negotiation of frames and foci, so that they have some idea of the intentions of the inductor and can evaluate for themselves the viability and validity of these 'external' goals. However, within the primary 'as-if' framing participants also need to understand, as far as is mundanely realistic, the intentional state of characters they are required to take on. It also requires Personalization (see Chapter 7).

3 'Involvement' in role arises from concern with the *particular* conditions of existence not from broad canvas goals.

4 Spontaneous action and feeling cannot be directly sought by actors, or stipulated as necessary by inductors, but only indirectly courted by concentrating on particulars and by having intentions towards particular objects.

5 An imaginary character cannot exist on stage merely by the actor's act of will. The character must exist in relation to context and objects (including of course other persons, and may only exist through them and with these).

6 Imagination must be active not passive, an active engagement with imaginary objects must be sought by the actor, in order that the actor should be able to suspend disbelief and fully immerse him/herself in the world of imaginary objects.

Summary of all the above guidelines

With the notable exception of Stanislavski, and the games and simulation authors referred to above, the contributions considered typically consist of isolated, conceptual and *ad hoc* statements about technique. There is no attempt to achieve a cohesive, systematic approach to technique. However, if we overview and aggregate the totality of work reviewed here we find some emerging common themes which give pointers towards the requirements of good induction technique. Table 4.1, groups together all those writers who have made particular comments about technique and which have a common focus – if not a common and/or fully articulated basis for the comments made. These are presented approximately in order of the frequency of mention and as can be seen at a glance the most commonly voiced technical concern relates to the need for detailed rather than minimalist inductions, followed by a degree of recognition of the value of using some level of the individual role player's personal experience to

Table 4.1 *Key induction concepts and relevant supporting work in psychology*

Use of/need for detail (Particularization)	Need for/use of personal expenses (Personalization)	Use of affirmative present context setting (Presencing)	Epistemological concerns (Action, knowledge and control)	Need for relaxation	Time considerations/concern with temporal build up	Need for credibility	Need to establish boundaries
Goldstein, 1973	Gabriel, 1982	Armstrong, 1982	Lauffer, 1973	Moreno, 1946 [1972], 1959	Benson et al., 1972	De Weerd, 1974	Gabriel, 1982
Klein, 1982	Gallagher & Hargie, 1989	Manstead, 1979	De Leon, 1975	Stanislavski, 1948a&b, 1968	Kern, 1982		De Weerd, 1974
Swink et al., 1984	Rhodewalt & Agustsdottir, 1986	Adams-Webber & Rodney, 1983	Bem, 1968	Baron, 1977	McReynolds et al., 1981		Moreno, 1946 [1972], 1959
Adams-Webber and Rodney, 1983	Rohrback et al., 1987	Moreno, 1946 [1972], 1959	Geller, 1978		Haney et al., 1973		
De Weerd, 1974	Stanislavski, 1948a&b, 1968	Stanislavski, 1948, 1968a&b	Swink et al., 1984		Olsen & Christiansen, 1966		
Benson et al, 1972	Smith, 1975	Ammerman & Hersen, 1986	Benson et al., 1972		Mixon, 1977		
Stanislavski, 1948a&b, 1968	Chiauzzi et al., 1985	Klein, 1982	De Weerd, 1974		Gabriel, 1982		
Lauffer, 1973					Lauffer, 1973		
De Leon, 1975					De Leon, 1975		
Mixon, 1977 (stipulated beliefs)					De Weerd, 1974		
Moreno, 1946[1972], 1959					Benson, et al., 1972		
Roman & Porter, 1978							
Forward et al., 1976							
Smith, 1975							
Oppelaar et al., 1983							
Moreno, 1946[1972], 1959							
Ginsberg, 1979							
Kelly, 1955a&b							

inform a role play. In Chapter 7 (and also in Chapters 6,8 and 10), where a theoretically grounded set of induction principles of Personalization, Particularization and Presencing are presented, it will be seen that these are consonant with the more informally articulated induction concerns of the writers reviewed herein. This strongly supports the contention expressed here that induction concerns are not arbitrary or unmatched by others' experience but actually experienced daily by many who already use role play but may not have a fully developed and integrated theoretical and technical stance or workbox of tools to use.

Before moving on to consider this fully articulated technical position it is useful to reflect in some detail upon the extant concepts of role and role play in role theories, which more often than not implicitly rather than explicitly have underpinned and informed the understanding of role play activities so far considered in this book. The relationship between these practices of role play is rarely explicitly informed by a formal alliance with role play and role theory terms; however, as we shall see, role play users take on a certain understanding of role play practice which is frequently grounded in misunderstandings or insufficient reflection upon the ramifications of using role theory terms to describe generated action within role plays. By focusing on some the definitional and conceptual problems within role theories we can begin to have a clear understanding of some the limitations of role play technique and also begin to form a clear picture of the direction we must take to address the current inadequacies in technique and understanding.

5

Reflections upon Extant Definitions of Role Play

One of the major difficulties bedevilling the use and the emergence of a satisfactory description of role play technique has been the failure to find adequate definitions for the essential aspects of such techniques. It is impossible to form a view of the technical requirements for setting up a role play if it is not clear exactly what is meant by 'role play', or if one's understanding is not congruent with the activities one sets up. For example, if the term role play is defined simply as the setting up of an 'external' imaginative environment, and if a conceptualization of role play that can extend to the person of the actor (and their experience) as a mutable factor within role play has not been provided, then one is unlikely to be able fully to exploit people as a resource within role play or to anticipate actors' induction needs. Equally, if the working definition of role play includes false contrast or identity with another technique, such as an experiment, then doubt must be thrown on the outcome of a role play which is thus grounded on false premises. Both types of example, among others, will be shown to be common through the considerations in this chapter.

It is most important to achieve a definition of role play that describes essential features correctly in order to provide the framework for an understanding of the requirements of successful technique. In Chapter 6, a new definition is offered which will hopefully provide this framework. First, however, it is necessary to consider extant definitions, and their inadequacies, in order to help the reader understand the bases of some of the limitations in technique as commonly practised. We need to commence with an initial understanding of role theories because many role play proponents have unwittingly taken on definitional problems by a loose allegiance to role theory terms – to underpin their attempts to comprehend role play.

Many of the role play definitional problems that are identified below relate to either the unthinking or, indeed, the inaccurate use of role theory terms. Rarely if ever are these terms – which are either explicitly or implicitly incorporated into role play definitions – subjected to critical analysis. Yet, ironically, within the domain of role theory concepts (and quite unrecognized) lies the key to many of the critical conceptual issues that role play users need to consider. Role theory itself has serious limitations; and these are unwittingly taken on by all those theorists and practitioners who implicate role theory in their intuitive or formal understandings of role play technique. It is important to understand these limitations, because not only do they throw light on important issues that are neglected in role play techniques, but also on what must be included in a definition of any role play in order fully to exploit its potential and recognize any limitations. Hence, prior to the development of a definition for this text (see Chapter 6), and prior to providing an exposition of extant role play definitions, we will first consider role theory terms – particularly with respect to their epistemological range

Role theory terms

It has already been suggested that many of the reasons underlying the difficulties in defining role play relate back to difficulties surrounding definitions of the pre-existing concepts of role. Here, we will briefly consider the major theoretical perspectives on 'role' and allied concepts, and their limitations. These major limitations will revolve around: definitional diversity and different units of analyses; social determinism; performative emphases; and lack of a personal and experiential dimension.

Broadly speaking, the term 'role' was first used technically, in the social sciences from the 1930s onwards by such theorists as Linton (1936), Mead (1934) and Moreno, (1946[1972] and 1959). The etymology dates back to classical Greek theatre. The dramaturgical connotations remain, indeed are central, particularly to the seminal works of Goffman (1959; 1961) and McCall and Simmons (1966); however, the understanding of what constitutes 'dramatic' has been highly particular, concerning almost exclusively 'performance'. (This latter understanding of theatre process will be addressed later in this chapter.)

Linton's early work (1936) on 'role', and its prolific extension by other sociologists, is perhaps the clearest in its denotative clarity despite its explanatory limitations. Linton was a structuralist, interested in the organization of society, which is seen as to a large extent determining individual behaviour. Hence, 'role' is located in the *society and the demands of social organization rather than in the individual* as a personal attribute or experience. Role is argued to be the 'dynamic aspect of status', the latter being defined as a 'collection of rights and duties' which are necessary components of societal organization which individuals take on in order to participate in the functioning of society. Similarly others, such as Heading (1972), define role as 'the active dimension of a social position'.

Later structuralists both redefined 'role' and 'status', even interchanging the terms. None the less, *'role' came to be viewed, above all, as a static concept*, equivalent to the above understanding of 'status' or of 'position'. A new term, 'role playing', 'role-taking' or 'role enactment' was, therefore, needed and hence was created to capture the dynamic phenomena associated with the 'enactment' of a role (see Coutu, 1951). Others such as Merton (1968 whose work was the most significant contribution) broadened

Linton's work by introducing the idea of individuals having role sets, but of course retained the social determinism and static nature of the concept of role. From such definitions it is easy to see that, in addressing role play as simulation, people might confound the idea of acting out a social status or position with the more amorphous idea of generating some individual action. At first sight Mead (1934), the founder of symbolic interactionism, used 'role', rather differently – seemingly dynamically and interactionally – within the context of describing the communication process that he posited as central to socialization and community. Role, here, has as its starting point the dyadic interaction.

There is a also a particular problem here in that Mead's use of 'role taking' was restricted to quasi-cognitive activity and 'role' is almost entirely replaceable by 'attitude' or 'position', indeed Mead used them interchangeably. Moreover, the 'other' is not a *particularized* other, but a generalized other and the *self* is seen to arise out of the child's growing ability to take the role of the *generalized other*, which is defined as: 'The organized community or social group which gives rise to the individual, his unity of self may be called the 'generalized other', (Mead, 1934; 154). Indeed, Mead did not define 'role' separately from this. Thus, this concept of 'role' with its apparent dynamic and interactionist advantages, was actually grounded in social determinism – 'the generalized other' – and in this sense was not to be distinguished from more structuralist accounts. What Mead's definition points to but does not develop, though it is echoed and expanded most significantly by social and developmental psychologists (for example, Flavell, 1968; Piaget, 1926), is the cognitive interpersonal aspect of trying to understand the other through a form of quasi-empathic process. To this extent it is potentially quite distinctive from the traditional sociological concept of role, and detaches itself from pre-existing socio-logical theories by pointing to an experiential empathic aspect.

Goffman (1959, 1961), who followed Mead's work as a symbolic inter-actionist, used 'role' much more particularly to emphasize, besides infer-ential aspects, the dramaturgical aspects of social behaviour relating to the presence of audience; that is, he propounded the idea that most of our behaviour is about 'impression management' – the deliberate attempt to construct an impression for an audience, through social performance. (Note here the continuing performative denotation.) As with Mead, Goffman's starting point was face-to-face interaction, but, also as Mead did, he changed the ground, finally encompassing a traditional sociological orien-tation by viewing the individual as comprising units that are functional for, and determined by, the larger society. In this view, roles are seen as *constitutive of and prior to the individual* and even Goffman's (1961) apparently liberating concept of 'role-distance' – that mechanism by which individuals separate themselves from their roles – was argued by Goffman to be analysable in terms of roles.

Mead's work is interestingly parallelled by the psychologist George Kelly (1955a and 1955b). Although he polarized away from social determinism,

Kelly also used 'role' figuratively and descriptively and describes the process of interaction by explicity suggesting that an individual may play 'a role' in a social process, involving another person in relation to the extent that one person construes the construction processes of this other play. This general use of 'role' as alluded to above is entirely replaceable by 'part'. It neither describes nor distinguishes any behaviour within its own ground – the two person interaction – and does not relate the individual to the society as Kelly made claim. (Kelly, as Moreno, seeks both to conceptualize 'role' and to construct a role play technique for therapeutic ends. None the less, it does again suggest, albeit unclearly, the fact of a relationship between empathy and experience, and role).

There were early attempts to integrate structuralists with more interactionist or dynamic views of 'role' to account for individual action (for example, Levinson, 1959; Sarbin, 1954; Turner, 1968), which was outside the remit of early structuralists. However, Levinson has been strongly criticized for his unitary view of 'society' (Holland, 1977), and Turner's view of role can be argued to be both a reification and to allow the individual very little freedom. Sarbin (1954), who made claim to present an integrated psychological approach to role theory, substituted the term 'role enactment' for 'role playing' by which he meant to refer to the motoric behaviour associated with social positions. His second concept, also derived from sociological theory, was 'role taking' by which he meant to denote cognitive, and inferential activity. Sarbin's approach represents a rather awkward attempt which not only reflected a naive understanding of sociological approaches to 'role' but also gives a very inadequate view of interaction, *where the enactor is doomed to meaningless action, that is motoric behaviour, and the recipient to attempts at meaningful construction of these meaningless motions.* (See Yardley, 1979, for an early critique of motoric constructions of social interaction.) Hence, meaning is not created within interactions or dependent upon the rich diversity individuals bring to interactions, but merely attendant upon an interplay of concretely generated and understood gestures, which exist prior to the individual. Again there are evident problems in trying to combine a more psychological and experiential model with a more performative and structural model.

More recently, Turner (1987) and Stryker (1987) have continued the theme of integrating structuralist and interactionist perspectives. Stryker has introduced the concepts of commitment and identity salience to role theory, where individual people's identities are defined as 'internalized role designations corresponding to the social location of persons'. Turner (1987) has considered the necessity of a self concept in conveying an idea of personal autonomy and agency in relation to simple role determination, although this concept of self involves some ambiguity in terms of whether it is essentialist or socially constructed (see Honess and Yardley, 1987). Notwithstanding these integrationist developments, both these retain *the key notion of role itself as being highly socially determined and determining of the individual, and as predominantly a performance concept.* Precise definitions of role (and role play) are especially rare within clinical literature, with authors generally assuming that the activity is well understood. Exceptionally and most notably, Moreno (1959) offered definitions of the underpinning concept of 'role'. Moreno is, for the purposes of the discussion here, a significant theorist. He is unique among role theorists in that he was centrally concerned with the technique of role playing, otherwise called 'psychodrama' or 'sociodrama', yet also had broader interests in larger social psychological issues (see Moreno, 1953). Further, much of his theory arose from, and returned to, the therapeutic encounter. His major theoretical construct was the principle of spontaneity, that is, the creativity of human beings. We will return later to his specific definition of role play technique, concentrating here on his definition of role.

Unfortunately, Moreno's definitions of 'role' were extensive, and involve multiple theoretical contradictions which were not addressed by him. Hence, even on one occasion, within one attempt at definition, he defined role as: 'a theatre part and imaginary person which may be a model to existence or imitation of it . . . [and] . . . an assumed character or function within social reality the actual and tangible forms of the self the final crystallization of the situations in a special area of operations through which the individual has passed.' (1972, Vol.1: 153). Here we have a range of definitions which encompasses highly disparate theoretical realms. For example, the concepts of 'role' and 'self' are usually viewed as inimical, especially by psychodynamics theorists with whom Moreno would broadly have wished to align himself. This is precisely because 'role' has performative connotations (as indeed is made explicit in other of Moreno's definitions above), whereas 'self' is generally viewed as a place of agency, self reflexiveness and spontaneity (the latter being most centrally and highly valued by Moreno). Indeed, on another occasion he did try to pull all these disparate dimensions together by defining role as 'an interpersonal experience' and as 'a unit of synthetic experience into which private, social and cultural elements are merged' (1972 Vol.1: 184). He failed, however, much as later practitioners fail, to endorse any particular definition of role, or to justify his attempts at definitional synthesis. Thus it is impossible to understand in any way other than the intuitive, the conceptual grounds of his techniques or the practical implications for these. Despite this over-inclusiveness – and paradoxically in some ways because of it – Moreno's technique is superlative among role play techniques; arguably, it is Moreno's theoretical greed to incorporate everything that led to his strength as an artistic and creative synthesizer. Further, despite the apparent focus on 'role', his writings and the practice to which these give rise constantly reflect a profound concern with the individual, identity and experience.

(There are a few somewhat more isolated psychological approaches to 'role', such as Berne [1968]. Berne, who created Transactional Analysis as a form and later a school of psychotherapy, used the concept of 'role' to refer to 'fantasy intrapsychic structures which give rise to individual action, and which finds expression also in role characterized behaviours [1969: 41]. Such a definition is distinct from all the work discussed above, with the partial exception of Moreno, grounded as it is in the world of the deeply psychological and intrapsychic.)

General definitional issues

Issues surrounding the varying definitions of 'role', 'role playing' and 'role taking'

It is clear from the discussions thus far that 'role', 'role taking' and 'role playing' cannot be viewed as having any agreed referents. Consistent with this view is that expressed by Coutu (1951), who indeed made a plea for clarification. He suggested using 'role taking' to refer to the inferential activities of understanding the other, 'role play' to the performance of functions connected with a status; a further suggestion was that a distinction should be made between 'playing a role' and 'playing at a role' – with the latter including an element of deceit. His advice has not been heeded, but this perhaps is not altogether surprising. As others since, Coutu failed to offer any thorough conceptual justification, which would have necessitated tackling the fundamental theoretical problems attached to the propounded differential use. Dewey (1969) also comments powerfully on this semantic and conceptual confusion, stating that even individual writers are inconsistent and 'most commonly, the writers are unsure whether one *plays* a role, *occupies* a role, or sees in role the *expected* behaviour or the *actual* behaviour'. Hence it also can be seen that the units that role theorists seek to relate to each other (for example, society, reference group, individual, self), and the ground from which these are seen to emerge, are exceedingly varied and occur at different levels of analysis. Thus some theorists, such as Linton (1936), have used the term 'role' to relate parts of the social structure to each other via the medium of the individual; this is in sharp contrast to those who merely use 'role' interchangeably with 'part' or 'attitude' in a two person interaction, and in even greater contrast to idiosyncratic psychological theorists such as Berne (1968), who used 'role' to describe intrapsychic relationships.

Role is almost always used to isolate a feature of social life in relation to a metaphorical or fictional whole. For the purpose of analysis, the infinite interdependence of systems, units and situations is denied by the establishment of boundaries – these boundaries delineating for instance the society, the reference group, the dyad, etc. To use the term 'role' at all, the appropriate 'whole' must be chosen for the desired usage and context. This suggests particular caution is required when being applied to the *generation rather than the* post hoc *analysis of behaviour, and the way in which frames and foci are established* (see Chapter 6, Definition 6). For, perhaps with the exception of formal episodes (see Harré and Secord,

1972), the 'wholeness' of an event, its boundaries and any definitive status are rarely perceived by individuals except with hindsight. Where and when boundaries are seen, these are likely to differ from the analytic boundaries assumed by the experimenter, clinician or theorist. Hence, the 'whole' implied by distinguishing the role experientially may not exist for individual 'role players' and, therefore, the meaning of individual acts differs between experimenter and subject, therapist and client.

Social determinism of role theories

A major feature of the principal role theories, whether grounded in classic structuralism or symbolic interactionism, is their social determinism; that is the units of behaviour or society are seen to be prior to, and constitutive of, the individual. Even Goffman's (1961) apparently individually liberating concept of 'role distance' is finally analysable by recourse to 'roles'. *Further individual experience and action is most often seen as outside the theoretical realm of role theories.* Thus Merton (1968) argued the individual to be the limiting case of his role theory and Dahrendorf (1968), who clearly supports theoretical determinism, acknowledged the gap between **homo sociologicus** and the *experiencing person.* For, all role theories are concerned above all with the *observer's* analysis of social behaviour and social systems, rather than the experience or agency of the individual person. Hence, role theory units of analysis are *post hoc* abstractions that inevitably reify and stereotype that which they seek to describe. *Such terms are not intended, nor are they adequate, to describe either the generative acts of individuals or the nature of individual experience and agency.* They may, of course, form the basis for an analytic model. Further, *such terms are not prescriptive enough to function as sufficient instruction for individuals to act.* Telling someone in a role play to play the 'role' of a police officer or 'everyman' is not a sufficient basis for the personal action; and from a methodological point of view, such an instruction which denies the personal is equivalent to the assumption that individual difference is 'error', and that 'roles' can be construed as independent variables (see Chapter 6, Definition 7).

In brief, when someone is asked to play a 'role' in a role play, it is usually loosely capable of being substituted by the term 'part' in the sense of being a participant in an event. However, if 'role' is intended to have a sociological meaning, asking someone to play the role of a teacher bears on the functional aspects of behaviour in relation to a larger societal organization – and it restricts the focus to that expected behaviour and relationship. Unless the researcher is interested in the impact upon the individual of his or her role as teacher or vice versa, the enquiry is narrowed down and little is expected of the role play participant other than a stereotyped delivery 'performance'.

Messinger et al. (1962) wrote of the use of role terms in everyday discourse, and argued that most frequently individuals use role terms when they are communicating their own experienced alienation from behaviour performed. Thus to 'play a role' or 'play at a role' separates the individual from his or her acts in a manner that is felt to be artificial, hypocritical and dislocating. If individuals do not normally describe or ascribe their own social actions in terms of roles but arguably in terms of actions, feelings, volitions, expectations, demands and the like, it is clear that engendering action in a role play should take account of this.

Theatrical root metaphors

Further light may be thrown on the inadequacy of role theory terminology to describe *generative* action – that is, spontaneous and experienced action as 'produced' by purposive human beings, rather than behaviour that is the result of following a script or responding without volition to a determining stimulus – by considering the theatrical metaphors from whence most role theories have arisen.

Extensive use has been made of theatrical analogies or dramaturgical models but, first by misunderstanding the theatrical event and then by confusing metaphor with identity, the language of drama has been mis-applied to role play phenomena. Hence, role plays are supposed to be adequately generated and analysed by attention to 'scenario', 'scene', 'props', 'character', 'role' and so on. However, these terms are *theatrical shorthands, which are intended to characterize an event from a particular technical perspective. They neither intend to, nor can they, adequately communicate an event or even give it substance or life.*

Consider 'role' more particularly. It is assumed by role theorists and role play proponents that 'role' in theatre refers to the *performative* in the actors' behaviour and/or to the functional in terms of the plot or motivational structure of the whole play. Consider, for example, the following: in essence the role perspective assumes, as does the theatre, that *performance* results from the *social prescriptions and behaviour of others*, and that individual variations in performance, to the extent that they do occur, are expressed within the framework created by these factors (Biddle and Thomas, 1966: 4). However, 'role' is only used in this sense, in the theatre, from an analytic or critical perspective. Crudely speaking, such an analysis in terms of the function and performative characteristics of roles is made to reveal the intentions of the playwright. Hence, the playwright is seen to have a view of the world, or a point to make; he or she unfolds a motivational structure via roles and actions that fulfil the task of reaching an end-point. Clearly, this process can be compared with the experimental social psychologist using a demonstrative technique to achieve a predicted outcome. The experimenter, clinician or playwright controls the total scenario in a manner quite distinct from the real world of more haphazard events.

Yet, as has already been stated, the above is a crude analysis of a script. A more sophisticated viewpoint would be that the script of a play cannot be treated as an object reification but must be taken as the necessary agency for the interaction between playwright/director/actor. Certainly the script may be analysed using terms like 'role', to perceive the functional aspects of the play's structure. Certainly 'role' can be seen to distinguish certain acts which should be performed in front of an audience. However, the phenomena of theatre are not adequately described nor can they be generated by reference to dramaturgical terms any more than social behaviour is.

At the final point of intersection of the play as written and the social context in which it appears, we have the actor. The task of the skilled actor is not objectively to declaim that which is given (even if this were possible) but to *embody* and elaborate the 'role' or 'character' to personhood, using certain expressive conventions appropriate to the social context of the event. (This assumes the more usual naturalistic/Stanislavskian approach to theatre. Other approaches, Brechtian theatre for example, theoretically illustrate the reverse case.) The actor must find for him or herself the source of action within the scripted words. The actor must come to know the kind of person who could utter such words and carry out such actions, and must know the part of him or herself (in the mundane sense) that can incorporate or extend to such action. To put matters another way, the actor must find the situation ecologically valid, and the audience must perceive persons and situations, not roles and scenarios.

All the above issues become particularly salient where Bronfenbrenner's (1977) reconceptualization of ecological validity ('the extent to which the environment *experienced* by the subjects in a scientific investigation has the properties it is supposed or assumed to have by the investigator') is considered in the context of role play literature today. This is particularly incongruous when one considers that many of the arguments advocating the use of role play emanate from supposedly humanistic intentions.

Explicit attempts at role play definitions

Mann and Mann (1956), a social psychologist, provided one of the earliest formal definitions of role play itself, unreflectively using role theory (sociological) terms. It is historically important because it is commonly referred to, both by clinicians and researchers, and yet is virtually unchallenged. Mann defined role play thus:

> (1) where a person is asked to perform a role which is not normally his own,

or

> (2) is explicitly asked to perform a normal role but not in a setting where it is normally taken.

Mann did not further define 'role' but seemingly relied on the reader's familiarity with the term, as if there were agreed referents. Therefore, it is unclear as to what areas of social behaviour are intended to be *generated* or analysed, by recourse to the use of the term 'role'. In a later article (Mann,

1959), where he and his co-author did in fact make a specialized distinction in using 'role', their role categories were drawn from a highly particular study of Benne and Sheats (1948), which described the behaviour of small groups in seemingly *ad hoc* terms. The difficulty here is that in failing to define 'role' more thoughtfully, there is no clue as to precisely what one might ask of an 'actor' required to generate action, and no consideration of what the 'actor' might need to 'engage' in such action. There is also the specific problem that implicit adherence to quasi-sociological terms conceals the gulf between the requirements relating to observers analysing behaviour, rather than actors generating behaviour, a problem to which we shall return shortly.

Without in any sense challenging such early definitions of role playing, the extensive social psychological debate of the 1970s over the use of role play did focus some deliberate attention on description and theory, particularly among role play proponents. *Aspects of this particular debate will be important for us to consider as we proceed, because it represents the only extensive and significantly focused discussion upon the usefulness and validity of role play which draws upon conceptual and definitional matters.*

Within this debate, Movahedi (1977) continued upon an earlier socio-logical theme of Coutu's (1951; see below), in criticizing the semantic confusion among role play proponents. Specifically, Movahedi attacked Mixon (1971), a recent leading and influential role play exponent within social psychology: 'for bastardizing the theoretical constructs of "role" and "role playing" by reducing them to cognitively meaningless figures of speech by violating the principle of non-vacuousness of contrast' – a somewhat strong attack on Mixon's apparent tendency insufficiently to distinguish what he means by his use of either term.

Movahedi's work has been concerned with advocating a particular use of role play in relation to assessing individual's attitudes, but, despite the above scathing attack on Mixon, Movahedi is open to his own criticisms concerning lack of differentiation between the concepts of 'role' and 'role playing'. Movahedi did acknowledge that 'role' is employed differently in social system theories than in role playing; however, he did not attempt to define role playing, despite his attention to the concept of 'role'. Secondly, he misrepresented sociological structural theories of 'role' (see below); and, thirdly, he set up a false antithesis to Mixon, based on this misrepresentation of the structuralists. Thus, Movahedi defined the social structural concept of 'role play' thus: 'Role . . . represents the pattern of behaviour that the incumbent of a social status has to negotiate with the incumbents of a set of complementary statuses in an ongoing interactive process of coping with structural exigencies in a given culture' (Mohavedi, 1977). Here he misrepresented structuralists (he does not cite individual theorists) as having a unitary and consensual approach to 'role' – that is, a common understanding – and thus collapsed the extensive distinctions which existed between structuralists (see below). (For example, reference to a 'set of complementary statuses' appears to allude to all structuralists but in fact is very much an individual stance of Merton, (1968). Negotiation, as used here, is typical of the very distinct approach of the symbolic interactionists (as opposed to the structuralists), who are indeed concerned with the co-construction of meaning. Movahedi then placed this idiosyncratic and inaccurate definition of the structuralist 'role' as diametrically opposed to Mixon's 'role' in the latter's 'role–rule' model of social behaviour. In fact, it may be argued that the reverse is the case. *Mixon's role–rule model bears a remarkable resemblance to the early structuralist and rather mechanistic view of the springs of action, and is, for that reason, ill-equipped to explain individually generated action.*

In rejecting Mixon's approach to role play, Movahedi (1977) also rejected Mixon's (1972) idea that role play can be used to explore **the critical social processes of interaction**. He suggested instead, that role play should be used to assess 'individual's attitudes towards the incumbents of certain social positions'. Although it is never made explicit one must assume that this suggested use of role play is directly related to Movahedi's definition of 'role', with its implicit dependent assumption that *role play technique equals the sociological playing out of roles* – an implication which he never examines and which, it is proposed here, is untenable. For, sociological roles are analytic and reductionist concepts which do not provide adequate explanation of the 'springs' of individually generated action. This is recognized by the influential contemporary sociological theorist Dahrendorf (1968), who acknowledges the gap between *homo sociologicus* and the experiencing person.

The above is simply an example of the all too frequent failure to consider, even at the most pragmatic level of analysis, *what role play techniques actually involve.* Such a view of role playing as involving the playing out of social roles is by no means rare, and much of the clinical and training literature encompasses such a view, even where actual practice contradicts such a simplistic perspective.

Mixon has been much commended by both the influential philosopher and the social psychologist, Harré and Secord (1972), among others (see also Ginsberg, 1979), for providing a radical alternative to other social psychology techniques, particularly in the area of replication of social psychology experimentation, which allows a more agentic approach to understanding. Indeed, his work has been the basis for other recent role play work in social psychology such as Manstead (1979) and Smith, J.L. (1975). Unfortunately, despite this, Mixon neither formally defines 'role' nor 'role play'. Yet, some of his language and description of his goals with respect to his four role playing conditions implicate a definition: 'devise a scenario that will prove so compelling to the actor in one or all four role playing conditions that the actor perforce duplicates the known outcome'.

Unfortunately, from the perspective held in this text quite clearly 'stimulus–response' might well replace 'scenario', 'performance', etc. Any notion of agentic individuality (which is at the heart of Harré and Secord's, 1972, concerns) is far from evident given the concern with producing conditions that are so 'compelling' as to override individual differences. Indeed, if one next considers Mixon's definition of his four role-playing conditions, the individual moves even further from sight. These conditions allow the role play to be performed or imagined, and the actor to be a specific character or 'everyman'. There is no mention of the individual playing 'self' here – or indeed another person. Character seems to relate to very superficial descriptors of human beings and the idea of an 'everyman' – a consensual mouthpiece – is quite unrealistic and certainly does not conform to the way in which individuals have a marked experience of individuality, unless psychopathologically damaged or 'engineered' into anonymity by extreme situations or by manipulative others. Above all, Mixon never actually defined what he meant by 'roles', nor did he define the activity of 'role play'. Hence, it is impossible to 'know' his analytic framework and, therefore, to place this apparently narrow technique into perspective. It seems unlikely that an humanistic or person-centred science can emerge from the above.

In particular, the implications of 'devising a scenario to achieve known outcome' are that validity is to be assessed in relation to outcome (functional validity), rather than to the proceeding process or to the experience of individual subjects (ecological validity). The role play generated is thus no more than a model, albeit a working model, analogous to aspects of social interaction but not having ecological validity as a necessary quality. Such role plays fall within a demonstrative paradigm; for, in Mixon's case, not only is validity achieved in relation to outcome, but given that role play is an intended simulation (see Mixon, 1972) of a conventional experiment (Milgram, 1963), there is a basic acceptance of Milgram's results and the positivistic methods used to achieve these.

The demonstrative nature of such positivistic social psychology experiments (see also Chapter 2) has long been asserted by writers such as Gergen (1978), McGuire (1973) and Rychlak (1977), who have argued that the main skill of experimenters is not scientific rigour and the true testing of hypotheses, but skillful stage design and scenario construction, to ensure that the hypothesis is demonstrated to be true, because the ability to control circumstance is deliberately (relatively) absolute compared to mundane interaction. Other social psychologists have based their work on that of Mixon (for example, Forward et al., 1976; Manstead, 1979; Hamilton, 1976; Baron, 1977). The latter added to Mixon's *conditions* for role play the 'role of self', but did not define 'role' or 'self'. Here, also, there was no examination of what role play *is* save that Baron asserted it is not a unitary phenomenon. Thus, the particular conceptual reasons for claims for using *role play* to explore 'self-presentation' strategies and cognitive mediators, and what these reveal about the social system and social reasoning, are not elaborated.

Forward et al. (1976) favoured the term 'role enactment' instead of 'role playing' (after Sarbin, 1954). Yet an almost identical set of problems are attached to both terms and Forward et al. did not elaborate on their reasoning for such terminology. Although they also failed to come to grips with technique, as Hamilton (1976; see below), they did appear to come close to a conceptual breakthrough. Thus, Forward et al. defined role plays as sharing: 'the common feature that subjects are asked to act *'as-if'* they were engaged in specified social context that are largely outside of the specific social context of the experimental situation' (1976; author's; italics). Yet having made this statement, they passed on, and although the above emphasis on social context is inaccurate, *the implications of the 'as-if' are profound and should have been confronted* (see Chapter 6).

Other 'as-if' definitions

Hamilton (1976) defined role plays as being situations in which 'the experimenter asks a subject to act *'as-if'* some condition or conditions obtained which in fact do not'. She emphasized that the essence of role play is the *'as-if'*. Hamilton's overall aim was to put into perspective the role play and deception controversy. In so doing, she drew up a schema intended to describe the varieties of role play as practised. It is unfortunate that she partly added to the terminological confusion despite the greater thoroughness of her approach. For example, when considering the 'content' of role play versus the 'form', she put forward the following features of content:

1 persons as Self or Another;
2 the role played within the investigative context, for example, as laboratory subject or other role;
3 context of performance;
    (a) elaborateness of scenario;
    (b) involvement of experimenter, assistants and subjects in complementary roles;
    (c) absence or presence of audience.

Exactly what she intended by 'role' or 'person' is not made clear and, therefore, one cannot be certain about the kind or range of discrimination being made. Nor did she reconsider these in the light of what we shall argue to be the essence of role play: the 'as-if'. Therefore, although the above – figuratively and loosely understood – may indeed describe aspects of role play, such a schematization does not elucidate the conceptual basis of, or methodological implications for, role plays.

Geller (1978) also defined role play with respect to *'as-if'* behaviour. However, he did not explore this further, preferring to draw upon Hamilton's descriptive schema for elaboration. He also added considerable chaos by following Coutu's (1951) distinction between 'role taking' and 'role playing' to distinguish active from passive role playing. For the purpose of role play Geller defined active role playing as 'imagining what another would do' and passive role playing as, 'behaviour of oneself enacted in a given situation' (this, it must be noted, a distortion of Coutu's position). Thus, Geller used 'role playing' ambiguously to refer both to the technique and self behaviour. If he had wished to be terminologically consistent then to consider a person actively taking the part of another in a role play he would have had to call this 'role-taking-playing' or 'role-taking-enactment'.

Lastly, Hendrick (1977) sought to criticize the existing literature and to defend the potential of role play. His central criticism of the contemporary role play literature was its apparent failure to consider the concept of 'role taking'; although it might be observed that within much of the clinical role play literature (for example, Kelly's Fixed Role Therapy, 1955a and 1955b) this principle was viewed as axiomatic. (Moreover, it will be argued below that the unreflexive use of 'role' is misleading and inappropriate, given its existence within a quite separate domain of theorizing.) Citing Mead (1934), Piaget (1926) and Flavell (1968), among others, Hendrick defined 'role taking' as the cognitive activity by which one infers the interactional cognitions of the other. He claimed to relate this cognitive activity to role play, which he defined – also after Coutu – as the 'overt enactment of one's role as appropriate to a given situation', with 'role' here referring to a reciprocal social position and appropriate behaviour being the product of consensual prescription. Hendrick, unlike other writers, thus did make a distinction between 'role playing' and role playing (technique), the former being equated with Coutu's 'playing' a role' and the latter with his 'playing at a role'. Hendrick then claimed that 'role playing' and 'role taking' are the two sociological concepts that account for the bulk of human interaction. Unfortunately these concepts emerge from different theoretical grounds. Further, this claim describes the full extent of his attempt to relate these concepts.

Hendrick also provided a schema for describing role play, although it is also a schema which is said to include any social psychology experiment. Even more confusingly, it was named the 'Role Playing Model'. Within it more important conceptual distinctions are blurred. For instance, he described the individual subject's behaviour as exemplifying 'self role' or 'other role' behaviour, which he stated are equally epistemologically valid. However, it is not clear what a 'self role' is, except a convenient *ad hoc* distinction. Thus, he also ignored all the theoretical problems concerned with the relationship between self and role, and all the methodological problems of generating and sustaining action rather than analysing it.

We have already considered Moreno's extensive and over-inclusive definitions of 'role', which it might be assumed underpinned his understanding of role play. However, Moreno also offers distinct explicit definitions of role play, which he described as arising from the individual's 'natural role playing'. 'Role playing' is seen as a naturally occurring process that is emergent in the earliest mother–child matrix of interaction (1946[1972], Vol 1: Section 10); and which culminates in the 'personification of other forms of existence through the medium of play' (1959, Vol 2: 140). Role play *technique*, which Moreno implied arises from natural 'role playing', is defined as consisting of: 'placing individuals (the actors) in various situations – *alien* to the situations in which they live – and in various roles – *alien* to their self and its private roles.' (1959, Vol 2: 146). Once more, there are difficulties in rendering compatible ideas of 'personification' and 'being in a role or situation', especially given that Moreno's understanding of the meaning of 'role' is so various. Nor do these definitions integrate those imaginative and other steps that are required of an individual in a psychodrama.

Neither Moreno's concept of 'role playing' nor that of 'role' is anywhere criticized or scrutinized by his followers (for example, Williams, 1989; Holmes and Karp, 1991), yet they are, as we have seen, highly various and conceptually inconsistent. None the less, and despite his terminological inconsistency, Moreno does provide more insight into technique (with the exception of Stanislavski) than any other role play proponent. Much of this is handed down within active training of psychotherapists, rather than through reflective reading. However, the limitations in his theorizing, indeed his grandiosity of writing, may have impeded the development of psychodrama or role play in other more conventional settings precisely because it is not communicated well through indirect means such as writing. On the other hand, the divergence of definition above is also indicative of Moreno's more realistic and creative ability to use all the available means and levels of human experience, for the purpose of setting up a psychodrama. This creative ability is absent in other role play user's work.

Conclusions

Those who have attempted to describe role play, and who inevitably directly use or allude to role theory terminology, do not seem to have recognized the profound conceptual problems outlined in this chapter, or their implications. Unfortunately, even after redefinition (see Chapter 6), we are left with some terminological dilemmas. Ideally a severance from role theory terminology, is required, so that all simulation role plays would have a different descriptor such as 'as-if methodology'. However, role play terms are used so ubiquitously that we cannot merely abandon them, but rather must learn to use the terms without taking on the conceptual burdens of role theory which are so often attached, principally those burdens of 'performativeness', reductionism and determinism.

In Chapter 6, we shall consider what is missing from all the above conceptualizations of role play that would pre-empt many of the conceptual and terminological tangles described. The aim is simply to provide an adequate description of what role play is, of what actually happens in an event for it to be called a role play.

What is essential and distinctive in role play will be argued to relate to the 'as-ifness' that Hamilton (1976), Forward et al. (1976) and Geller

(1978) all touched upon but did not fully explore. However, role plays are not adequately described solely in relation to this 'as-ifness'. Hence, all the necessary features of a role play will be described and discussed. Comparisons will also be made in relation to general experimental and therapeutic technique. Thereby, it will become clear, that in many ways role play is not distinguishable from other exploratory or didactic techniques, except with respect to the absolute essential identifying features of secondary 'as-ifness'. Moreover, adequate conceptual description of role play will be demonstrated to need no recourse to role theory terms.

6

Redefining Role Play
and General Methodological and
Technical Considerations

In Chapter 5 some of the pervasive terminological and conceptual difficulties in extant descriptions of role play, and their bases in role theory
terms, were outlined. These, it was shown, resulted in deterministic and
performance-oriented accounts of human action, which are then often
taken on inadvertently by role play users, and which have impeded a full
development of subsequent dependent role play technique. It is, therefore,
of the utmost importance to attempt a definition that not only avoids these
major pitfalls, but also provides a viable basis for generating practice
guidelines. The attempt made in this chapter is presented in the form of
eight descriptive principles or definitions, which seek to formulate the
necessary and essential features of any role play. These principles should
facilitate a better understanding of the conceptual confusions surrounding
arguments over the efficacy of role plays, namely: the assumption that
role play techniques are necessarily humanistic techniques; the assumption
that role play techniques are intrinsically antipathetical to deception techniques; and the assumption that role play techniques are intrinsically
antipathetical to conventional research techniques. Above all, the discussions around these propositions are grounded in this book's stated
critical stance towards conventional methodology within pure and applied
psychology (see Chapter 2).

Such a definition as is attempted here should also allow closer scrutiny of
the methodological implications of different role play designs and techniques. (There is particular reference to the literature of the social psychological debate of the 1970s, because it was in this debate that most concern
was expressed and issues optimally clarified, despite the severe limitations of
even these attempts at elucidation.) Only one of the definitions (Definition 2)
absolutely differentiates role play from any other exploratory or learning
situation (see Yardley, 1982a); all the other seven characteristics are,
however, necessary to the activity of role play.

The descriptive principles

Definition 1: An initial framework is set up that serves to separate the events occurring within it, from events occurring outside it in the mundane world – primary 'as-ifness'

This framework is usually called role play or simulation. It provides a separation of the 'inside' world of role play from the outside mundane world. Just as any experiment in psychology or any therapeutic encounter, behaviour rehearsal or game activity, the framework symbolizes and draws upon the common socially constructed assumption, that there is a discontinuity of cause and effect relationships from the 'outside' world. There is here a **primary 'as-if' status**.

If John is rude to Jane within role, within a role play, it is not expected that this 'rudeness' will have consequences for their relationship 'outside' the role play. This framework in itself does not distinguish role play from conventional experimental methodology or from any psychotherapeutic episode where, between therapist and client, a world is created within a world.

Such a framework creates the opportunity for role play facilitators to control aspects of the mundane world, more strongly, consistently and systematically than usually occurs in the outside world. A world within a world is constructed which purports to limit consequences for participants, and thus in turn – perhaps most importantly – to limit consequences and responsibility/liability for the instigators of the role play. To the extent that this world is seen or presented as discontinuous with the 'real' world, there is a lack of need for accountability and the complete involvement of all concerned.

Reality status and methodological implications However, despite their primary 'as-if' status, role plays, games, therapeutic episodes and conventional laboratory experiments are, as Movahedi (1977) cryptically states, 'real inasmuch as not imaginary'. Certainly they exist as *part* of the mundane world and, as such, are subject to the same social processes and motivational structuring as other events. Within social psychology there is a well established literature on demand characteristics, that is the phenomenon of 'subjects' in experiments trying to meet the assumed expectations of the experimenters. Within psychotherapeutic and behaviour therapy literature there is a growing awareness of the importance of the real person and the real characteristics of the therapist, and the impact of this on process. Hence, in terms of the setting up of role plays for research, clinical or educational purposes, this points to the clear need for the role play facilitator to know, and/or to examine, the purposes for which the role play is being carried out. This must involve a rigorous examination of the extent to which the facilitator is 'manipulating' the content and structure of the role play in relation to the achievement of specific ends. For example, the goals of didacticism in social skills training versus exploration in psycho-drama, implicate very different strategies in relation to the depth of action to be generated, the information to be stipulated or elicited, and the analytic focus to be adopted. And both these goals lead to quite different technical requirements in the setting up of a role play. (These will be considered in some detail in Chapters 8 and 9.)

Much of the strident debate of the 1970s concerning the reality status of role plays *vis-à-vis* conventional experiments has obscured this primary shared identity. This has occurred largely because the grounds of theoretical differences, about the nature of 'reality', implicated in these arguments, has not been explicitly clarified, and because primary 'as-ifs' are not distinguished from secondary 'as-ifs' (see Definition 2 below). For example, Miller (1972), Freedman (1969), Cooper (1976), and Aronson and Carlsmith (1968), argued that role plays lack realism and the involved participation of subjects, compared with conventional experiments. On the contrary, as argued above, both approaches are based on a primary 'as-if'. Moreover, the relationship between an 'as-if' proposition and the 'reality' of the ensuing behaviour depends in the first place on one's definition of reality. For example, the most common view of reality, held by methodological behaviourists, lies in the simulation and generation of independent variables which have a lawful relationship to generated dependent variables. Thus, more subjective and phenomenal issues such as subject involvement are, in fact, redundant and outside their area of concern.

Forward et al. (1976) and Geller (1978), countering this position, suggested that role play is more real because more phenomenally involving of participants. Their vision of reality, however, in contrast to that posited above, lies in the phenomenal and subjective sense of reality as held by the participants. Mixon (1977) and Hamilton (1976) tackled the issue of reality in social psychological experiments rather differently, by asserting that both role plays and conventional experiments are *simulations* of the real world, and that on those particular grounds neither is to be preferred. Although this has some congruence with the primary 'as-if' status, as explored above, Mixon and Hamilton do not consider, in depth, what is or is not intended to be simulated in either case. Further, a secondary explicit level of 'as-ifs' occurs in role play but not in the conventional experiment, which has not been recognized (see Definition 2, below). Mixon (1977) and Hamilton (1976) went on to say that role play is likely to be more effective because it is potentially more complex, and more capable of involving a greater number of variables. But the view supported here is that this spuriously relates the degree of reality to the degree of complexity of an event.

The issues surrounding 'reality' and 'involvement' can, therefore, be seen to be pseudo-issues in that these terms appear to have different connotations for different authors, in addition to which they are inadequately clarified. Role plays cannot be distinguished simply in terms of their reality status. If, however, role play proponents intend role plays to be humanistic and 'realistic', whether for research, therapy or any other applied task, certain considerations follow. For example, the degree to which the primary 'as-if' frame separates the experimental or therapy world from the mundane world might be explored with participants. Can participant Z engage in a role play where they are the 'subject' of sexual harassment without being negatively affected by the role play in a manner that extends outside the role play itself? Will participating in a role play where an attitudinal position that is normally rejected is 'played out' actually lead to a change of attitude (as the Janis and King, 1954, evidence would suggest) in the mundane world? It is likely that if greater involvement is required from participants, this boundary may need to be highly permeable; which, in turn, would require accountability and the possibility of 'real' or mundane consequences for participants and experimenter, therapist or teacher. Then experimenters and others would have to review the assumption that role play necessarily (whether it involves deception or not) protects participants from unpleasant and real consequences. It is this tension – between consequence and lack of consequence – which is differentially exploited in therapy. For this reason, in general the therapist would hope for 'real world' consequences; however, if a role play demands one participant enacts very pathological behaviours, how is the therapist to guard against generalization of such behaviour rather than desired behaviours? In chapters 5, 8 and 9 we consider in more depth these issues of real consequences and their benefits and disadvantages.

Definition 2: within this initial primary 'as-if' frame some of the constituent conditions (frames and foci) have a secondary 'as-if' status, demanding that an alternative perception be made from a normal perception

These secondary 'as-ifs' are the only features that distinguish role plays from conventional experiments and conventional therapeutic encounters. Although, among others, Hamilton (1976) and Geller (1978) recognize that role plays have an 'as-if' quality, the nature of this 'as-ifness' is not examined and thus the dual aspect within role plays of 'as-ifness' is not discovered. Hence, its importance and consequences cannot be realized. Role plays contain explicit and implicit secondary 'as-ifs' within the primary 'as-if' frame of experiment or therapy, or other procedure. For although it has been argued that both conventional and role play experiments and therapies commence from an initial severance from the mundane world (see Definition 1), it is only in the role play that there are explicitly embedded secondary 'as-ifs' in which the participant is enjoined to act 'as-if', given certain conditions described by terms using the person/situation dichotomy; for example, 'you are yourself, with, however, the following traits . . .', 'you are Mr X . . .', 'your partner is a nuclear physicist . . .', 'that piece of paper is an electric shock machine . . .', 'it is a summer's day . . .', and so on.

The kinds of secondary 'as-ifs' present in role plays are extremely varied in both content and presentation and open in themselves to methodological considerations such as are particularly contained within Definitions 6,7 and 8 below. Their superordinate importance, however, lies in the *fact* of their existence, particularly in relation to the issues of participant involvement or engagement. Further, this important distinction between primary and secondary 'as-ifs', unrecognized by other writers, lies at the root of the controversy over the 'involvement' of participants. For when opponents of role play, such as Miller (1972) and Freedman (1969), talk of role plays leading to lack of spontaneity, self-consciousness and uninvolved deliberation they are, in effect, objecting to the explicit presence of secondary 'as-ifs'. For proponents, it is exactly co-operation at the level of secondary 'as-ifs' which is seen to lead to subject involvement and spontaneity – although the case on either side is never argued. Bearing in mind our earlier discussion on underlying conceptions of reality (see Definition 1), if we take as our criteria of reality and involvement the participants' phenomenal sense of these, certain technical problems arise concerning the establishment of actuality, particularly via the secondary 'as-ifs'.

Frequently and incongruously involvement is equated with activity rather than passivity by role play proponents (For example, Hamilton, 1976; Mixon, 1971; Baron, 1977). However, the problem with what are labelled passive role plays, such as paper and pencil tests, is not that they lack active performance or overt behaviour, but that they do not partake of the necessary and paradoxical secondary 'as-ifs'. That is to say, they remain *conditional* not actual (see Chapter 7 on Presencing). The subject is not instructed to *be* in the present, within the secondary 'as-if' frame or transformation, but merely asked to respond intellectually to conditional matters – a logical and predictive task. The experience of the 'as-if' may, however, be strong and valid even though physically passive – as in the world of the dream. Similarly, in active role plays, subjects are not technically aided to engage in the actuality of the secondary 'as-ifs' but are instructed merely as to the conditionality of the event.

Engagement with the secondary 'as-ifs' is crucial in determining the experiencing of reality on the part of the participants. The quality of this experience and the precise nature of the secondary 'as-if' objects to be engaged differentiate, not the role play from the conventional experiment etc., but the humanistic role play from any other role play (see Chapter 8 on Particularization and Personalization). This technical development and awareness is essential for the advance of role play, whether or not the theoretical context of role play is positivistic or humanistic, to increase the efficacy of role play.

Definition 3: for the purposes of investigation, separation is made from the stream of social action which is seen to have boundaries that delineate it from that which it is not

The term 'role play' indicates that some psychological/social material is being given an 'episode' status: for example, *a* bank transaction, *a* meeting between friends, *an* argument between lovers. The seeming coherence and unity of an event is thus detached from the stream of ongoing social life. This separation may appear self-evident in relation to formal events such as a wedding (in Harré and Secord's (1972) terms, a wedding would constitute a formal episode) but is clearly more problematic around less formal interactions, where the segmentation of experience becomes increasingly arbitrary (see Definition 4).

For the purposes of analysis, the infinite interdependence of systems and situations is denied by the establishment of boundaries; these, however, may be permeable boundaries (for example, a parallel problem was identified in Chapter 5 on role theory terms). Events are presented as having clear beginnings and endings; even with a formal episode this is problematic, as a wedding may be defined in religious terms as commencing with the reading of bans, but in psychological or indeed social terms may commence at very different or very indeterminate points in time. Considering a more informal episode, such as 'getting to know someone', the definition of this context will be highly shaped by the individual's understanding of what it means to get to know someone, and so on.

The extent of permeability of boundaries in role play is thus clearly related to the degree to which the boundary structures allow the participant to negotiate or change the initial definition of the situation. For example, where an instigator asserts, 'This is a role play on anxiety', boundaries are maintained and asserted by the instigator alone, unless a participant is able to redefine the situation or to elaborate another context for its exposition. This, in turn, may introduce new factors, unforeseen by the instigator, such as: 'this is not a situation in which I feel anxious' or 'it simply wouldn't happen like that'. The permeability of boundaries may also be challenged by a participant, for example: 'I cannot separate this situation from another. There is no clear beginning or end here'. Clearly many role play situations involve presenting participants with a predetermined scenario, which is felt to be entirely consistent with the aims of the role play instigator and his or her aims for participants. However, participants may – and frequently do – complain of the lack of personal validity to which such predetermined scenarios give rise.

Paper and pencil role plays, those which simulate conventional experiments and those tied to positivistic methodology in general, do not allow any challenges to boundary maintenance. Such a challenge would be a necessary feature of a truly humanistic approach. Clear boundary maintenance is almost entirely dependent on the way in which the instigator asserts and defines the situation. From a positivistic point of view this is a necessary precondition for experimental rigour, yet there are many arguments for suggesting that more meaningful and humanistic research and learning experiences might arise from negotiation of definitions (see Harré and Secord, 1972). Negotiation can be easily incorporated into role play techniques, as is done informally in psychodramatic role play, by concentrating on individual interpretation and creation of situation and scenario, rather than assuming that situations can be standardized without the participants' explicit co-operation. Thus, within the latter, what might be common to individual and social actions would be grounded in individually *generated* richness and diversity, rather than in parsimonious a priori analyses or hunches, mediated through supposedly interchangeable individuals.

Definition 4: this separation appears to contain, or may yield, some internal logic, identity or coherence, in terms of the goals of the investigator – a separation that may be presented as 'open' or 'closed'

This initial separation by the role play instigator tells us little about the methodology underlying it. What is more important than the separation itself is the rationale behind separation. Thus, a separation which involves the inclusion of 'complex' social behaviour is not necessarily to be preferred over one which involves 'simple' behaviour – a reason for superiority often put forward by role play proponents. The same episode, for example confronting a workman over poor workmanship, or participating in a Milgram experiment, may be seen by an experimenter using role play as *the* appropriate episode, having face validity in terms of a hypothesis about assertive behaviour or, conversely, by another researcher as constituting a fairly arbitrary separation, having only facilitatory status with regard to the purpose of understanding an individual. In the former, symbolic interpretation of the event is unimportant compared to the 'reality' of the independent–dependent variable relationship, within an experimenter defined 'assertion situation'. Hence, given that the definition and possibilities of this situation have been predetermined, a **'closed'** experimental or therapeutic event or episode is constituted. All behaviour and action will be judged against a criterion relating to assertion, whether or not mundanely justifiable; for example, these situations may be redefined as events concerning social class differences rather than as situations normatively prefiguring assertiveness as an independent dimension. In the latter case, where the situation is viewed as having only facilitatory status, and given that symbolic interpretation of all elements of the 'situation' is paramount, this may be termed an **'open'** episode. This allows redefinition and negotiation of meaning to take place, in so far as the experimenter does not pre-empt the possibility of alternative meanings emerging. The participant or observer may wish to consider different judgement criteria for good or poor workmanship, the particular frames of mind that impact upon the person's ability to deal with a potentially confrontational situation, the personal agendas involved in winning or losing an argument, the strategies of negotiation available and used, the impact of dealing with persons known versus those unknown, and so on.

Where the role play instigator chooses the episode and defines it as closed and not open to redefinition, it has a demonstrative aim and is associated with the goals of prediction and control. Many role play experiments have followed this model, in particular those that are concerned with replication or verification of experiments otherwise 'conventionally' carried out (For example, Mixon, 1972; Strickland et al., 1976). Both Rychlak (1977) and Gergen (1978) have argued that experimental social psychology is traditionally demonstrative and consists of finding contexts or scenarios which demonstrate the experimenter's hypothesis to be true rather than truly testing such hypotheses. Even Mixon (1972), who has been viewed as a radical social psychologist, worked within such a framework and, despite his more interesting use of role play in experimentation, aimed to create and demonstrate scenarios that would determine outcome. Similarly, role play assessment techniques which purport to measure social skills or assertion skills are closed with respect to definition.

In the social and mainstream clinical psychology literature on role play, negotiation is not a salient feature. The frequent espousal of honesty rather than deception involves stipulation, not **negotiation**. For example, in a Mixon-type role play, the beliefs that are necessary for the action to take place may indeed be communicated openly to the subject, but whether or not the client is willing and able to accept these stipulations is not queried. For instance, the participant is told that he is 'everyman' and that he is taking part in a jury trial; thus, no negotiation can take place. If humanistic aims were to be pursued, attention would have to be given to the possibility of the participants' knowing not only the hypothesis, but of recreating the hypothesis, negotiating the choice of a suitable context and negotiating the meaning of *all* the actions then ensuing. This type of approach would distinguish humanistic role plays from conventional role plays. For example, a researcher might be interested in the impact of being a victim upon making a jury decision concerning a similar crime. If the experimenter arbitrarily decides that the victim crime to be role played will be that of having been mugged, some individuals may have actually experienced this or something similar, while others may not; those who have not shared this experience may or may not be able to reach a sense of the likely consequences for themselves. However, the participant may well be able to identify a 'victim' event of similar seriousness that *they can relate to*.

Definition 5: the ways in which individuals are led to participate in role plays (or other procedures) are importantly related to the motive structure of the whole role play enterprise (or other procedure)

Role play proponents have often argued that their techniques, of necessity, make use of the 'whole' person. This is nonsensical. Just as in any other methodology, the 'whole' person in a role play is used, only in the gratuitous sense that physically the person is presented with all his or her potentialities. Obviously not all of a person's experience and behaviour repertoire can be called upon at any one time – these are infinitely embedded and also creative or emergent. What is more important is the way in which one uses individuals: whether at one extreme as mere agencies of, or means of prediction for, the experimenter by which he or she can establish general laws or whether, at the other extreme, they are used as agents and final causes in themselves for the purposes of understanding each individual separately. In the latter case, the experimenter or therapist is at least figuratively moving towards understanding the impossible – the whole person – because more of the control of the ongoing situation is placed in the subject's hands.

Role plays can and are used for both purposes, but most frequently the individual is viewed as agency not agent, and often at a very trivial level despite the contrary intentions of social psychologists, for instance, particularly when using role play for replications or behavioural assessment (for example, Greenberg, 1967; Holmes and Bennet, 1974; Willis and Willis, 1970; see also Chapter 3 for details of current research strategies). These give only three- or four-line instructions to role players. The terseness of these instructions conveys the impression that the experimenters expect role play subjects to be able to plunge wholeheartedly into the role play without knowing clearly their own situated identities, the full circumstances in which they are involved, or the environment in which they are present. In such cases, evidently very little is demanded of the individual in terms of personal resources and creativity. Given minimal instructions such as, 'role play being afraid/a naive experimental subject/a parent/a prisoner/an 'everyman', all that is demanded of the subject is an ability to provide consensually mediated stereotypes in line with the demand characteristics of the experiments, which are and seek to be depersonalized and depersonalizing.

As was considered in some detail in Chapters 2 and 3, this is equally the case with most research and clinical practice role play strategies to date. The most typical paradigm is probably that of the assertion skills role play, where again there is a minimalist induction approach involving a one- or two-line context setting followed by a one-or two-line prompt, from a therapy or research confederate, to be followed by a one- or two-line response from the subject/patient. Even the 'style' of delivery of information to be imparted to the participant impacts upon the meaning of the final role play event. Hence, giving one participant information 'secretly' and away from another participant constructs a context/framing of distrust; or emphasizing the imaginative nature of a role play in the induction, rather than its to-be-shared actuality, can construct a role play in which the actors feel depersonalized.

Clearly, for the most part, role play inductors adopt a minimalist, conventional context stripping and reductionist methodology. This is far from the humanistic greater emphasis upon individual subjects participating in the development of appropriate research questions and methods, or treatment goals and strategies. No use is made of subjective experience and individual ability to comprehend aspects of social being and interaction. Rarely is there any concern for meaningful material which might incorporate the intentions of the participants. Only psychodrama and a handful of other insight-oriented role plays prove to be exceptions to this dominant and restrictive methodological orientation.

Definition 6: each boundaried situation contains frames and foci which arise from an interaction between the initial definition and framing of the overall context (see Definition 1) and the ad hoc *definitions of both inductor and participant*

'Frame' refers to a definition of the situation which gives meaning and direction to the actions that occur and to objects that are present within its psychological boundaries. This frame separates one zone of meaning from another and is not usually consciously held. 'Focus' refers to a highlighted detail of awareness or action necessarily occurring within a frame. The terms are problematic as frames are infinitely embedded in other frames and may at any point become foci. Further foci are suggestive of and engender other frames. Frames carry assumptions which give rise to a varying motivational structuring of events that may be intentional or non-intentional. The framing and the foci may be implicitly or explicitly conveyed by the investigator to the participant and may or may not be resisted by, or negotiated with, the participant.

Typically within psychology, frames and foci are defined with reference to, for example: patterns of behaviour; self-presentation strategies; personal and social roles; cognitive activities; interpersonal skills and strategies; situations; etc. The degree to which framing or focusing is forced upon the participant alters the nature of the 'scientific' or therapeutic enterprise. Demonstrative aims involve a tighter control on frame and focus: the episode is defined, certain features highlighted that might normally remain unobtrusive and certain actions are prescribed.

In contrast, the more diffuse humanistic goals of exploration and under-standing necessitate allowing individual participants greater choice in selecting areas of relevance, and greater opportunity of redefinition and multiple and changeable focussing. (This is an essential element of psycho-dramatic role play.) To the experimenter or didactic therapist, the latter approach may seem to weaken the role play and confuse the design, but the former approach runs the risk of obtaining superficial and/or meaningless results, or non-generalizable therapeutic experiences.

Deception within experiments (or within systemic therapies) involves participants operating with frames and foci that differ from those of the experimenter. Some have argued that role plays are a methodological alternative to deception. However, as Cooper (1976) asserted, deception is not a methodology in itself and does not distinguish role play from more traditional approaches. Even more to the point is the simple fact that while deception certainly involves definite methodological problems concerned with differential focusing and framing, role plays themselves may involve deception – perhaps even unwittingly. For example, Holmes and Bennet

(1974) carried out an experiment to compare and evaluate the efficacy of role play *vis-à-vis* traditional experimentation, and argued that it demonstrated negative findings for role play. But participants were told that the focus of the study was their role play skills, in spite of the fact that it was role play that was being evaluated, not the individuals. The implications of this differential focusing on the part of participants and experimenter obviously should be considered in evaluating the validity of a role play.

Role play experiments that replicate other experiments differ in the extent to which they give participants detail, but all set out to give frames and foci; but rarely, if ever, are frames and foci negotiated and drawn from participants' experience, despite the desirability of this from a humanistic and methodological perspective. Role plays used in didactic therapies and applied situations, such as social skills training, also involve the therapist or leader predetermining focus and framing.

Most role plays in social, applied and clinical psychology, therefore, can be seen to work within a traditional demonstrative approach.

Definition 7: the action of the episode must be established by stipulating some conditions and leaving others free. The relationship between numbers of conditions established and the 'freedom' of the participant is paradoxical

When critics, of whatever methodological orientation, complain that participants are not free or able to be spontaneous they usually appear to be referring to the individual participants' experienced lack of freedom. This is usually understood to relate to an overbearingly high degree of stipulation on the part of the experimenter or therapist, leaving the participant little choice of action. However, equally important but almost totally neglected is the lack of freedom or choice occasioned by *lack of stipulation* on the part of the researcher or practitioner.

Fiske (1978: 114), in considering the problems of adhering to his strict positivist research methodology, raised a related paradox. His thrust did not concern the *experience* of subjects but their interpretative actions. He argued that both too great abstractness and its opposite, too great detail, threw the individual back on his or her own resources and interpretive style. This diagnosis is agreed with here but, given a positive evaluation of using the individual's resources, we would seek different remedies. When, for example, a role playing subject is given insufficient information, either for lack of information or because of too great a level of abstractness, then certainly the individual is thrown back on his or her own resources. Faced with little or vague information, what typically happens is that the participant responds at a rather crude level to the assumed demand characteristics, and draws on stereotypifications and even acts on these. Illustrations of this are presented in detail in Chapter 9; see also the Stanford Prison Experiment (Haney et al., 1973; see critique in Chapter 4), where the evidence or 'realism' proffered is likely merely to reflect gross acting out on the part of the participants.

Providing too much information may produce similar results if participants are given no appropriate strategy for dealing with the information, forcing them into haphazard selectivity, anxiety and either disengagement from the role play or inadequate performance.

To avoid such problems and at the same time pursue humanistic aims, the role play inductor should demand specificity of detail related to the focusing and framing of the event. Such detail should be constructed with the co-operation of the participant so that what is commonly and objectively understood has roots in individual experience. Hence, in a role play it is not sufficient to give a detailed script that bypasses the individual or to demand a 'free' improvisation based on a minimal scenario that gives no sense of direction. The individual must be able to see the situation posited as 'his or her own' situation. If the individual is unable to do this, it must be achieved by eliciting elaborations from the participant while openly maintaining any imposed definition that the experimenter finds necessary to his or her purpose. This definition must, however, be feasible, given the participant's views. Failure to achieve any such agreed definition would suggest that the experimenter's own assumptions embedded in the created situation are erroneous. For example, if the researcher or therapist's chosen situation is a husband–wife confrontation with the aim of either measuring or teaching assertion skills, and if the researcher or therapist views the situation as typical but the subjects or clients view it as extremely unlikely, then clearly some readjustment is needed. Moreover, if participants' views are not elicited on this matter and the role play continues, then 'objectivism' has been maintained at the expense of 'objectivity'.

Definition 8: the conditions stipulated are established through the medium of what is conventionally named the person and/or the situation

The establishment of these conditions through the person–situation dichotomy is a convention that needs examination, in all experiments, therapeutic encounters and role plays. It involves the implicit or explicit attribution of motives, reasons and causes to specify agents or agencies (see Burke, 1969 for extensive treatment of motivational language). In the traditional experiment the accounting style primarily concerns situations or environments. The theoretical emphasis is on environmental manipulations and the subject is instructed to concern him or herself with the situation and not with the self or personal experience. Other persons are seen as part of the situation but the person as agent is not usually involved. Similarly, despite an avowed interest in the person in role plays, the emphasis is generally upon the situation or scenario. Even where a character or role is played, given the lack of specificity that is usual to the induction of these, the role is not integrated into the subject's own experience. Thus, most accounting in both the traditional and the role play experiment is heavily biased towards the situational, with consequential implications for behaviour and experience.

In particular, as has already been argued in Chapter 5, advocates of role play typically draw or rely upon sociological role theory – a form of analysis that is rooted in situationism and determinism. More significantly, those who seek to exploit traditional role theory make no attempt to develop a separate analysis of the psychological *technique* of role play. It is precisely such an analysis that focuses on the generation of action by individuals, which, as we have argued, is beyond the scope of sociological role theory.

If humanistic research, in particular, is sought by role play proponents, *then induction techniques must be sensitive to the requirements of generating individual action.* This in turn necessitates a more sensitive vocabulary, analysis and understanding of the nature of role play. It requires the recognition that role playing with respect to the technique does not equal the playing or taking of roles, except at the most banal level, where 'role' is loosely used and interchangeably with 'part'. Even here the term 'role' should be used with circumspection when communicating with participants. For as Messinger et al. (1962) point out, the words 'playing a role' in mundane existence convey overtones of the individual's experienced alienation or intention to deceive another. Above all, the confusion in the literature over 'role' has detracted from the analysis of what it is that really distinguishes role play, and it is to this fundamental distinction that we now turn.

Although the secondary 'as-if' features of role plays have been asserted to be the only distinctive aspect of role play, users cannot be content with their technical mastery alone. All eight methodological issues have profound relevance in choosing the kind of research style and content that may be covered by the umbrella term 'role play'. Role plays as used in social psychology are conventional and, far from offering an alternative to more familiar experimental techniques are typically limited by the same positivistic aims and methods. Commonly, as has been shown, role play users favour experimental control, demonstrative selection of material, situationism and subject subordination to experimental goals over negotiation of meaning, personalization of experience and openness – which might be seen as true humanistic goals. Thus role play in a humanistic sense has by no means been given an adequate trial as a research approach. Role plays as used within psychological therapies and similarly based in positivism are also equally limited, where the therapist's definition of situation, and control of frame and foci is over and above the client's subjective experience. Some forms of clinical and applied role plays such as psychodrama are not limited in this fashion and, as we have seen in Chapter 4, they have much to offer (consistent with the technical approach advocated here) that might enhance role play methodology, notwithstanding a very different set of goals to more conventional behavioural/cognitive therapeutic orientations.

The conceptualization of role play as essentially distinguished by virtue of its secondary 'as-if' status leads us next to consider how best to engage participants with these secondary 'as-ifs'. We need first to consider the nature of involvement and engagement in more detail. Three critical induction processes – **Personalization, Particularization** and **Presencing** – will then be put forward, all of which will be grounded initially in an epistemological rationale and positioning.

Note: This chapter is based on an article entitled 'On distinguishing role plays from conventional methodologies', *Journal for the Theory of Social Behaviour*, 12 (2): 125–39, 1982.

7

On Involvement, Engagement and Technique in Role Plays: Conceptual Underpinnings of Three Key Induction Principles

As we have already seen, any role play may be conceptualized as requiring two levels of conditionality. The first level of conditionality, the *primary* 'as-if', is common to all experiments, therapies and rehearsal activities, including role plays. This applies to the general framing of the event, which serves to isolate it from mundane consequences. This thus reassures all parties that their personal responsibility is limited, while seeking to elicit their willing co-operation in these circumstances. The second level of conditionality, the *secondary* 'as-if', alone distinguishes role plays from other activities, that is, *in the role play, and only in the role play, particular and deliberate perceptual substitutions and reconstruals are required of both a situational and personal nature (the secondary 'as-ifs')*. Thus, for example, a research laboratory is to be viewed as a hospital consulting room; the confederate is to be viewed as a medical consultant; and the protagonist, normally healthy, is to view him or herself as physically diseased. All the terms commonly used to describe aspects of 'as-if' experiments such as, 'role', 'character', 'person', and 'scenario' can be reconceptualized as, and further broken down into, these secondary 'as-ifs'. Hence, the role of policeman, where minimally described by simple reference to this role label, is nevertheless posited upon an assumed tacit grouping of identifying factors (secondary 'as-ifs' – a person in uniform, a person whose job is to uphold the law, etc.). The role may be a little more explicitly detailed (although still minimalist), for example a sergeant, that is someone with a certain level of authority; a traffic policeman or a plain clothes detective – all of which secondary 'as-if' details are signifiers of meanings held relevant by the person describing/inducting the role play.

Problems with the Concept of 'Involvement'

As we have seen in earlier chapters the question of systematic technique in role plays is seldom addressed directly by researchers or therapists. The closest approximation to any focused concern with technique has been that expressed within the 1970s' social psychology debate on the issue of subject involvement within experiments, often the cornerstone of arguments and counterarguments on the general efficacy of 'as-if' methods. Greenberg (1967) appears to be the first social psychologist to have suggested that subject involvement might be a crucial variable in role-play simulations of experiments. Since then, Geller (1978), Baron (1977), and Alexander and Scriven (1977), among other role play proponents, have stressed the importance of such involvement for 'realism'. Mixon (1977) has queried whether involvement is necessary for simulations although on balance he appears to favour it. On the other hand, Miller (1972), Aronson and Carlsmith (1968) and Cooper (1976) have asserted that role plays lack involvement in comparison to traditional methods.

The concept of involvement is, however, variously comprehended and hinges on a prior, and invariably implicit, understanding of reality. Thus the arguments concerning involvement are mostly founded on those concerning 'reality status'. To summarize briefly (see also Chapter 6), reality may be viewed at one extreme as the phenomenal experience of the participant, and, at the other, as something that is expressed in the independent–dependent variable relationship, which can be said to be contaminated by subjective experience and which can only be inferred through consensual validation provided by 'objective' observers. From the extreme phenomenalist/humanistic perspective there follows a very close relationship between reality and the experience of involvement. Conversely, from the extreme empiricist position, there follows only an indirect and tenuous link between the two. Therapists are engaged in various positions along this curve, with cognitive-behaviourists and indeed classical psychodynamic thinkers lending weight to the view that clients' behaviour and thoughts stand in relation to 'external' reality; whereas latter day psychodynamic thinkers such as Stolorow et al. (1987), and evidently humanistic and existential therapists, put the weight of value on subjective validities.

Nevertheless, whatever the therapist or researcher's assumptions about reality or indeed about the nature of the source of action (independent controlling variables, subject plans, unconscious forces, role–rule models, etc.), *all researchers and therapists share an interest in the participants or clients being phenomenally involved in the overt task, although for different reasons.* Hence a methodological behaviourist may be interested in ensuring that the manipulation of particular features of the environment is achieved without the subjects' conscious awareness – or at least without their awareness of its significance. A humanist might be expected to attach greater importance to the process of involvement itself and to the objects of involvement.

Generally speaking, critics of role play techniques, both those who have used role play and those who have not, espouse conventional empiricist methodology whereas proponents of role play claim more humanistic intentions. Despite the latter's stated intentions and their particular claims about the superior involvement of subjects with respect to role plays, the experience of phenomenal involvement does not appear to be explored theoretically or even, more importantly, by talking with experimental subjects. Geller (1978) makes some attempt to investigate the phenomenal involvement of his subjects but does this by means of a simple rating scale, and indeed appears to give more credence to indirect and 'objective' measures. Furthermore, Forward et al. (1976) and Geller (1978), for example, suggest that the achievement of involvement may be a matter of choosing skilled individuals or giving participants appropriate training. In particular, Geller (1978) suggests that training might proceed by exposing unskilled actors to training films of 'as-if' situations where the actors are skilled and their performance convincing, implying that involvement is performatively evident and can be externally modelled or learned. Such an approach was earlier espoused by Goldstein (1973) in his structured therapy, where he advocated inducting 'novice' clients into appropriate therapy/learning behaviours by exposure to films modelling such behaviour. Such constructions of involvement as convincingness, in terms of external performance criteria, are contrary to a humanistic construction of involvement, which lays emphasis on individuals' phenomenal experience.

Most commonly, the technical problem of client and subject involvement in role play is sidestepped by leading the reader to believe that involvement equals physical activity, an extremely naive belief in post James-Langian psychology. It is argued (Baron, 1977; Hamilton, 1976; Mixon, 1971) that the sheer activeness of role play methods leads to subject involvement and thus distinguishes active from passive role plays. Obviously, however, an act of pure imagination such as day-dreaming may be as involving and realistic in the subjective and phenomenal sense as any overt act. Indeed, even behavioural desensitization to decondition anxiety relies on the client's capacity to become 'involved' in an imaginative set of actions (secondary 'as-ifs'). Hence, where passive imagining is being passed over in favour of overt activity, something different from subject 'involvement' is expected, which itself needs the more precise presence of 'real others' – other participants who place external demands on the subject by interacting with him or her and thus countering purely autistic involvement.

In qualitative research carried out by Yardley (1984b) and integrated into Chapter 9, it is clear that participants have a more sophisticated view of the concept of 'involvement' than many researchers or practitioners, and these views embrace some of the distinctions made above. For example, most role play participants – whether working within a minimalist role play situation or within more fully inducted, especially personalized and particularized, role plays – understand 'involvement' and 'reality' almost solely on criteria of mundane equivalence and ecological validity. Only very occasionally, and always within a minimalist scenario, does it appear that participants evaluate 'reality' and 'involvement' with the experience of any marked emotion. Interestingly external judges are completely different in their evaluations, almost always being concerned with performance and dramatic and stereotypical actions as the hallmark of reality and involvement, a distinction entirely consistent with the observer observed phenomena described by Jones and Nisbett (1972).

We commence by considering the epistemological basis and rationale for the three major induction principles put forward here. The complementary technical position on these induction processes is presented in Chapter 9, and supported by other role play practitioners' technical guidelines (see Table 4.1) and by the empirical investigations reported in Appendix 3.

The Concept of Engagement

Because the concept of involvement is problematic in the literature, the term 'engagement' is proposed here to throw emphasis on the objects of engagement, rather than on internal and physiologically grounded states. Thus one is not merely 'involved' in some free floating state or whatever, but is engaged with some*thing*, some*body* or some *event*. Apart from representing a phenomenological approach, the above conceptualization provides a more objective basis for an assessment of 'involvement'. One may more easily enquire as to the 'objects' of an individual's engagement than one may elicit descriptions of the subjective state of involvement. For what matters, methodologically speaking, is not necessarily the *degree* of subjects' involvement, but what objects the subjects are involved or engaged with (whether these be externally visible things, people or events; or internal things, people or events). In an 'as-if' experiment based on conventional methodology it should not matter that person X is more or less 'involved' than another participant. However, it does matter that both participants are engaged with the *intended* objects (secondary 'as-ifs') of the experiment. In a deception paradigm, for example, the experimenter intends that these objects are different for him or herself than for the subject. In a humanistic enterprise one would expect these objects, in principle, to be accessible to both.

If the experimental or therapeutic role play is intended to have ecological validity (role play proponents claim that role play facilitates such validity), other factors regarding these objects also need consideration. First, participants must *feel* that the quality of their engagement with the objects of the role play situation is roughly comparable and equivalent with that which they would experience in mundane reality. Secondly and relatedly, subjects must *recognize the objects and their juxtaposition to be likely or at least possible objects of their mundane world*. This argument evidently finally develops into a strong humanistic/phenomenological position, where the engendering of objects absolutely appropriate to the individual would be paramount. Such research moves into the examination of these objects, as constructed and experienced by individuals, and to the search for the general grounded in the idiographic; such therapy moves into the examination of these objects as constituted and experienced by the individual and the search for significance in terms, for example, of psychopathology or potential for growth and change.

Particularization

The discussion above clearly has implications for technique. Thus, the first task of the person employing 'as-if' techniques is clearly to establish what objects should be made explicitly known to the participant. Whether or not the researcher or therapist intends to deceive or hold back information from participants, those objects which it is intended that the participant shall know should be stipulated clearly. *Quite frequently researchers and therapists take it for granted that participants 'see' the intended objects or 'know' the purported situation, which may not be the case.* (Even worse, inductors often do not appear to have made any decision as to whether a situation is supposed to be familiar or not to participants.) In an 'as-if' experiment, for example, all the objects, even where these are to be perceived as they naturally occur (thus a chair remains a chair), need to be made known to the participant in the experiment.

The process by which it is suggested that the above should be achieved is that of **particularization** – *the explicit detailing of all the secondary 'as-ifs' (thus a chair is a car), so that all these objects are brought into awareness in order that they may be known. This necessitates some discussion about the relationship between 'knowing objects' and 'being aware of objects'.* (More crudely defined notions of the need for detail by other role play proponents have already been discussed in Chapter 4 and were presented in summary in Table 4.1.)

In the theatre, for instance, realism is achieved for the audience, by *attention to detail*, so that they may enter the state that Coleridge, talking of poetry, called 'the willing suspension of disbelief'. The actor has similar problems which are tackled in depth by Stanislavski (see below). The problem is not in *remembering* or being *constantly aware* of secondary 'as-if' conditions, which would focus the participant's attention on these to the exclusion of everything else, but in the *knowing* of these secondary 'as-ifs'. Speaking mundanely, one must know something very well before one can be spontaneous, casual or skilled with or within that something. Objects that are supposed to be familiar, whether tangible or intangible, must be intimately known even to be disregarded in an 'as-if' situation. There is a parallel here with Polanyi's (1966) concept of 'tacit knowing' where an object that is focused upon and to be known, is made known indirectly through the medium of knowledge or experience which is at that time covert. This knowledge itself may also sometimes be the subject of focal awareness (although there are categories of knowledge which are never open to focal awareness). In this way a blind person, for example, knows or perceives the world through the medium of the cane, being focally aware of what the cane comes into contact with, yet without direct awareness of the cane itself. At another time the cane itself may be the object of focal awareness.

The differential need for different levels and degrees of Particularization is also significant (see the detailed exposition in Chapter 9). If we recall the Stanford Prison Experiment here (Haney et al., 1973) the inductions there totally neglected the normative fact that individual prisoners have very different biographies, and would have very different levels of knowledge about prison culture and procedures depending on their own histories. Not only should participants have been given detailed particularized inductions but these should have been differential not universal.

Presencing

If action is to occur in a supposedly known environment, then for it to occur 'as-if' in mundane reality, all those features of the environment that bear physically and psychologically on the actor must be *known*. *This must take place first, by making these objects direct objects of awareness. This awareness must be sufficiently detailed so that the objects feel familiar, known, and are taken for granted by participants.* At the physical-spatial level, for example, where a laboratory or group room is meant to represent a prison, the physical boundaries must be sufficiently known in their new symbolic status – they must be particularized. *Secondly, these objects must be made present and actual so that they are perceived as 'out-there' (part of the 'situation' or 'other person') or 'within-here' (part of the 'self').* In practice, this entails that the inductor who sets up the 'as-if' event must also work *actually* within the conditional frames that he or she expects the participant to use. For example, the inductor does not say in his or her instructions, 'This is supposed to be a waiting room . . . Will you act as if . . . ?' but rather 'This *is* the waiting room . . . You are . . .' The inductor thus conveys a personal familiarity with the scene by the assertion or expectation that the scene is familiar and actual to the participants. This process, termed here **'presencing'**, constitutes the second major induction principle or definition. Presencing is clearly interdependent with Particularization, either given or elicited; where Particularization provides the contents, Presencing provides the style of communication of those contents. For objects' 'actuality' to be enhanced those objects must first be 'identified'.

As we saw in Chapter 4, others have inadvertently used this induction method of Presencing (see Table 4.1). For example, Manstead (1979) used a second person and actualized form of induction. Above all, Moreno and psychodramatists almost inevitably incorporate such a tactic (although without a theoretical or technical rationale) in their inductions, both by the therapist 'sharing' and 'co-constructing' the role play space (see also Definition 4 in Chapter 6), but also by the use of the present actualized form of grammatical expression. Stanislavski also, as evidenced in his theoretical writings and through his demonstrative anecdotes, makes it perfectly clear that it is 'actuality' of performance and experience that he demands, a process which is mediated through actors' ongoing interactions as well as through individual work in rehearsals and performance.

To return to the last point in the section on Particularization in this context, it may be noted (see Chapter 5) that Alexander and Scriven (1977) have suggested that detailed particulars should be given to subjects by an experimenter, to establish a common interpretation of events. However, there is evidently a problem here which Alexander and Scriven do not address. Where too great a burden of detail is imposed upon the subject, selective attention and differential salience will probably result in an increase in variability of interpretation and response, as the participants struggle to simplify over-complex but not 'owned' information (see Definition 6, Chapter 6). Such considerations probably led Mixon (1977) to caution against stipulating beliefs in too complicated a form, since, as he is interested in normative roles and rules and determining causes, his intention must be to iron out individual variability. This points to two options: on the one hand, one may give subjects strategies to deal with this detailed information and thus more tightly control the proceedings; on the other, one may merely provide this detailed information, exploit the variability of individual interpretation, and thus encourage idiosyncratic experience. The major methodological problems following the need for Particularization are to determine from whence the particulars emanate, and hence the degree of subject Personalization and the degree of Particularization.

Personalization

The degree of personalization, the degree to which particularized material or objects are drawn from the subjects themselves, might be argued to be a solely methodological issue related to the objectives behind the role play procedure. Yet it can be stated unequivocally that even where the objectives of the procedure remain covert; and where a situation is presented via 'objective' and physical objects, even the slightest degree of Personalization of the mere physical environment would improve the quality of individuals' engagement with the environment. For example, if the event is to take place in an imaginary post office, asking subjects to set out the physical space themselves (counters, doors, etc.) will undoubtedly improve their comfort in this environment. Further, the space will become more vivid and more meaningful.

In, for example, role play experiments, to date, the personalization of secondary 'as-ifs' is almost entirely absent. Role concepts are used which depersonalize both the subjects and situations, according to the role theories which are held by the experimenter. Hence there is absolutely no attempt explicitly to call out the individual's idiographic experience in such a way that it can inform a standardized situation. This is also generally the case in role plays used in therapies and training (with the exception of psychodrama). We have already considered the minimalism of these in Chapter 4. In a humanistic context it is particularly desirable to call out such idiographic experience, but in practice it is rarely done. (There are a few notable exceptions who do use or prescribe the use of individualized experience [see Table 4.1] but these are very much in the minority.)

In contrast, if one turns to a theatrical event which is highly scripted and where one might, therefore, expect a low degree of Personalization one finds the opposite. The importance of the personal experience of the actor and the individual's ability to personalize are paramount.

Stanislavski (1948a; 1948b; 1968) has founded an extremely precise technique for acting based on this observation which, although using different concepts and vocabulary, is highly relevant to the three main induction principles of Personalization, Particularization and Presencing. Stanislavski's emphasis is on the actor's intimate and meticulous knowing of the 'given circumstances' and 'objectives' of the play and on the search for dynamic roots in his or her own experience to be specific and make these actual. He is emphatic that the naturalness and spontaneity necessary to bring the text to *life* cannot be directly sought but only achieved indirectly through precise consideration of the concrete details of an event to a degree not common to mundane observation. For Stanislavski, the processes involved in the induction processes of Particularization and Personalization (as put forward in this chapter) would be seen as interdependent since meticulous consideration of the circumstances (secondary 'as-ifs'), both those given to and created by the actor, must be integrated into the actor's own emotional experience – often, indeed, by the conscious attempt to remember a similar or related emotional experience. This meticulous consideration may be passive and contemplative, or active and improvised, with or without the presence of real others.

Stanislavski is occasionally cited by psychologists but frequently misunderstood. Geller (1978), for example, in his paper on role play while recommending Stanislavski's method intimates that the 'Method' (as it is commonly known) is almost mystical and irrational, stating that absorption is not achieved through conscious thought but at the 'threshold of the unconscious'. Stanislavski does indeed refer to the ultimate creativity of engaging the subconscious but, as we have seen, this state is to be achieved through conscious and particularized work.

A brief but interesting paper by Sturm (1971) suggests integrating Stanislavski's technique (and, to a lesser degree, Moreno's) with those of behaviour therapy. Sturm posits a parallel between Stanislavski's operational concepts, that is 'given circumstances', 'objectives' and 'results' and those of behaviour therapy, 'cue', 'reinforcement' and 'response'. However, Sturm fails to understand that for Stanislavski these considerations are not analysis of what is objectively given but part of the process of rooting specific detail in individual experience itself. Thus, to reiterate, each *particularized* detail either must be created by the actor or, if already given, must be assimilated into personal experience by the actor.

Lastly in relation to Stanislavski here, Moreno (Vol. 1, 1946 [1972]: 153), in comparing psychodramatic acting to theatrical acting, completely misunderstands the role of the personal in Stanislavski's Method. Thus, Moreno says of a Stanislavski actor: 'An actor taking the part of Hamlet has to suppress or reduce himself as a private person out of official existence, but the degree to which a given role can replace or fulfil the space of the private person of the actor is chronically incomplete'. Although the latter half of the statement can, at its face value, be concurred with, the former part of the statement is diametrically opposed to what Stanislavski was about. For a Stanislavski actor does not merely play with a skeletal role but integrates him or herself with the role and *personates* it within an 'as-if' framework, bringing the role to vital embodiment. (See also Stanislavski in Chapter 5, on technique.)

Moreno Despite his criticism of Stanislavski, Moreno evolves therapeutic techniques that are in practice very similar in emphasis to Stanislavski's but lack Stanislavski's precision and clarity. In Moreno's psychodrama there is considerable emphasis on the 'warm up' or 'induction of role players'. This generally also involves processes akin to *Particularization* and *Personalization*, so that the context and background, or an event and its people, are clearly detailed and drawn from the protagonist's experience. *Presencing* is also achieved by the protagonists using the first person, 'I am', when rehearsing and even when listing factual details about their parts – 'I am 60, tall, happy, etc.' (evidently in more detail). Further, the director engages in the actuality of the 'as-if' event by the way in which questions or assertions about the situation are framed, that is, in the present assertive grammatical form. (See also section on Moreno in Chapter 5.)

Interestingly, neither Moreno nor Stanislavski impose superordinate central hypotheses about human nature or theories about the minutiae of interaction upon their actors. In Moreno's case this situation may be said to arise out of theoretical inconsistency rather than design. However, for both authors the result is that they do not impose an oversimplified and unworkable motivational model as a supposed grounding for action. Thus information given or elicited, although not haphazard, is not logico-analytic but perhaps what might be termed 'empathic-analytic'. The lack of controlled consistent demands allows and encourages participants to generate their own objects and to use their own inconsistent, empathic-analytic categories and perceptions, their own knowledge of self and others, to generate the minutiae of interactions and experience.

Toulmin (1977) had made two observations consistent with the above ideas concerning our knowledge of self (and thus, by extrapolation, of others). He states that this knowledge is of a personal kind based on direct experience of, and interactions with, specific human beings. It is neither strictly intellectual nor cognitive, not arrived at by distancing but by interacting. Secondly he states that human beings normally deal with one another in ways that engage their entire personalities without regard to abstract distinctions between cognition, affect and the rest. Thus, to consider the setting-up of a role play, if one asks a subject either to be himself or to be someone else, then special considerations follow for the way in which particularized information relevant to either of these demands is given or elicited so as to take account of the nature of personal knowledge. To engage a person in any 'as-if' conditions, one must be sensitive to the mundane demands of perceiving self or another. These demands may be, and are very likely to be, quite distinct from the demands of analysis and experimental evaluation.

It has been argued that participants can only be appropriately engaged with role play objects through the processes of 'Particularization', 'Personalization' and 'Presencing', put into effect via certain technical practices. These practices have parallels in theatre stagecraft and psychodrama but have until now been almost entirely absent from role plays in experimental social psychology and most conventional clinical role play practice. Certainly no systematic and well-developed guidelines have been provided which focus on these, despite informal support for these processes (as has already been considered above).

The three major induction techniques put forward in this chapter have been argued principally on the basis of conceptual and epistemological principles; however, they are also rooted in a wealth of practical experience and supported by reference to the practice guidelines of Chapter 9. In Chapter 8 all those principles which relate to the satisfactory setting up of a role play are expounded and illustrated with reference to individual case examples and vignettes. The focus is upon practical application of the methodological principles and definitions expounded in Chapter 6. In Chapter 9 a more detailed and practical application and exposition of the major induction principles of Particularization, Personalization and Presencing is presented, together with additional relevant induction guidelines. Thus Chapters 8 and 9 provide a relatively comprehensive guide to inductions, supplemented by detailed case material in Appendix 2.

Note: This chapter is based on an article entitled 'On engaging actors in as if experiments', *Journal for the Theory of Social Behaviour*, 12: 291–304, 1982.

8

Overview of Practical Implications for Good Induction: 1

In this chapter we reconsider and overview the strategies of questions and decisions that role play users should take on board, in relation to the essential technical defining features of role play that were proposed in Chapter 6. Specific applied, clinical and research examples will also be considered in relation to each defining feature. Although there are some distinctive features in, for example, a clinically oriented role play versus a research example, and even further distinctions within specific domains such as cognitive-behavioural interventions as against psychodynamic interventions (see Appendix 1 for worked examples of both), there is little to be gained here from trying to provide exhaustive examples – although necessary distinctions will be drawn. Hopefully it will be clear to the reader at this stage that much of the technique within the approach advocated rests on a common overarching strategy, one which is less concerned with the specific effects of paradigm distinctions than with fine analysis of the requirements of, and attunement to, each individual role play event. The essential decision-making strategy, if not the specific practice, should be common to all types of role play applications. The selected examples that follow are not part of an exhaustive and comprehensive guide, rather they are indicative. Further detailed vignettes are provided in Appendix 2.

Details of all the three major induction techniques of Particularization, Personalization and Presencing, and additional, induction principles, have already been elaborated in Chapter 7, and will be further elaborated in Chapter 9. And as we stated in the introduction to this book, there are no recipe book solutions or shortcuts that can be taken to avoid thorough and careful analysis of role play induction requirements. Each new role play situation – whether for education, training, therapy or research purposes – must be individually tailored, and requires adapted techniques of induction, based again on a thorough understanding of the principles outlined within this book.

Moreover, throughout the following chapters, it is hoped to conduct a relatively thorough critical explanation of conceptual, methodological and experiential aspects of role play induction procedures. It is intended that the reader will thus be sensitized to the complexity of some of these issues, yet will begin to have a more focused grasp of the necessary induction procedures pivoted upon Particularization, Personalization and Presencing.

Methodological principles revisited (see Chapter 6)

1   An initial framework is set up that serves to separate the events occurring within it from events occurring outside it in the mundane world: primary 'as-ifness' (the primary 'as-if' frame)

In setting up any role play and thus giving the 'contents' of the role play **episode status**, the inductor must first ask: What am I *intending* to communicate about the relationship of this episode to the 'outside' world in terms of 'actors' responsibilities for their actions (both verbal and non-verbal)? Is such an intention sustainable, useful or valid in this instance? If my aims are broadly cathartic – as they might be in psychodrama psychotherapy – is it reasonable to assume that John screaming at Mary that he hates her 'while in role' will not adversely affect Mary, or indeed John, out of role? And what other steps might I have to take to 'protect' Mary, or to ensure that John is sufficiently and appropriately responsible. Is a *post hoc* debriefing, and bringing people explicitly and clearly 'out of role' sufficient (see Appendix 1)? Do I as an inductor have a responsibility for all that goes on within a role play? Would I be comfortable as an ethical researcher about setting up another Stanford Prison Experiment? Following on from this, if I do not want a confusion between 'mundane real life' and the 'constructed role play prison domain', how can I facilitate the appropriate engagement of 'actors' and yet reduce the risk to them? On the other hand if, for example, my aims are to retrain actor-participants in certain skills using role play, do I want such a clear division of 'real' world versus 'unreal' world, and how might I weaken or blur the boundaries so that learning is transferable from within the role play to without?

ORGANIZATIONAL VIGNETTE: 1

Ms S., an organizational psychologist, has been contracted to provide a training session for middle managers on stress control and managing difficult situations. Her principal chosen methods will be role play techniques. Training provides in itself a **primary 'as-if' framing**, as participants and trainers *know* that there is no evaluation of their performance to be made in terms of the organization for which they work. This knowledge provides the *initial framework which separates the events occurring within from those without*. The degree of permeability is, however, both an objective and subjective matter. For example, even where it is stated that there will be no institutional evaluation, individual participants may well not believe this to be the case – perhaps the organization has a poor record on broken promises, or there may be an inevitable subjection to peer evaluation within the training. Clearly, also, participants will bring their own self-evaluations to bear, in an manner that crosses the boundaries of the event, that is the institution may not have a memory of the event but the individual/s are intended to have a memory of the training event.

    Too great a separation of the learning task will be seen on both sides as an irrelevance and thus non-motivating; too little separation will be likely to be perceived as threatening and not allowing for mistakes or loss of face. How can this be addressed? Insofar as the material chosen to work upon has a high salience for the training group, the boundaries will be less impermeable. However, it is crucial that the trainer controls the permeability and this is probably best achieved by a combination of a strategy of introducing role play situations of graded salience in step-like progression, strong prior boundary construction distinguishing between the mundane world and the 'as-if' worlds in order to make the role play safe for participants to 'experiment' within, and, finally, following each role play exercise, direct links should be made to facilitate the crossing over of learning from role play to mundane existence, within a general context of good and sensitive teaching skills. Role play technique alone does not, of course, replace the need for sensitive communication strategies by the inductor. These should include explicit discussion of the limits of boundary maintenance for participants, especially in relation to their organizational status. Even so, clear beginnings and endings of role plays, with adequate debriefings and bringing people 'out' of the role play are also essential.

CLINICAL VIGNETTE: 1

A therapeutic space is normatively constructed as a safe space, where individuals may safely express, experience and experiment without fear of immediate repercussions in the 'real' world outside therapy. A role play space within such a context shares, indeed accentuates, this initial framework. None the less, the arbitrariness and fragility of the separation of the role play space is even more marked within such a context. For not only are clients' own boundaries often very fragile at the point they are seeking therapy, but, also, there is in contrast to the 'safe space' idea of therapy an equally powerful normative expectation that therapy will impact significantly – and probably even powerfully – upon clients both within and without the therapy space.

If Mrs D. comes to therapy because of social anxieties about eating in public places, and if it is appropriate to deal with this problem symptomatically at face value, then the consequences of setting up a role play of a restaurant and of Mrs D. becoming 'involved' and therefore highly anxious in a 'real' manner, are – barring the unexpected – of some consequence but unlikely to be traumatic. However, if a cot-death scene is 'recreated' for the therapeutic purposes of helping the unresolved grief of a bereaved mother, the situation is clearly more fraught with danger for the client. With respect to the latter, the ability to demarcate the role play as not current, not real in the here and now, and capable of being ended as a 'provoked' experience is paramount. The clinician here would not only have to create particularly strong symbols for the encapsulation of the scene as 'apart', but also judge the capacity of the client to be able to 'usefully' engage in such a trauma and to be able to disengage, and not to be overwhelmed. It behoves clinicians, in particular, to be very careful, clear and honest about the intent in using an 'as-if' technique such as role play. Fuzzy ideas about catharsis are neither justifiable nor sufficient. Beginnings and endings must be clearly and strongly marked, through Presencing. Clients must also be given, above all and under most circumstances, expressed permission to control endings themselves. The clinician's expectations of impact should be conveyed, so that clients may be confident about entering role plays, and be able to concede or refuse to be impacted upon. Above all, because the framework is in the final analysis illusory, the construction of this framework must be carried out affirmatively, creating a space apart from the mundane world. Such needs may legitimately modify the induction principle of Presencing. In accordance with the capacity of the client to cope with full engagement and withstand a full immersion in the 'actuality' of this 'recreated' trauma, it may be necessary deliberately to create distance from the event during the 'replaying' of it (for example by using the past tense in the induction rather than the present tense), while still affirming the encapsulation of the role play event from mundane time and space, a 'real' world which will soon be re-entered leaving the painful role play behind. Here the inductor must particularly recognize a responsibility for the role play's final participation in the world of consequentiality, while actively limiting its effect through the induction procedures. For therapists, this space can also be viewed as a transitional environment between 'solid' reality and its dangers, and the apparent safety of intrapsychic fantasies of containment. The transitional environment can offer safety; however, in the final analysis, neither cot blanket, toy nor role *play* space offer any ultimate safety.

RESEARCH VIGNETTE: 1

A researcher is interested in the effects, over real time, of the process of a three-year nurse training programme on the relationships between its multi-ethnic participants. The researcher's prime interest is in the latter, not in nurse training, which is seen merely as a vehicle for the provision of close contact within learning, occupational and social domains. A decision is made that role plays will be used to understand multi-ethnic relationships within contexts of assumed (on an a priori basis) differing levels of social intimacy. With respect to the initial primary 'as-if' framing of the event, a decision has to be made whether or not to share the purpose of the research with the participants, or, whether to deceive them as to its true intent. Clearly, what is being researched is real in the sense that it is a real part of participants' lives, and the potential impact upon real lives is evident if, for example, the very act of focusing upon ethnicity alters the relationships between people, particularly if detrimentally so. The level of permeability between the research world and the mundane world is likely to be very high, particularly where the participants are explicitly made aware that the focus of research is ethnic relationships. However, although deception of participants – for instance by misinforming them that they are taking part in an experiment on general social anxiety – may initially reduce the permeability between 'real' and 'constructed' worlds, it may have very significant effects at debriefing, where subjects are likely to feel deceived in a very sensitive area of social being. A more general strategy of asking subjects to 'go with' the experiment, without being furnished with a very precise rationale, might provide a middle ground but, even here, the researcher will need to bear some responsibility for the potential for exacerbating ethnic difficulties.

If we reconsider at this point the Stanford Prison Experiment, it is equally evident that it can be crucial to confirm to individual participants the precise point at which they enter the 'as-if' world. In the Stanford role play experiment participants did not know whether they were in 'reality' or 'make believe' and, as has been argued in Chapter 3, this may have had serious real world consequences for them. And it must be noted that the experiment was prematurely abandoned over and over again, because of the distress caused to participants. The participants seemingly became victims of their 'captors' in a very real sense.

2   Some of these conditions are said to have a secondary 'as-if'
status demanding that an alternative perception be made from a
normal perception

As indicated above, scrupulous attention is needed both to what the inductor sets up as secondary 'as-ifs', and also to what the actor brings to the role play by way of attendant and emergent 'as-if' assumptions. It is here that the major induction principles of **Particularization, Personalization** and

Presencing are oriented, and to which we will return below to consider in more detail.

In a role play some of the actor's impact emerges from taken-for-granted 'real' characteristics of the actor. It is in practice very difficult to differentiate between what is absolutely taken on by an actor and what 'belongs' – even perhaps as a potential – to an actor. However, in creating or constructing particular aspects to a character or situation the creator is seemingly stating that these aspects have some significance over and above the usual flow of aspects and events. It is evidently also the case that where a choice is made about who plays a certain role certain other important aspects are being made significant about that person/role, although these are generally taken for granted. It is important for inductors to be clear about the significance of these, both at the actual taken-for-granted level and at the explicitly secondary 'as-if' level. For example, if the interview situation in the organizational vignettes is to take place in the executive suite, then the physical characteristics may well be important and the inductor needs to be clear that the complainant may be affected by this and the 'role player complainant' needs to know that the classroom is not now the classroom but an executive suite with particular characteristics. The specific induction into the secondary 'as-ifs' will not be pursued here but the reader is referred to Chapter 9 and to Appendix 2. More general issues relating to secondary 'as-ifs' are subsumed by consideration of the other methodological principles (3 to 8 inclusive) in this chapter.

3   In delineating an episode, the part that is separated from the stream of social action is seen (presented) as having boundaries that delineate it from that which it is not

The major decision to be made concerns who is going to define the boundaries, the instigator and/or the participants. It can often be highly difficult to decide *when* and *where* a situation starts. A behaviourist may look for contiguous cues within an already (a priori) pre-established beginning, in a role play on social anxiety. However, a research participant here, or indeed an analytically oriented psychotherapist or client, may focus on cues around an earlier significant and 'marking' encounter or relationship as the starting point for the social anxiety.

Will the start point for the role play be the delineation of contiguous cues in a predetermined but concurrent social situation, or will the start point be a preliminary 'engagement' of the major protagonist's internal world which may need a re-evocation of the past? Who will define which time and which space is important? And indeed, who will decide what it is that is separable from the flow? Will the role play be limited to a unity of time and space, or will it allow movement between times and spaces, in relation to the defined area of educational, research or clinical interest? Role play users must decide upon these questions.

ORGANIZATIONAL VIGNETTE: 2

Ms S. has, prior to the workshop and together with senior managers, decided to focus a major part of the training on managing issues concerning sexual harassment. In presenting such material to her learning group she will be focusing upon episodes of sexual harassment and upon the managers' attempts to investigate and discipline these, while particularly attending to the stress of managers in following procedures through. Insofar as she determines that episodes initially will be categorized and defined by such terms, and mindful here that she will use role play to enact such episodes, she needs first to consider whether or not the boundaries around the event are sustainable. For example, it is possible that 'learners' will wish presumptively to challenge her categorization. Her learners may well wish to press a case for sexual harassment being merely an example of the firm's rather conservative authoritarian and patriarchal house style – a style which affects all employees, male or female. Should she now, in setting up a role play, allow this construction to redefine the role play episode, taking it away from explicit sexual harassment as separately definable; should she allow this construction to enter into the interpretation and debriefing of the role play event *post hoc*; or should she didactically disallow any such interpretation and reconfiguration of boundaries. This methodological consideration has precise technical implications for the setting up of the role play.

CLINICAL VIGNETTE: 2

Finding the beginning of a problematic situation in a therapeutic context is more often than not complex. Even approaches – such as cognitive and behavioural ones – which do not seek to address historical causes in any active sense (indeed, often dispute such historicity within a context of psychogenetic explanation) need to find a starting point for an episode characterized as containing the social anxiety. A highly pragmatic approach might suggest commencing the role play for our phobic client in busy restaurant X and dealing with what arises within it. However, in so doing, the therapist has predefined a beginning and an end – a separation from the flow of other experience – that may have no equivalence for the anxious client. Antecedent events may be defined as within-episode by the client and unless there is good reason the therapist ought to respect the client's partitioning of events for role playing. This does not mean that the therapist might not continue to segment experience into role plays on the basis of his or her criteria, but at the very least the client's own partitioning should be actively acknowledged. For example, the therapist could expand the restaurant scenario to take on earlier events, a separate 'antecedent' role play could be set up to encapsulate these or, in terms of economy of time, the role play induction in the restaurant may quite simply involve acknowledgement of the antecedent events, for example: 'You have spent the last couple of hours at home trying to get ready to go out to dinner but considerably distracted by worrying about how you are going to feel when you are out. Your husband and son have become increasingly irritated by your frequently expressed anxiety. You are now in the restaurant, sitting at a table near an exit . . .'. The latter approach acknowledges the seamlessness of actual experience and the historicity of events.

RESEARCH VIGNETTE: 2

Here the researcher has already decided to set up role plays in the following contexts and always involving an ethnic mix of participants: a coffee bar break with colleagues, a restaurant meal in the evening, a date, an invitation to a neighbourhood social event, and an invitation to a family gathering where the invitee does not belong to the same ethnic group. The contexts are constructed by the researcher to function at seemingly different levels of social-emotional intimacy. Participation in this series of role plays is to be repeated over the three-year training period. Evidently, with respect to each role play, the idea of a beginning and end to the episode has already been established by the researcher and, insofar as he or she is not interested in each individual participant but in establishing some very general principles, then very individualized constructions of beginnings and endings may not be necessary. However, the inductor/researcher might wish to do some bridging work with participants, so that they can make the episode their own to some degree. Overall, the beginnings and endings – the type of separation of event – are here determined by the researcher's a priori research focus which is categorizing certain types of experience as relevant foci for research and leads to stronger demarcations of beginnings and endings than would be the case where the prime focus of concern was individual subjects. However, satisfactorily to induct participants into such a role play, some leeway may be necessary for redetermining a suitable beginning or ending to facilitate the participants' experience of a sense of engagement.

4   This separation from the stream of social action appears to contain, or may yield, some internal logic or coherence in terms of the goals of the investigator. This investigation may be presented as open or closed

Demonstrative or didactic aims lead to closed role plays. Here the instigator chooses all the content in relation to a specific set of goals, based on a particular and a priori understanding of the relationship between these. If the instigator aims to teach a discrete set of skills of relatively low symbolic status, that is not open to carrying a heavy burden of meaning, then such an approach may be valid. However, the instigator must then consider whether he or she is able to specify the optimal contexts for the optimal or sufficient display of these skills. Can such a context be created or recreated? At what level of precision should the instigator *particularize* the role play context and its moment to moment content?

The instigator must consider the following issues and questions. For example, if I am trying didactically to teach a formal set of skills, for instance table etiquette, it is likely that I can specify to a high degree the relevant factors. However, if I am trying to teach conversational skills at table, can I recontextualize these from specific known circumstances; or, at the other extreme, must I anticipate, with the 'apprentice' all possible interlocutors to fulfil the task? Do I assume, rightly, that an agreed inadequacy in conversational skills in my apprentice is best contextualized within the time and space of a dinner party? Shall the other role players merely enact predetermined demands from the instigator, or major protagonist, and follow a highly predictable script; or are others allowed to bring unpredictable spontaneity to the role play? Does the situation need defining and controlling in relation to the perceived learning vulnerability of the client? If I am carrying out research, is the separation an ecologically valid one, that will be recognized to be so by my 'subjects'. These are pedagogical and methodological matters, which must be addressed.

ORGANIZATIONAL VIGNETTE: 3

Ms S., as already stated, has a set of working principles and goals related to alleviating stress in managers dealing with difficult situations, and is particularly interested in the extent to which decision making in organizations is compromised by particular agendas which arise when individuals are under stress. She is keen to provide participants with additional resources, has a cognitive orientation, and is also concerned to view herself as efficacious and increasingly able to deal with 'difficult' challenges. Thus, her goals also include a personal agenda. For the sake of argument, we shall assume also that her initial decisions have a face validity, in terms of the organization. The organization has a broad concern with producing better managers, believes in the factor of stress as counterproductive, and is content to leave her to decide upon specific aims and methods.

Ms S. has worked in the organization before and, therefore, believes that she has knowledge of the situation which she has judged likely to be common and problematic to all middle managers in such an organization – that is, *disciplining an individual over a sexual harassment misdemeanour*. There are well-established management practices within this organization, reinforced by abundant written text. She assumes knowledge of these texts and practices also to be common. She also assumes that personal agendas held by these middle level managers will have a high impact on the conduct of such interviews and that stress is an inevitable feature of such situations. Moreover, she believes it likely that decision-making processes will reflect a general lack of sophistication in terms of cognitive strategies. On these bases, as already pointed out above, let us suppose that she pre-emptively decides upon an illustrative scenario and defines a minimal script and skeleton characters. She has thus created a *closed situation*, certainly at this stage, not open to redefinition or negotiation with the participants. The pitfalls are hopefully evident. To create an 'open' situation the inductor would need here to negotiate both the goals and the situations which would be seen by all parties as validly illustrative or representative of the area of concern. The details of the situations are equally important and need negotiation.

CLINICAL VIGNETTE: 3

If you have a highly circumspect goal and only want to teach a client to use eye contact more positively when talking to more powerful others, a role play that has already been predetermined or highly scripted (a closed role play) is likely to be useful, certainly as a starting point. It matters little if the client is not likely to meet a very similar situation, if the intention is to teach didactically a set of learnable – and to some extent decontextualizable – skills. However, if Mr P. is fine until he meets a highly particular set of circumstances, and if he already has the appropriate skills but cannot use them in certain circumstances, then the need for using a more open, personalized set of role play circumstances within a negotiated set of goals is paramount. The latter cannot be achieved without his active co-operation and, probably, at quite a high level of resolution of detail. Generally clinicians are very good at relating to the individual as individual, particularly when they eschew rigid techniques of therapy. Role play has unfortunately been used rigidly, but it has the potential to be an enhancing extension of more individualizing clinical skills if used in this way. Hence, Mr P. should be asked to offer a situation that he feels is representative of his difficulties (whether or not on a graded basis, if an element of desensitization is called for). The situation should be examined with him for important detail and for its impact upon him in terms of the logic of *his* experience – not the logic of the therapist. Such an examination would provide an 'opening' up of the scenario. And, because role play is essentially a dynamic process and leads to unexpected consequences or unremembered aspects, it may be that a new situation or role play episode is called for after commencement of the original role play – one which does more justice to the matter of concern.

RESEARCH VIGNETTE: 3

In contrast to the clinical vignette, the choice of contexts and research goals is already determined and somewhat narrowly defined in this case, by the researcher, although the outcome of the research may indicate that these situations were poor choices with respect to the area of exploration. It would of course be possible for the researcher, prior to constructing these, to engage in some preliminary 'opening up' research with the subjects to check out the 'local' validity of these contexts in terms of his or her goals. Whether or not these situations will contain the necessary 'ingredients' that the researcher assumes is linked to the extent to which the group of individuals he or she is researching can share the assumptive world of the researcher. The variety of social experience may be so great, and even the ethnic diversity so great, that the assumed relative social-emotional significance of these different contexts may differ considerably for each individual. This throws us back on the need to be constantly vigilant about the extent to which one can generalize from the particular without qualification. A sensible strategy in these circumstances would be for the researcher to adhere to the strategy of using the same situations for all participants, but to open out the research and check out the meaning of the event with each participant through qualitative feedback at the end of the role play, in addition to the gathering of attitudinal observations and whatever other data the research has fixed upon as the significant data to be measured by whatever chosen means. The finer the analysis, and the more detailed the research questions, the more likely it is that participants will have to be involved in setting up appropriate scenarios. Further opening up may involve individual participants going on to construct their own role situations, stimulated initially by the researcher's contexts. This would allow much more ecologically valid research to occur. Whether or not participants would share the researcher's goals, or find them to be valid or significant, is yet another matter.

5   The ways in which individual participants are led to participate in role plays and enact their roles are importantly related to the motive structure of the whole role play enterprise

If you are to give role players only very minimal information about their roles and the situation, are you going to tell them *why* the information is limited? Is the information limited in order that they may spontaneously generate and create their own action and interpretation, or is it merely to confuse them and keep them in the dark, or perhaps to force an interpretation upon them? If there are several 'characters' within the role play, will their inductions have equal weight and equal access to self-definition (Personalization) as compared with external definition (Particularization)? For example, if the role play 'belongs' to one participant's experience, what level of autonomy will other actors have; will they merely provide a foil? If the episode 'belongs' to the inductor, not any participant, again what level of freedom or constraint is expected and why?

    Are the participants to be relatively passive experimental or therapeutic 'pawns', or are they to be involved as fully agentic and self-reflexive human beings? If they are to be kept in the dark, in terms of the instigator's intentions, what is the effect of different states of knowledge on the action? Are these intentions legitimate? Do these different states of knowledge have different mundane validity?

If participation is to be built in, how will the factor of having many participants with different interests, experience and abilities be addressed? Is it to be a role play for everyone, for particular actor or actors, or for the investigator? How will information be given or elicited that addresses these different participant positions? Whose view is to determine the setting up conditions or the analytic conditions? Who is allowed to change or redefine a role play? Who has the final say in resolving differences (see Menzel, 1978)?

ORGANIZATIONAL VIGNETTE: 4

Ms S. decides to move quite quickly into setting up a role play interview situation and chooses participants on a relatively *ad hoc* basis. There is little time for discussion beforehand for the consideration of aims and methods, apart from a brief didactic introduction into the area of sexual harassment at work and the manager's role in disciplinary procedures. The participants prove somewhat resistant and unco-operative. Their experience of the role play induction mirrors that of the organization, where they feel they have to carry out tasks they have not been well prepared for and over which they have a good deal of discomfort. Ms S.'s expectation of working to 'unmask' personal agendas at this stage clashes with a middle management view of organizational insensitivity to their needs. A concern for the participants as fully agentic, sentient human beings demands that the manner of induction into the task is scrutinized. It is unfortunately not unusual for someone with avowedly 'humanistic or person-centred' aims to treat individuals in a cavalier manner for the purpose of achieving some greater good. This is somewhat typical of much of the 1960s and 1970s encounter movements, which led to a good deal of negative evaluation of those same movements.

Equally, if the induction of particular characters is cavalier, this treatment or attitude towards the character, as expressed by the inductor, is likely to be assimilated into the character and into the responses to the character. For example, if the complainant is described by the inductor in a frivolous tone, or in a sympathetic tone for that matter, that attitude towards the character is likely to taken on by the role player and/or the role play partners.

CLINICAL VIGNETTE: 4

At a very strategic level, a therapist might well want to use induction to heighten certain features. In our example, where the historicity of the restaurant event is recognized, this might be indirectly intensified by the therapist conveying impatience to the client in the manner of his or her induction. This is, however, a highly strategic manoeuvre and would need both a therapeutic rationale and a good deal of caution – because it deliberately brings together and confounds 'reality' and 'role play' and this necessitates great care concerning the client's sense of safety (see 1 above). However, the manner of induction – the treatment of the client by the inductor – is a salient aspect of reality which needs must impact upon the client. Hence, various stances towards the client are possible here, ranging from empathic and client-centred to strategic and manipulative. If the inductor sounds very sympathetic when inducting Mrs B. into her role, but is quite antagonistic in describing the behaviour of the husband or waiter, then the inductor should take account and be aware of this.

There may be again strategic reasons for 'sharing' the experience of the client in viewing and co-constructing the world as hostile, but this may also not be in the best interests of the client if it is intended that a wider perspective should be brought to bear.

RESEARCH VIGNETTE: 4

Student nurses are thrown together by virtue of their training programmes. One may assume that these individuals would not under other circumstance have been as likely interactionally to engage. Throwing them together in various role plays may mirror this quality, and may be seen as an acceptable extension of the original scenario or may, more worryingly, be seen and experienced as more a matter of coerced fraternization – which in itself may engender some feelings and behaviours. Giving students choice here of which group to work in would give a more co-operative basis for working. This of course might mitigate against the revelation of more negative aspects of ethnic relations because choice might exclude working with 'problematic' others. However, the researcher must make a judgement and each decision will then limit some aspect of the research findings, a limitation which should be taken into account in the design. Within this organizational setting overall, one can remain consistent to the organizational rules and in a manner contiguous with the house style or adopt a different house style for the purposes of research. Hence, in the latter case, the researcher may work with volunteers only and share all the research designs with them, including the choice of appropriate contents; alternatively, he or she may mimic the organizational house style and dictate the terms of participation on the same basis as their working situation, and thus predetermine all the contexts for discovery.

6   Each boundaries situation contains frames and foci which arise from an interaction between the initial definition and framing of the overall event and the ad hoc *definitions of both inductor and participant. (The foci, in particular, are mediated through Particularization and Personalization)*

Is there to be deliberate deception in the role play? How will this affect the validity of the event and the interpretation one might put on it? Does a close scrutiny of intentions behind the role play and the methods being used for induction, together with scrutiny of the contents of induction, produce a corrigible and congruent overall picture? Are the emergent *ad hoc* definitions of participants and instigators harmonious or discordant? Does any discrepancy facilitate or debilitate the role play and its validity?

ORGANIZATIONAL VIGNETTE: 5

The scenario as described by Ms S. uses the example of a male work supervisor who frequently makes salacious remarks to junior female staff and frequently puts his arm around women when he is talking to them. Several complaints have been made and one complainant suggested that Mr T.'s hand had, she thought deliberately, touched her breast during such an encounter. The role play participants are given a scenario and character descriptions, with a good deal of stipulated detail – Particularization. The message carried within the framing and focus of this information is that the major complainant is truthful and has no ulterior motives, and that Mr

T. has in fact been sexually 'abusive'. The induction assumes, via its narrative structure, that facts are established and that the participants will concur with this rendering. The induction neglects that each of the participants would mundanely already have heard and/or believed a different version of this apparent truth, and that the personal agendas are already present. In attempting to define a play-like narrative with unity and cohesiveness, Ms S. has lost her first training opportunity and unwittingly encouraged resistance to her training goals. The interactive consequence is a hardening and polarization of attitudes around the implicit agendas and framings that have not been negotiated prior to the 'educative' role play.

Any attempt to encourage 'engagement' with the role play is relatively hopeless at this point. No matter how much attention Ms S. pays to Presencing, Particularization or even Personalization, she has set up the initial stages of the training event and the role play in such a way as to undermine the very induction procedures that she now seeks to use as tools.

CLINICAL VIGNETTE: 5

Inappropriate focus in a therapeutic episode, especially one of high emotional significance such as in the cot death bereavement example, will potentially lead to the client becoming retraumatized and/or disengaging. Role plays of highly traumatic events demand particularly sensitive negotiation with the client to establish the appropriate level and type of framing; for example, moving from a superficial, fact oriented or even peripheral establishment of episode towards a more subjective and in-depth focus as and when the client is ready. Quite simply, the closer the awareness of the baby is – even descriptively – 'forced' here, the greater the danger to the client and the greater the revocation and indeed recreation of uncontrollable trauma. Equally, insisting upon dealing with the peripheral and the trivial when the client is ready and needing to deal more directly with the central horrors of the episode can be similarly damaging. The need for the therapist to judge the emotional tenure of the deliberate aspects of construction of the role play is a therapeutic desiderata of all therapeutic interventions and the skills are those of the therapist. However, role play concretizes these judgements and reduces ambiguity. In a sense there is less margin for error in that the potential power of mobilization of role play is considerably greater than in more reflective activities.

RESEARCH VIGNETTE: 5

If the participants do not know that the object of research is ethnic relationships, they will not be able to inform the researcher of the significance of their actions in the role plays. Hence, if the researcher were to focus upon physical proximity as a significant marker of intimacy, it may well be that this focus is misleading. Lack of consultation will lead to inappropriate frame and focus since the marker of intimacy within a specific ethnic or, indeed, family culture may not be easily observable by an outsider. One can also see that openly sharing the framing and concealing or deceiving the participants about the framing can be equally problematic. The traditional concern from a positivistic approach will clearly be that sharing the framing in terms of the intent behind the study may lead participants to shift their behaviour in specific directions. However, we also know that participants try to read intention behind an experiment and only come up with behaviour that affirms the experimenter's hypotheses, when they have guessed or read these accurately (see Orne, 1959). The compromise step may well be to keep individuals in the dark – with their consent (certainly not to deceive them as this is likely to distort their behaviour and its significance even further) – but to keep a much more open mind when exploring the behaviour that does occur and reconsidering its significance against many contextual considerations informed by very full accounts elicited from subjects. Hence, any piece of empirical work should open up many understandings not move towards inappropriate, and finally unsupportable, 'proofs'.

7   The action of the episode is established by stipulating some conditions and leaving others free. The relationship between number of conditions established and the 'freedom' of the participant is paradoxical

Inductors must not only consider the level and amount of information they give actors or elicit from them, they must also consider the likely and actual response of actors to detail. As we shall see, generally speaking, actors crave detailed information (Particularization) and feel freer to be truly involved in the secondary 'as-if' conditions when they are well inducted into these. Leaving actors 'stranded' leaves them feeling self-conscious and unable to attend to the hoped for interaction with others.

There is, of course, the possibility of overloading actors with information; in practice, however, this rarely happens. Where it does, generally speaking, actors will select individually what they are best able to make use of, as mundanely occurs in interactions. If it is intended that some information is of far greater significance than other information, then the induction must look to the normal methods of presenting information to auditors, in order that its significance is noted.

Inevitably, the formalized presentation of information to actors is rather different to the mundane emergence of 'information' for individuals in the everyday world. Regard might well be given to this latter factor when making sense of the action that then occurs in the role play. Attention must be given to situation (past and current, and, if validly anticipatable, to the future); to the individual 'characters', again in terms of past, present and future; and to what is significant to the purposes of the role play. Attention must be given to what it is that is significant for actors so that they may ground themselves, for the purposes of the role play, in a manner that addresses mundane experience, personhood and agency.

Judgement is needed to achieve the right balance of stipulated conditions against 'free' conditions. If didacticism is desirable and workable, much of situation and events can be stipulated pre-emptively. Even if there is a need to personalize the role play or indeed to collectivize a description that has emerged from discussions with the participants, there is still a need to decide how much freedom of construction of the event will be allowed to emerge 'spontaneously' as part of the dynamics between participants in action. However, giving either too little or too much information can lead to similar, and probably undesirable, outcomes. Where individual role play participants have minimal information they will tend to stereotype and 'act out' rather than 'act in'. Equally, if inductors overload participants (particularly with irrelevant information) or demand the elicitation of too much information, participants may respond 'catastrophically', by holding on to gross facts only, and produce equally stereotypical action.

ORGANIZATIONAL VIGNETTE: 6

If Ms S. spends 20 minutes describing redundant information about Mr T. or gives a minimal description of him: '40, fat and too intimate in his behaviour with women', a stereotype is likely to result. In the first instance the role play will be overloaded so that the participant role player is forced into simplyfing the detail, and, because the detail has low significance differential the role player will move from simplification to stereotypification. In the latter case, given too little information the role player will be forced into a crude reading of the inductor's intentions and perceptions and translate this into crude characterization. The latter leaves the participant insecure and directionless because, if all they know about their character can be reduced to one sentence, the freedom of action that can be engaged in without a secure basis of clear identity is limited. Who is Mr T.? How on earth can one engage in the behaviour that is not restricted to be being 40, fat and too intimate? What does such a man talk about, how does he walk, is he good at his work, is he happy, is he an angry man? The inductor might expect the role player to fill in the gaps, without explicitly asking for this or suggesting how to achieve this. In such a case the instigator is asking for a caricature and making it likely that the actor quite simply will 'dry' for lack of anchor or a purpose. If, however, participants are encouraged to personalize the character, to provide a level of detail with which they can personally connect, this gives them both a level of freedom in terms of self and character determination, while placing a demand for particularity of behaviour that will enable them to engage more fully.

If Ms S. has indeed set up a role play concerning sexually inappropriate office behaviour, and if her initial assumptions here are acceptable to the participants, what is her purpose in setting this up? If she is interested in participants really connecting and making sense of the role plays and in taking highly discriminating action with respect to individual differences, then participants must be helped to mutually co-determine the level of their induction needs. If she is merely to teach an inflexible strategy, based on a simple set of rules, the extent to which participants are left floundering with stereotypes or assisted only to provide the caricature performance of their lives may be matter of less significance.

CLINICAL VIGNETTE: 6

As in all role plays, ongoing sensitivity to individuals' induction needs is demanded. In a role play, whether relatively impersonal such as the setting up of a restaurant episode for the client who is phobic about eating in public or more intimate such as the cot death example, the extent of information needed cannot always be accurately predicted in advance. Some clients will swing into action easily and immediately engage with the action; others will need considerable facilitation via Particularization, Personalization and Presencing, possibly because they lack knowledge, familiarity, personal relevance or simple imagination. Insensitivity to such inabilities – or indeed insensitivity to an individual's ability to engage, for example, by insisting on belabouring the induction – is ineptitude on the part of the inductor. It may also be important to 'insist' on providing high levels of externally stipulated Particularization and not eliciting high levels of Personalization to ensure the client engages fully in experiences not too close to core issues which might expose too much vulnerability.

RESEARCH VIGNETTE: 6

The question of the extent of stipulation to and the extent of drawing out of particularization from participants as against leaving much unstated or unelicited is based, above all, on an idea of external validity within a research context – a question related to the researcher's decisions about the need for 'rigour' and external equivalence of one role play to another. However, it is evident that lack of detail undermines a role play and too much detail and lack of purpose can have paradoxical and somewhat unpredictable effects, as argued above.

For some nurses in our example, lack of knowledge of a particular context may be of little significance if the context relies on relatively general social behaviours and mores, such as a staff disco. However, one might assume that a more intimate episodic setting, such as eating a family meal, will provide more challenges to knowledge – no doubt relating both to ethnic diversity and to highly individuated family culture. Inevitably, providing more and more relevant bridging information may 'contaminate' the 'purity' of a research endeavour, but it is even more likely that useful knowledge will arise from contrasting the effects of 'bridging' gaps of knowledge against leaving 'performers' in the dark.

8 The condition stipulated is established through the medium of what is conventionally named the person and/or situation

Mundanely speaking, as already discussed in Chapter 6, many of our person/situation distinctions here are arbitrary and *ad hoc*; and many of our distinctions are part of deliberate or undeliberate warranting and accounting strategies, certainly not rooted in any understanding of absolute causality. Explanations invoke socio-cultural and personal constructions of events, the legitimacy of which may be more or less convincing but always open to reinterpretation. Given the power of description to shape events, this is certainly a major factor in role plays, and inductors must take note of the warranting and accounting practices emerging through their own set-up induction descriptions and procedures. A role play, set up and pre-emptively described, is a piece of social reality already interpreted, with certain possibilities of action and interpretation removed *de facto*. If Mr Smith is described as selfish, or even merely as loud, those descriptions will have consequences, and it may well be that another interpreter of the putative Mr Smith would not have described him in the same terms. (Psychotherapists, excluding perhaps recent family therapists, especially as expressed in theory, have been particularly blind to the co-construction of a social world by therapist and client – despite their generally greater commitment and sensitivity to meaning.)

ORGANIZATIONAL VIGNETTE: 7

Ms S. is interested in the effect of stress on decision making, as is the organization who has contracted her services. If she sets up a role play scenario where she asks participant K to role play the part of a highly anxious senior manager, and if she describes the role in such terms without indicating the reasons for the stress, then Ms S. is probably making some relatively unthinking ascription of stress to an individual state of mind – it is constructed as person-based. What this may neglect is either the individual's experience that the anxiety/stress is, in fact, organizationally caused, or, whether experienced or not, that it is organizationally based. The level of change necessary may be personal or organizational, and required as a matter of principle or pragmatics. However, a role play that ascribes states unthinkingly to either individuals or organizations is likely to obscure problems through the inevitable increased stereotypification that follows in the acting out of unreflective, undetailed premises. If the ecological basis and validity of ascription are weakened in a role play, any learning or change intended to follow from it is bound to be compromised.

CLINICAL VIGNETTE: 7

Ascription of significance to personal characteristics of an individual rather than to external situational factors is a highly salient area within clinical and therapeutic practice and judgement. It is indeed at the fulcrum of social, moral and diagnostic tensions. And putting aside here those instances of sheer incompetence, ascription in relation to these areas is always fraught with difficulty. It is mundanely of significance and value, and very much the stock-in-trade of therapists, to aim to help clients discriminate between 'inward' state and the impact of their own actions, and external 'reality' and the impact of others and aspects of the environment. There are, of course, no absolutes here. Hence, pre-emptive ascriptions to either persons, others or environments need care. Such ascriptions cannot be entirely abandoned otherwise description would not be possible.

For example, a role play is set up with our greiving client related to the separate visits of two midwives following the tragedy. One health visitor is presented by the client as brusque and unsympathetic; the other as gentle and empathic. A sensitive role play will accept the client's descriptions as the reality initially. If there is a need to be more reflective about her own contribution to this perception, a later role play might challenge these perceptions – and provide a context for considering whether or not her perceptions of difference were related to her relative state at either time.

RESEARCH VIGNETTE: 7

Again ascription of meaning to persons or environment needs care. 'Accurate' ascription will require local knowledge of a particular ethnic culture – for example, is certain behaviour normatively assertive or aggressive within a given culture? With an already stipulated set of social episodes the researcher is already ascribing considerable weight of significance to external situational variables and has privileged this area of explanation over more person-centred, individualistic conceptualizations.

However, the matter of degree remains pertinent. Will the researcher ascribe and convey personality characteristics to other role players that would be better attributed to situation, and vice versa? Will cultural stereotypes invade more individually significant acts? Will Mr S., described as the 'head' of an Asian family, take on characteristics consistent with those attributes that might be implied by using such a term in relation to a European family? Will an Italian mother be described as loud and effusive, and, if so, what does that signify in terms of stereotypification or individual character?

9

Overview of Practical Implications for Good Induction: 2

We have considered induction needs from a methodological perspective in Chapter 8 focusing on eight descriptive principles. We have also considered the conceptual and epistemological underpinnings of the three major induction principles of Personalization, Particularization and Presencing, with some broad descriptions of the technical requirements of each principle. In this chapter we will review each of these latter three principles in more technical detail, and with a much more pragmatic intent. The text will draw heavily on the subjective accounts of role play participants; upon observed role plays which are presented as vignettes to illustrate technical points; upon systematic studies (two sets of studies are drawn upon: one set of empirical studies, outlined below and in Appendix 3, and one set of qualitative systematic workshops, see also Appendix 3); and also upon the author's not inconsiderable experience of role play procedures. Technical induction principles will also be enlarged upon to include a few remaining categories of induction considerations, some of which are entirely complementary and some of which fall outside the principles of Personalization, Particularization and Presencing but hopefully contribute towards a comprehensive picture.

Personalization and related induction principles

In Chapter 7 it was proposed that even in role plays designed to be constructed outside the control of participants – possibly within a positivistic experiment or within a context of didactic teaching of, for example, social skills training – a degree of personalization in constructing aspects of the role play in question would be an important factor in establishing a taken-for-granted level of knowledge against which participants can 'act' with confidence and with a sense of meaningfulness. When actors are asked to give general feedback on a role play example, the most frequent comments made relate to the personal validity of a role play and the extent to which they personally feel the role play is real or not.

The general feel of the situation

Inductors need to pay attention to the quality of the general *experiential* feel of the role play situation for actors since, generally speaking and almost without fail, the yardstick of *personal experience* emerges as the most powerful criterion, for actors, for evaluating role plays as 'experientially' real, involving and engaging. Even in situations where actors are not required to relate any of the role play experience to their own and there is no explicit demand for Personalization – indeed even where it is clearly the case that a role play situation is quite alien to them – subjects continue to use their own experience as the yardstick of credibility and make frequent, unsolicited direct comparisons. This is commonly expressed in terms as vague as the 'general feel', but may also be expressed in terms of 'accuracy' of the other role, or in terms of the credibility or predictability of the other role.

This general feel is also sometimes expressed, by actors, in terms of 'reality' being facilitated by the *correct dynamic* being created between themselves and another actor, producing an emotional state akin to an original similar experience; and that 'reality' is saliently compromised when these feelings and dynamics are not recreated, especially if the 'target' role play is supposed to an explicitly personally owned/or known situation. This presence or absence of such a dynamic can be further accounted for in terms of inadequate 'acting' of the 'other', or insufficient information (Particularization) being made available to the 'other actor', preventing them from faithfully carrying out the role. The general issues of 'acting' and 'adequate information' (Particularization) are dealt with more fully below.

Nature of involvement and reality for actors

It does appear that, just as researchers are conceptually confused about the nature of involvement in 'as-if' experiments, and have proffered such explanatory concepts as 'arousal' and 'physical action' (Yardley, 1984a), so a small minority of actor-subjects proffer parallel understandings. For this small group, comprising overwhelmingly *only* those actors who *do not* have personalized inductions (that is, they are not undertaking a role play of personal relevance or where personalized inductions are lacking), 'involvement' can and does equal the experience of *any* marked emotions and the greater the arousal or emotional volume, the greater the sense of reality and involvement.

However, unlike most role play researchers, most subjects do in fact offer understandings of 'involvement' and 'reality' which primarily take on board the necessity of mundane equivalence, or ecological validity, as their hallmarks. The prime importance of the re-creation of the familiar, in terms of experience or perception, that runs through the vast majority of the actors' explanations and accounts, may be construed in terms of both appropriate external and internal objects. For some actors even the credibility of the 'props' as external objects is important, but most actors speak of recognizable internal or interactional experiences, which do not challenge the actors' credulity, past experience or knowledge, or sometimes capabilities – especially 'acting abilities' (see below). This does appear to be the major aspect in creating verisimilitude for actors, and cannot be conceptually equated with arousal. Boredom is perceived to be as real an experience as ecstasy; and arousal *per se* is never used as a criterion for reality or involvement by those actors who receive personalized inductions.

Creating the familiar

The question of creating the familiar as against the unfamiliar and unpre-dictable is, of course, highly problematic. First there is the central question of defining whose 'familiar' we are talking about. This question must be addressed, however, if experimenters and psychological therapists are to know the extent of application of their findings.

The question of what is legitimately to be *unknown* in an 'as-if' experi-ment (role play) purporting to have ecological validity, seems even more complex. Unpredictability cannot be legislated for except at the level of 'leaving spaces'. Yet the known and the unknown are deeply interdepen-dent and bear a parallel epistemological burden. This concerns the nature of the relationship between knowledge and action, particularly as pertains to the distinction between tacit knowledge, and knowledge that is directly in awareness. Each experimenter or therapist, whether using role play or other techniques, makes assumptions about this relationship which are rarely examined. Practitioners of applied role play techniques frequently 'know' about these conceptual, and indeed practical, quagmires yet gloss over them by heavily restricting the range and focus of a simulation. 'Actors' must be given permission to experience 'unknowns' in role play as they mundanely might.

Personalizing role plays as problematic

Although Personalizing role plays is without doubt more successful in terms of establishing engagement and ecological reality, there are some associated problems. First, role plays can become too personal and too revealing of individuals in the role play. Protagonists clearly can and do feel uncom-fortable revealing personal details (even where they have spontaneously volunteered these) about themselves, their friends, and family members and may discontinue when they feel too emotionally involved or when they feel other members of the group are embarrassed. Clearly notwithstanding the intent of the role play (for example, though many therapies will 'normalize' a certain level of personal disclosure, high levels of personal disclosure are not usually expected within research psychology), the manner in which the role play is made safe by the inductor, the extent to which group dynamics are taken on board, will clearly affect the sense of comfort of individuals in disclosing. Even day-to-day factors can change a group's willingness to disclose. If role plays extend over time, changes in group composition, occasioned perhaps by a particular individual being absent for one role play event, can facilitate or inhibit disclosure.

Identification with characters

It is interesting that one of the classic techniques of induction within psychodrama is the inductor's use of the *second person* in giving 'character' information to a participant, for example 'you are . . .'. Information delivered in the third person can, however, be advisedly used for the particular and expressed purpose of distancing a character. Presencing in the former sense also involves an appeal to Personalization, calls upon a 'whole' person response or integration of information to person. Why should this be? Why should the mere technical utterance of something in the second or first person have such a distinctive impact over something express in the third person? It would seem to indicate something about the power of selfhood and invoked selfhood, as quite distinct from observable self and others; something well beyond the power of social constructionism to explain, but quite ontologically and phylogenetically primitive, which positions the individual in internal relationship to an ultimately vulnerable but emergent and creative self, that paradoxically and necessarily finds itself within action not within exteriorized scrutiny. Hence, if one believes that in general terms individuals position themselves within action – at the very least in internal relationship to themselves – then one needs to call up this mode of being rather than the mode of external observer in demanding a role performance. The use of second person language to achieve this may merely be permission to call up this way of being, but it is clearly necessary as a perceived act of commitment by the inductor.

The actors' own experience may inhibit or facilitate identification with a character

'Mr Plod is a very belligerent angry character who enjoys humiliating Noddy'. Clearly this description may be problematic for participant X and it is certainly a common experience that some individuals 'refuse' to take on such a role as they find it outside their own emotional range or find it threatening. No matter what the boundaries established by role play inductors, no matter how seemingly 'safe' role plays are, different individuals will find that the calling up of certain behaviours for them intrudes upon self experience and values and cannot be sufficiently 'as if' detached to be performed.

The character to be enacted may facilitate or inhibit identification

See the discussion above on 'identification'. The 'nature' of the character to be played can strongly influence whether or not an individual role player can satisfactorily identify with the character and hence become engaged in the 'enactment'. Not infrequently participants are unable to 'engage' with a 'part' because they feel so at odds with the value system of the character and are, for example, more keenly aware of the judgement of their peers, uneasy that they should be seen to take to a role too well. For example, the espousal of sexist or racist views may be highly sensitive in a group; an assumption of heterosexuality is often evident in the role plays between participants and between roles, though it is highly unlikely that all members of a role play group would ascribe entirely to heterosexual values. Although this might be argued to be no different from any other mundane presumptive construction of 'normality', there is extra significance to the 'demand' for certain types of behaviour to be enacted or taken on, when the normative assumptions imposed do not accord with the personal position of individuals.

Particularization

We have already considered in detail the conceptual underpinnings of the induction need for Particularization in Chapter 4, and the summary in Table 4.1 also suggests support for detailed inductions from other workers. Moreover, all the evidence of the studies reported in Yardley (1984b; see Appendix 3) powerfully supports the unidirectional usefulness of increasing the levels of Particularization (and indeed Presencing and Personalization) to individuals' experience of reality and involvement. More complex issues surrounding Structure and Particularization are dealt with later in this chapter and in Appendix 3.

The need for sufficient information

Actors frequently complain about having insufficient information, when asked to enact a role play that is not 'owned' by them or personalized. Complaints about information overload do occur, but only usually in a highly personalized context of another actor, such as in a psychodrama. Faced with insufficient information about the *purposes* of a role play, its *setting* or its *characters*, the vast majority of 'actors' feel forced into random and meaningless activity, and most frequently can be observed to fall into highly stereotypical activity. Lack of information is experienced as a source of intolerable ambiguity, not freedom, and participants do not know whether to attribute this ambiguity to inadequate induction or to a 'realism-driven' aspect of the 'as-if' situation itself – another example of frame elision.

For example, if Mr Plod is described as short, fat and bearded, with an avuncular appearance and disposition, is this all we need to know about him for the purposes of the particular role play, or is that all there is to know about Mr Plod? And who is it who is doing the knowing? Is the choice of information based on the inductor's purposes or the result of ill-conceived instructions? Is the information based on Noddy's description, the Tops', the Golliwog's, Enid Blyton's, a particular reader's, and so on? How much information is the player of Mr Plod expected to create for himself?

The lack of detailed information, indeed the stereotypical nature of some situations, can be experienced as positively liberating for some role play participants

In contrast to the above, but somewhat rare in occurrence, is the experience of a very few actors that less information means more freedom. In experiments and workshops, and indeed in therapy, some participants express a sense of safety in playing roles where there is no personal commitment or revelation. This does not lead to a sense of authenticity in ecological terms, but to an existential or regressive freedom to express feelings and values normally rejected or anxiety provoking, which we might otherwise define clinically as 'acting-out'. From a psychodynamic perspective, it is plausible to understand here that individuals untrammelled by realistic or quasi-realistic constraints (whether internal or external), are liable to 'act out', giving free range to normally suppressed or repressed impulses, and to behaviours normally denied to the self. This can clearly be seen in the Stanford Prison Experiment (Haney et al., 1973), and such phenomena are indeed relied upon for certain aspects of psychodrama. However, such freedom does not lead to the experience of ecological validity.

VIGNETTE

A role play is set up centred around a youth club in a socially deprived area. The role play inductor, a youth club leader, is interested in using role play as a training medium to resolve issues around controlling anti-social behaviour among a small group of 'problem' children. Armed with very little information about the children concerned, participants are asked to take the roles of these children.

The central problem is set out which involves giving details of an aggressive bullying encounter between 'bullies' and a 'victim'. Although, interestingly, the youth leader feels that a close simulation has been achieved, the participants have principally acted out aggressive and disruptive behaviours with very little sense of how the 'real' children would have behaved. And although there is a congruence between the youth leader's state of knowledge about the children and that of the actor-participants, little understanding of the phenomena can be achieved because the actors so poorly understand their characters.

Note here that the externally validating perspective, that of the youth leader, is limited because his original perspective is external: he has almost no knowledge of the individual identities of the children. He gets back from the actors precisely what he has put in, and there is little or no potential for developing an experientially informed understanding of the events, through which he might be able to get more control of the situation. Interestingly, other observers and indeed the actors do not give equal credibility to the action, and it might be interpreted that the role play has re-created the 'protagonist/inductor's' own experiential state at its most extreme, with heightened awareness of **the problem**.

Acting out, it might be stated, within such a youth club setting, is characteristic of youth. Such a poorly personalized role play does perhaps highlight the problems of controlling behaviour when such children are indeed relatively anonymous – which was the status of all children at the youth club, so again is in that sense structurally consistent. However, it restricts diversity of perception and view. Moreover, as already implied, there is here a problematic tendency to caricature, exhibited by both inductor and actors alike. Of note here is the role cautionary non-stereotyping approach of Jessee and L'Abale (1981) warning professionals against the over-pathologizing of clients.

Predictability

This is not a concept that relates to an experimenter or therapist's ability to predict or control the outcome of a role play. It refers to the extent to which one actor can predict the likely actions and behaviour of the other actor/participant. This is an interesting and frequently mentioned theme among participants in role plays, but is expressed mostly strongly and most consistently in role plays where the role played situation is not personalized or particularized for all the actors in a role play. The more open-ended and less particularized the role play situation, the more concerned actors appear to be that the other actor/actors is/are unpredictable and, because of that fact, problematic. But even in some situations where the role play is not explicitly personalized for either actor, where the situation at a general level is familiar to participants, unpredictability remains a problem insofar as the actor's own experience is used to project a character and set of behaviours onto the other role partner – from whence, clearly, prediction often fails. Thorough Particularization of roles and situations will modify problematic unpredictability, so that what is supposed to be known and predictable is known to the role players. Role play inductors must consider whether unpredictability is valid within the role play as a characteristic of the situation or relates to a failure of induction or actor selection.

Unpredictability, furthermore, is bound up with **frame confusion** (see 'frame' and 'foci', Chapter 8), as actors are frequently unsure of whether unpredictability arises from insufficient induction, insufficient acting ability, or from a 'genuine' characteristic of the character and role played situation. Interestingly, and relatedly, problems of frame elision often arise in inductions where participants are inducted separately and out of earshot of each other. These participants then worry whether some awful unpredictable event is to be sprung upon them as a result of collusion between the experimenter and the other role partner. This is pertinent to the likely frame confusion in the Stanford study already cited, where 'false arrests' of role play participants took place, as for real, in the middle of the night preceding the actual role play event.

Predictability is, of course, a problematic area epistemologically, as it raises the question of predictability in everyday discourse and interaction. Evidently ordinary interactions are neither fully predictable nor unpredictable. There is a dimensional or typological aspect here. In Harré and Secord's (1972) terms, 'formal episodes', those episodes which achieve a definite social outcome on the basis of the achievement of a particular social procedure, have intrinsic predictability; other informal episodes have very little predictability by comparison. Clearly the behaviour of a close friend is generally more predictable than that of a stranger. Predictability also adds a temporal dimension to Particularization, in the sense of determining *when* something occurs.

Clearly, Predictability and Particularization are strongly linked. Only where there is sufficient particularized information can predictability arise. If unpredictability is a target or a valid part of the role play structure, this must be clearly defined. However, whatever the level of particularized background information, unpredictability remains a mundane epistemological issue, whether or not the role play is highly scripted or open-ended, and needs careful attention.

Accuracy of enactment

Accuracy, as such, rather than general predictability, can only be a salient issue for participants where they are aware that there is an external criterion to be met. Where role plays are Personalized, and intended to replicate mundane reality for a participant, then the issues of accuracy of a complementary role became crucial. Inappropriate, even single behaviours and actions, can call up entirely inappropriate responses in the protagonist, and render a whole encounter meaningless and invalid. For example, in a father–son role play, where the action and 'roles' are personalized for the 'sons' but not for their 'role partner' actor-fathers, actor-sons frequently find that actor-fathers' performances fail to meet their expectations. In such a situation, actor-sons frequently report that they are put off their stride and find it very difficult to interact. Even in situations where a role play is not personalized for any of the actors, yet they are expected to take on a role/part that is normatively central to their own identities (in this case that of a son), there is a very strong tendency to be facilitated or not in their own roles to the extent that actor-fathers compare with their own fathers.

The induction requirement here is evidently that of sufficient Particularization in order to provide accurate and familiar interactions in relation to criterion values. Although there is an element of serendipity in the 'pairing' of actors who may or may not share similar social and parental interpersonal environments, the overwhelming need for an actor in a supposedly familiar role play environment is familiarity which allows a reasonable degree of predictability. As Rommetveit states of speech but is equally applicable to action:

> speech is continuously listener orientated and monitored in accordance with assumptions concerning *shared* and convergent strategies of categorization . . . and based on the tacit assumption that the speaker is monitoring what he says in accordance with what he assumes to constitute our temporarily shared social world. (1979:55)

This also provokes the need for **Bridging Particularization**; for inductors to sensitively assess the extent of the disjuncture between the actor's experience and the expectations of role, and the extent to which these disjunctures are salient and must, therefore, be addressed.

Structural issues

We now move on to consider other induction concerns which particularly extend the three basic induction processes of Particularization, Presencing and Personalization.

The way in which induction information is given to actors can itself be meaningfully assimilated by actors into the 'as-if' situation

As stated above (and discussed in Chapters 6 and 8), induction style can become part of framing confusion. This is an interesting and potentially powerful phenomenon, readily observable as well as commonly reported by actors recounting their experiences. The manner in which information is given to actors in the induction is readily assumed to have significance over and above what may be intended by role play inductors. Hence, for example, *separating* an actor-officer from an actor-inmate for the induction procedure of a prison role play is likely to be construed by participants as indicating that one person is to be tricked or unpleasantly surprised. In such role plays carried out by Yardley (see Appendix 3), participants frequently assumed that they were to be exposed to an unpredictable 'violent' act.

This is a particularly interesting case of frame elision, where the primary and secondary 'as-if' frames are confused or merged. (A powerful parallel case is explored in Chapter 4, in relation to the Stanford Prison Experiment.) Such suspiciousness, on the part of actors, must be anticipated by inductors, and decisions made about what information is to be shared between actors and what information is to be given in a differentiated manner to actors, and for what purpose. If there is a clear intention neither to create suspicion nor a problematic, planned unpredictable act, then inductors must be sensitive to any unintentional effects here arising from an inappropriate reading of the situation.

Structural compatability between mundane reality and role plays in relation to Particularization

Structural differences differentially affect roles. Although some aspects concerning Structure are implicit in the earlier exposition of induction processes (Chapter 5), this is dealt with more fully here. For example, in a role play involving a confrontation between a father and son over returning home late (see Appendix 3), the situation as *structured* is one in which conventionally 'father' has the interpersonal power, but 'son' has the knowledge power in that he is the only one of the dyad who knows where he's been that night. In such a role play – as carried out with 26 participants/dyads, across two role play situations with either minimal or enhanced induction conditions (with respect to Particularization, Personalization and Presencing) – all 'fathers' uniformly complained of lack of information, while 'sons' seldom complained in either condition, although clearly in the 'minimal' induction situation 'sons' were as bereft of information as the 'fathers'. Equally, in an inmate–officer role play, officers in the 'power' position complained of lack of information across all levels of induction conditions, whereas inmates did not.

What seems to happen here and elsewhere is that, where either the 'power' of the situation lies or the 'need for response' lies, it is the individual in that place who 'needs' the information and who has the 'responsibility' of acting upon it. Hence, 'sons' in the minimal induction role play of the father–son encounter (who uniformly sought to minimize an encounter universally interpreted as being with a potentially angry father, and who indeed sought to 'escape' the situation), took on a relatively passive role which called upon little in the way of resources. In contradistinction, the fathers (interestingly, the almost exclusive focus of external observers' concern to the detriment of 'sons'), needed information in order to be active and 'in control'. For, if the father–son role play situation is normatively most clearly defined as one in which the 'father' may be expected to take the initiative – for example, first because the 'father' stayed up to signify his alarm at the 'son's' late homecoming – then the control of the situation and the initiative must be seen as the 'father's'. The 'son' may merely respond to the 'father's' initiative. Moreover, the 'son' is free to 'create' any story that he likes about his lateness, within the bounds of the constructed skeleton plot; indeed 'creative' justificatory accounts are almost a 'demand' of the normative situation.

Lack of information is not such a problem, therefore, for an individual in a 'role' that is essentially that of 'respondent' rather than 'initiator'. But for an actor whose 'role' demands that he or she take the initiative, lack of information is highly disruptive – and is experienced as such. Where the 'respondent' actor is furnished with detailed information or has elicited detailed personalized information and the 'other' actor is deprived of information, this paradoxical state of affairs is even more incongruous and structurally inappropriate.

The above illustrates *the complexity of the relationship between action, knowledge and control* (see also Chapters 5 and 6, and Appendix 3), *which three factors impact upon, and indeed derive from, both the structural realities of the role play and the structural features of the 'as-if' framing.* Moreover, in an 'as-if' situation there are extra problems of knowing which state of knowledge belongs to which frame – that is, to the 'as-if' frame itself or to the induction frame external to the 'as-if' frame. We now consider a detailed example drawn from one of the workshops. (This potential ambiguity is also alluded to by Ginsberg, 1979.)

VIGNETTE

An interview situation is schematically outlined by one participant to two other participants. The inductor's task is to discover how, given a limited data set, the participants make sense of the role play. The participants are merely told that they are to role play a job interview, that one participant is to be an interviewer, that another is to be an interviewee, and the last is to be the secretary to the interviewer.

Given no other instruction, and given an empty space in which they are to act, all three participants remain standing throughout, and take no initiative to use any props. The interview commences and it becomes evident that no one knows what the job is or what position the interviewer holds or, indeed, even where the interview is taking place. However, as 'good' participants responding to the 'demand' characteristics of the total set-up, the role players struggle on. During the course of the interview the interviewer 'creates' a toy manufacturing company and a job for a design engineer, although she is clearly quite unfamiliar with the nature of such a company or job. Quite by chance, and unknown to the interviewer, the interviewee, in his real life, has a long standing interest in mechanical and electronic toys and thus has some background experience relevant to the job which he can, and does, draw upon.

None the less, the interview continues to stagger, as the interviewer finds herself in the position of not knowing where she is coming from; she has no actual knowledge of the 'product', 'industry', or 'job being offered' and seems unable to improvise. The interviewee, being more knowledgeable, 'helps out' the other participant-as-actor and, in relation to the interviewer's evident padding-out of the interview, offers more appropriate knowledge.

Here, the reversal of the social roles of 'who ought mundanely to know more', affects the expected and customary power relationship within the interview, thus skewing the interactions. Again, structural properties of the simulated situation interact with the 'real' knowledge status of the participants.

Clearly the formal properties of the event to be simulated here, do not correspond to the actual relationship between the participants. There is insufficient preparation and provision of induction information and this results in an unrealistic interview sequence. *The interactants reported that they were intent on padding out the scene to meet the perceived demands of the role play inductor, not the demands of an interview situation.*

Control as a structural issue

One person role plays   The impact of increasing levels of Particularization, Personalization and Presencing is especially marked in relation to single participant role plays. These are role plays where individuals are involved in an individual imaginative task, and are not required to interact overtly with another person in a role play, although they are usually required to make externally available responses. (These have been called 'passive' role plays elsewhere, see Chapters 5 and 6.) In such a setting, the effects of Personalization appear to be untrammelled by the limitations imposed, for instance, by another actor's acting abilities. The latter may diminish the credibility of an imaginative situation. Most importantly, the problematic issue of who controls the information becomes irrelevant, except in relation to information stipulated by an experimenter or role play facilitator, because the control of the imaginative internal act lies above all with the 'subject'. Such a focus upon individuals is more typical of psychodrama, than other role play techniques, where the particular intention will be to provide a projective exposition for the 'protagonist'.

Two or more person role plays   In two or more person interactions, the control issues become more problematic. It would seem that in situations where the 'character' would mundanely control the situation relative to another, then the actor playing that character **ought** to have greater control of the induction information for there to be *structural consistency*. However, the question of who mundanely controls an interaction, and/or information pertinent to that interaction, is an extremely complex one. Moreover, uncertainty is always a part of interactions, with the exception of highly formalized and ritualized interactions. It is rare for one actor to have an entirely predictable dominant control of information.

The above is clearly confusing for induction purposes. *Actors will not always, if ever, be able to decide whether inadequacies of experienced information and control belong to the induction procedures or to the situation or character being 'simulated'.* Personalizing the situation for one actor, but not another, introduces a particularly one-sided form of control, atypical of most mundane interactions which role play users need to examine.

In the example of the father–son experiment given above, it was possible to make some direct comparison between the processes of Personalization and Particularization. Whereas actor-sons, who had a personalized induction, were clearly and overwhelmingly more 'involved' in the enhanced condition than in either of the other conditions, the actor-fathers did not distinguish as clearly between the minimal induction (low Particularization, low Presencing) and the enhanced induction (high Particularization, high Presencing). Here again the factor of 'control' emerges. Severe limitations were placed on ecological validity by the actor-fathers' lack of informational control *vis-à-vis* the actor-sons. The latter owned, and controlled, the relevant information necessary for the enactment. Mundanely, the fathers would be expected to have control. This lack of control seems to have seriously impeded actor-fathers' sense of spontaneity and efficacy, and led to a certain disinterest in their role.

In a parallel experiment involving a role play situation between an actor 'inmate' and actor 'prison officer', where the prison officer had to give the inmate bad news about his girlfriend, neither actor was given or had elicited personalized information, so that for induction purposes the actors were in an equivalent position with regard to control of information. Here again the same control principles emerge, in that those actor-officers who had a more particularized and presenced induction as compared to actor-officers who had a low level of particularized and presenced information, experienced the 'as-if' situation as significantly more real and felt more involved. However, this was not true for the actor-inmates who had more information; these actors did not experience the 'better' inducted situation as any more real or involving. This is consistent with the father–son experiment, where situational and induction control factors appear to have interacted. Again, in the prison situation one would mundanely expect the officers to be in control. The induction, however, favoured neither actor-officers nor actor-inmates in terms of control. Although this did not therefore strengthen the structural position of the actor-officers, it did not undermine it (unlike the case of the actor-fathers). The relative lack of interest of the actor-inmates in the role play in either condition seems consistent with the passivity and powerlessness of their structural situation within the role play. It must also be remembered that neither group received personalized inductions and this may have had even greater negative impact on the 'inmates', given that the role play problem with which they were presented involved a situation that was supposed to be highly personal and salient for the 'inmate' rather than for the 'officer'. The qualitative accounts provided by both actor-inmates and actor-officers did, in fact, highlight *the lack of sufficient information.*

Of course, much of the control of the role play lies with the inductor, particularly where, in addition to setting up the induction parameters, additional induction material is introduced during the course of the role play.

VIGNETTE OF INDUCTOR CONTROLLING INDUCTIONS AS AGENT PROVOCATEUR

In a role play, an inductor sets up a relatively complex simulation of the control room of a nuclear power station. Having given a relatively full, particularized and presenced induction, the inductor leaves the scene 'to run' but uses an 'outside' imaginary telephone link to input new conditions/events. This stratagem parallels the conditions relating to unpredictability, with respect to events mundanely outside the control of the 'control room team'. The role play inductor has a 'hidden' ergonomic agenda, that of being interested in how such a team would handle crisis, and therefore for valid methodological reasons withholds that particular information. Hence, here the control aspects of the simulation do appropriately mirror the 'mundane' reality and are, therefore, unproblematic.

The actor's own world

Acting abilities: the other actor must be credible and at least partly predictable

Over and above the impact of Personalization, Particularization and Presencing, actors often express difficulty with experiencing role plays as real or involving because of the relative *acting* ability of their partner or partners. There is a perceived need for credibility of acting. Moreover, individuals are seen to have particular difficulties in taking on certain kinds of role. In complementary fashion, many participants assert their difficulties in playing certain kinds of role: either because they have insufficient experience of, or knowledge about, the sort of person they are asked to play and are, therefore, unable to creatively generate appropriate behaviour; or because they are uncomfortable about producing some kinds of behaviours or emotional states. (The latter will be explored in more detail under **'Identification'**.)

The question of acting ability has not been formally addressed in this text thus far, not because it seemed without importance, but because the thrust of any role play technique has to be focused upon *facilitating all levels of 'acting ability'*. Clearly, sensitive individually oriented inductions go a long way towards meeting individuals' induction requirements. However, there is no doubt that individuals are different in their experience; their emotional range; in the way they typically present and express themselves interactionally; and in the way they behave. For example, it is not unusual for actors to state difficulty in expressing rage, although they may feel that the 'part' demands it. It is clear from this example that, whatever the type of simulation, something is demanded from the actor-subject that would not mundanely be demanded or be experienced as a demand – something that does not mundanely 'belong' to the actor-participant's world. A disjuncture is further created between the experience of mundane impulse and behaviour.

Although there are many other mundane situations where 'performance' is demanded – that is, behaviour that we may not spontaneously feel – there is a consistency and degree of purpose in an 'as-if' situation that intensifies and formalizes this distance. Good actors, in this respect, may be those who can read and meet others' performance demands very well, without experiencing boundary confusion and hence distress. However, in considering the question of *demanding* performance, this once more raises the problems of asking who it is who controls and defines the situation, and to what purpose?

Considering acting as an ability does not appear, therefore, to sidestep or make redundant any of the other issues concerning definitional control. It does highlight the need for clear analysis of the actor's range when an inductor's 'legitimate' expectations are not met, and the need for individually oriented induction techniques to **bridge** the difficulty. And, if all else fails, a change of actor may be required to provide appropriate stimulus for another actor, or to achieve a particular result.

Acting ability is also likely to be related to Presencing (that external process through which the participant is collaboratively facilitated into creating the actuality of the role play environment and their own role play state of being). It is undoubtedly the case that good lay actors, and indeed professional actors, short circuit and internalize this process, rendering its explicit operation redundant. A similar 'external' procedure is carried out in hypnosis, where – without exception – the hypnotist induces an imaginative hypnotic state, partly by asserting the reality of this pseudo-reality. Thus the hypnotist, in a sense, takes responsibility for the initial 'imaginative' leap, reducing inhibiting self-consciousness. Indeed, much fuller such procedures are frequently carried out, particularly in regression inductions. Lay actors, just as hypnosis clients, will need help to take this imaginative leap in the form of Presencing.

The factor of *credibility* of one actor *for* another, as concerns the acting of characters, is commonly translated by actors into a need for consistency, translucency and explicitness of action. Such need for clarity of action bears a good deal of correspondence to the 'demands' generated by observers of actors. (In the experiments briefly summarized in Appendix 3, external observers of all the role plays – in complete contrast to the 'actors' – viewed the minimally inducted, highly stereotypical performances, as more realistic than the more highly inducted and, in terms of action, more highly differentiated role plays.)

Although actors inside role plays never come close to such stereo-typicality in their overall evaluations, detailed consideration of actors' idiographic accounts does commonly reveal that they expect more consistency of characteristics in others than they do of themselves. Once more we touch upon the profound epistemological dilemmas of inner versus outer reality, of observer–actor differences (Jones and Nisbett, 1972), and of inferential activity versus 'pure' external observation. (We shall revisit this point by later considering the highly differential perceptions of external judges in relation to the role play experiments, see Appendix 3.)

The pressure to perform

When given only *minimalist inductions*, actors usually experience a high level of performance demand. The simplest and most evident intention then arises of entertaining the audience and not boring them. This entertainment concept is often rather primitively understood to necessitate busy, super-explicit and interesting activity. Hence, silence is rare in minimally inducted role plays (not in fuller inductions) and participants are observably very 'busy' throughout. Amateur actors will know the syndrome well, as might many a suffering audience.

VIGNETTE

An individual actor is asked merely to role play 'waiting for a friend', without any further induction. This leads to several individuals giving highly expressive perform-ances of impatience, of watch-checking, foot tapping and excessive vigilance.

Something quite extraordinary then occurs. In behaving in this manner, under the experienced demands of '*showing* that one is waiting', the original 'other', for whom the actor had decided to role play waiting, becomes 'lost' to the waiting actor-person. A new imaginary character appears 'to be waited for', one who better fits the actor's expressed impatience. The waiting person then builds supporting rationalizations for their impatience into the character awaited. One role play participant in just such a situation, therefore, said:

The whole thing changed; I was waiting for X but I am used to waiting for X, he's always late, but because I thought that I had to *show* I was waiting, I behaved as if I was surprised at the wait, but I wasn't originally.

Again there are some parallels with mundane existence where at times it is felt necessary to give an expressive account of behaviour. For example, a woman waiting alone will give such signs so as not to be thought available for opportuning by a man, and thus give a performance.

Giving away self: honesty versus concealment

A frequent reflexive theme, for actors, is the extent to which one reveals self, either in the sense of 'giving self' or inadvertently 'giving away self'. Individuals believe themselves to be differentially opaque or translucent, and have different levels of concern or confidence about 'being seen'. Acting in this sense is not always viewed as sufficient concealment, although it may serve this purpose. The power of actors' characterization is definitely not simply a matter of assuming a face or a mask. This is witnessed by our everyday confusion when trying to infer characteristics of 'real' character from actors' acting. When a clear explicit relationship or set of behavioural 'evidence' fails to support such an inference, a deeper interpretation may then be made about, for example, 'repressed selves', with differing degrees of validity. Within this spectrum lies the old conflict between extreme behaviourism and extreme psychodynamic depth interpretation.

Concerns about being 'seen' are of course not restricted to 'role play' alone; thought provoking, in this context, are the views of the communication theorist Iser (1980):

> communication is a process set in motion and regulated . . . by a mutually restrictive and magnifying interaction between the explicit and the implicit, between revelation and concealment.

> contact in communication centrally depends upon (the thing in between, the nothing) filling in a gap in our experience. Dyadic interaction comes about only because we are unable to experience how we experience one another.

Induction contents of 'as-if' situations

Following on from the above, the question of what is to be made explicitly known to the actor in an 'as-if' experiment or role play therapy procedure is a highly complicated one. It demands that an inductor has a very clear idea of what it is that is being investigated, and the extent to which the actor-participant really needs to be in the 'dark' or to be left with truly mundanely unpredictable spaces to 'fill'.

Does the inductor's knowledge of a particular social world match that of the participants? And whose knowledge is to take precedence, and under what conditions? Whose judgement is to predominate on descriptions – the experimenter or clinician in stipulating certain 'facts' grounded in unarticulated premises, or the participant who says, 'Well it wouldn't actually be like that'?

If we are to re-create the intentional strategies, actions and reactions of self-reflexive and agentic human beings, it clearly makes no sense to impose the assumptive world of the researcher or clinician's intentions upon participants, 'as-if' they were mind readers of the inductor's intentions and assumptive state of mind; willing to pretend that they shared those assumptions, or indeed were of one mind with the experimenter or therapist, yet not privy to the crucial 'secret' areas that are seen as pivotal in 'manipulating' human behaviour.

An interesting study by Kern et al. (1983; referred to earlier), although not concerned with ecological validity, is useful here in that it substantiates the usefulness of clearly putting participants in the picture, when striving for external validity within traditional paradigm research. The experimenters found that in a specification role play, where subjects were told of certain dependent measures which it was important that they simulated accurately, there was a marked increase in target external validity as compared with both 'typical' and 'replication' role plays. This needs to be noted by experimenters and behavioural clinicians alike.

The characters and to some extent the situation should be perceived to be authentic and possible in the real world

Some participants 'demand' greater degrees of credibility in a character than others and actors are more or less willing to encompass the incredible or reject it. Particularly in a minimally induced situation, there are considerable individual differences in the amount of ambiguity or superficially contradictory information that participants can hold as valid without 'bridging' work. (Elsewhere, 'bridging' work has been defined as that Personalized or Particularized creation of links between material that cannot be otherwise accommodated, and the use of further material that enables the participant to make sense of the original stimulus material for the role play.)

Of particular relevance here, although not directed towards role play methods, Rommetveit (in his elegant treatise on language 1979 where he refutes Strawson's alternative dichotomous public or private domains for an intersubjectively established social reality) states:

> the need for a bridge from the here-and-now of the dialogue to some particular and unique event; can hence not be solved by any publicly valid general recipe for 'identifying descriptions'. Different constructions will be required depending upon what kind of foundations are available in the form of shared experience and strategies of categorization on the part of the participants in the dialogue. The bridge by which the novel information is linked to what was known beforehand and which it thereby becomes part of an expanded or modified social world will in each case be exactly as fragile as the pre-established commonality between speaker and listener upon which it is founded. (Rommetveit, 1979:32–3)

This underscores the idea that little can be taken for granted, relating to states of knowledge and social assumptions between participant actors. It is striking the extent to which participants bring entirely different assumptions about the 'real world', both subtle and gross, to any role play. Only the passage of time facilitates increased knowledge between participants, providing a counterforce to this continual state of things.

Similarly, Lewis and Antaki (1986) state of interlocutors, that:

Usually the speaker and listener will share a context in which each will know the other's frame of mind. The speaker can orient what he or she says to the particular assumptions of the audience. It is this metacognitive world of meaning that allows the listener to understand what the speaker says automatically without having to entertain all the possible interpretations of what was said. (1986:10)

The above cannot be taken for granted in a role play – it must be constructed piece by piece. And even though Antaki and Lewis were presumably referring to *mundane* social occurrences, they fail to describe those many events when these shared states of knowledge may not be taken as read. A more cautious analysis emerges from Atkinson and Heritage (1984), commenting on Garfinkel's research on conversations:

the studies demonstrate the staggering range of assumptions and contextual features which may be mobilized *ad hoc* to entertain a particular 'documentary version' of a sequence of events (1984:95)

and, similarly, Rommetveit:

Our immediate interaction with others is constantly based on the tacit and firm assumption of some commonality with respect to interpretation . . . as listeners, we are spontaneously acting on that assumption when listening to what is being said in accordance with the perspective induced by the speaker. As speakers, we automatically monitor what we say in accordance with what we assume to be the intersubjectively shared reality here-and-now. (1979:56)

VIGNETTE

Participant X is unable to accept his role fully because, unlike many of the group, he is not able to make sense of the role description/image of a shy unmarried woman, living with someone, and having a hobby of pistol shooting. These for him are such grossly incongruous attributes that he could not believe in such a character.

An interesting exercise can be carried out here to understand more fully the phenomena involved. Reported below are the results of such an exercise in relation to a specific description of character for a role play.

The original character description is read out to participants but only furnishing them with one piece of information at a time, in order to elicit the evolving experiences of participants of a character, and assumptions about a character. This yields particularly interesting results, in that attitudes towards clients shift dramatically in relation to each new piece of information. Part of an example follows:

Prompt: youngest sibling of wealthy family at Public School
Response: spoilt brat

Prompt: stammers
Response: he's a pretty anxious person generally, unconfident, wouldn't like to have a stammer in a public school . . . For him and starting to like him a bit.

Prompt: doesn't enjoy it or fit in
Responses: its obvious that he's an outsider, he's not going to fit in with anybody . . . desperately trying to fit in. He might not like rich people now

Prompt: performed extremely well, got into Oxford
Response: bit of a recluse, but . . ., not going out socializing, worked hard but
dropped out, I mean he went to University and discovered there was more to life
than just working and getting your exams, . . . he's somebody who can't take
pressure

Particularly problematic was the description of this man as a womanizer and a
misogynist; some of the respondents could make sense of this and could provide a
network of explanatory and consistent meanings, others could not make sense of
these particular facets at all and 'refused' to construct such a person.

Particular difficulties arise for a participant who cannot make sense of the
character given to him or her. What appears as most significant, when a character is
perceived as unreal, is that the actor-participant cannot find a central point of
identification with the character from which their behaviour might emerge. The
participant then adopts a rather Brechtian attitude towards their character, which
breaks the spontaneously experienced flow between experience and behaviour.
However, it must be stated that this 'alienation effect' is not exclusive to 'acting',
but is also part of normal mundane social interaction, where the break between
action and experience can be viewed as unwanted self-consciousness, bad faith,
inauthenticity, manipulativeness, etc. Where the other actor-character is not viewed
as credible, the first actor has to choose whether to take the behaviour at face value
as part of the naturally inconsistent character, or as being a result of poor acting or
interpretation, which needs managing by ignoring its inadequacy and by responding
to the more 'perfect' icon on which it is putatively based.

The situation must be credible

A flight departure is delayed because two thousand sheep are loose on the
main runway (workshop example) – credible or incredible? If the situation
is credible to the participants, they will be able to sustain their realistic
involvement in a situation? Is credibility a matter of the objective demonstration of fact or a question of sustainable belief?

Clearly, within mundane reality what is credible for one individual is not
for another, and the extent to which an individual experiences any social
purported fact will profoundly affect the actions of that individual. Role
play inductors must bear credibility in mind, not only at the general level
but at the particular level of each interactant. If only one or two individual
'actors' from a large credulous majority cannot find a situation credible,
how will other actors manage these two? Will they 'persuade' them by their
own credulous 'performances' or will they work with the incredulity and
treat it as part of the roles being played? What will the incredulous actors
do to sustain 'performance'? Or will they simply refuse to continue their
role play and/or sabotage it?

In an actual workshop individual actor-participants had different
reactions to the 'sheep on the runway'. Interestingly, however, one of the
few participants who could cope with the information, without breaking
out of the 'as-if' frame, was the actor who was playing the part of a
character who was drunk. The outlandishness of the information concerning flight delay was subsumed within the actor's general expressed state

of drunken incredulity and weakened grasp of external reality, with a licence, through drunkenness, to express strong reactions to all communication. However, most generally, credibility is facilitated by detailed sustained inductions via Presencing and Particularization.

The dynamics of the interaction between characters may be facilitatory or inhibitory either because incredible or because credible but rejected

Quite simply here, whereas individual characters may be viewed as plausible and possible to take on to role play, the interactive dynamic between those characters may be rejected as implausible or unacceptable to participants to enact. For example, with respect to the latter, a sado-masochistic psychological relationship between characters may well be rejected by role play participants as damaging to themselves to enact, or insufficiently warranted by the overall purposes of the role play exercise. In such an instance the inductor must negotiate safe boundaries for the participants, be prepared to negotiate the contents or, if all else fails and the role play is necessary, find different actor-participants.

Actors' personal experience may inhibit or facilitate identification with characters (cf Darroch and Steiner, 1970)

This is one of the most important and interesting features of reasons given by actors for their experienced inability to identify with a character, even when they have been provided with a reasonable level of induction information. (Interestingly, actors will provide more spontaneous explanatory accounts in relation to 'identification' and role play, than in relation to any other construct.)

Actors, when accounting for any inability in identifying with 'characters', *given a relatively full induction*, most commonly cite themselves as the limiting factor – that is, their own backgrounds and experiences are too distant from the characters for them to take the latters' positions. Conversely, *where information is lacking and inductions minimal*, failure to identify with a character is *not* usually reported in terms of actor 'failure'. Most frequently failure is attributed to negative characteristics of the character (which is an interesting example of negative, outgroup stereotyping).

For example, in the prison officer–inmate experiment (referred to above and in Appendix 3), under minimal induction conditions inmate-actors reported an inability to relate to the 'inmate character', based on the character's perceived aggressiveness and uncaringness, although such a description was not part of the induction. Quite simply, the more full the induction into a particular 'role', the more accepting and non-judgemental is the actor of the character to be played; the more minimal the induction, the more judgemental the actor. (Moreover, such distinctions are absolutely paralleled by observation of the content of such role plays.). There is a very clear message here for role play inductors.

One of the effects of 'Presencing' appears to be a binding of individuals more sympathetically to their characters   This is in contrast to the judgemental and polarized attitudes taken towards characters in poorly inducted role plays, without Presencing, of which the following are an illustration:

'My role as cast appeared to be that of a cold heartless warder.' (Minimal induction conditions.)

'I really hated the whole thing about the character I was given and tried to mellow it down a bit. I think perhaps in that respect it was unrealistic, expecting POs to show concern for human feeling.' (Intermediate induction conditions.)

This polarizing tendency, again referring to the inmate-prison officer role play experiment (see Appendix 3) in which warders were viewed as heartless or mean, *never* appeared where there had been a much fuller, particularized and presenced induction. Moreover, whereas in the enhanced induction condition, there was a good deal of consensus among the actor-officers that the officers were human beings who were at least attempting to be understanding; in the minimal induction conditions, this was not ever the case – callousness and shallowness predominated. Furthermore, actor-officers in describing their own characters did vigorously attempt to integrate the background information that they had been given. The net result generally was the mellowing of the actor-officer, despite the fact that no definite leads in this direction were provided via the inductions. This polarizing tendency was totally consistent with observations to be made about the content of the scripts. It was also entirely consistent with the expectation and experience, held here, about stereotypification in characters who are insufficiently inducted.

   It is of some significance to the critique of the Stanford Prison Experiment (see Chapter 4) that the processes described above mirror exactly the events of the Stanford Prison Experiment, where warders became brutal and inmates passive and despondent (Haney et al., 1973). Of further interest and significance is the related result that only external observers, and not actor-participants, overall viewed the more stereotypical behaviour as more realistic. This again poses questions about the validity of judging realism from an observer's perspective.

The dynamics of the mundane relationship and mundanely emergent relationship between participants has a profound effect on role playing activity

'I'll get X back in the next role play for that' or 'You always put me in a trouble-making role . . . he must be a natural.'

Particular relationships are 'played out' within the medium of role play, and add a layer of enrichment or complexity to the understanding of any 'as-if' event. Participants may and do repeat antagonistic dyadic relationship within a role play, either being 'cast' in those roles by others or by spontaneously creating them. This clearly needs sensitive handling by role play inductors, who may need to positively 'hold' and use these real relationships, or defuse and redirect them. Much will depend on the ego-strength of individuals, and the overall Gestalt of benignity or malevolence of the group *and* the inductor; and this is clearly sensitive in role plays used in clinical practice, particularly within the powerful medium of psycho-drama, where action and affect is commonly and deliberately heightened.

A group, of course, changes over time. Frequently, in experiments or therapy, individuals came together mostly as strangers or relative strangers, sometimes as acquaintances through work, but certainly not usually as close friends or intimates. Over the hours or weeks, stronger relationships are forged; sometimes more positive, sometimes more negative. A number of individuals will leave a group entirely, some because they are not comfortable with their general membership of a particular group of people. The evolving relationships, and the inevitable progress of self-disclosure and 'visibility' through acting, become both more and less problematic.

For some individuals, there will be a wish to trust each other more and reveal more about themselves, playing roles that deal with highly personal issues. Others will wish to increase or stabilize interpersonal distance, and perhaps to use role plays as a more utilitarian device to solve cognitive or technical problems, or to comply with experimental purposes.

Hence, inductors need to give careful attention to the social and inter-personal dynamics of a particular group and check to see if there is broad congruence between the group's purposes and capabilities, and those necessitated by the inductor's particular purposes. We are reminded that the primary 'as-if' frame (see Chapter 6) of the role play is not a watertight guarantee of nonconsequentiality. This also applies equally powerfully to the next induction theme below.

Another dimension – Time

Time passing helps immersion in 'as-if' situation

Participants, particularly in the workshops but to a greater extent following the more Particularized inductions, mentioned the extent to which time passing within a role play facilitated participation and the experience of reality. Evidently extended time was not facilitative when individuals did not have sufficient induction information, and 'ran out'. This aspect had not been specifically anticipated, and is not directly accounted for within the induction principles outlined in this text. It is entirely consistent, however, with the principles of experiential familiarity upon which all three induction processes were built: *that time should allow the experiential accretion of resources (including experiential knowledge resources) for actors*, and thus be an important factor in subjects' experience of involvement and reality (see also Baron, 1977; Ginsberg, 1979). Moreover, in an interactional context both actors mutually support each other in this regard by providing an ongoing interactive Presencing. Conceptual issues around the time–space relationship and role play are considered below.

Time–space relationship

It is generally accepted that thought and action have different temporal characteristics. Notwithstanding their deep mutual interdependence and co-constitutiveness, thought is fleeter than action and unbound by the mundane space–time constraints to which action is, of necessity, subject. In addition, and in general, thought is held to be prior to action, although there are clearly circumstances when thought follows reflex behaviours or action, as with acts of reflection. But no matter what the ordinal relationship, thought resides – as does the dream – in a distinct time–space domain.

If we can indeed conceptualize reflective thought and action as temporally distinct, there are inevitably frequent and continuous temporal lags between the two, no matter how small the lag, whether microseconds or hours (though usually within an interactional flow involving seconds rather than longer temporal units). Research which involves the *post hoc* gathering of accounts hugely enlarges this gap, no doubt causing subjects to lose much of the salient detail of their experience, and leading to summaries that distort and under-report subtleties and intricacies. Role play methods are, potentially, particularly adept at narrowing (or indeed enlarging) as far as possible the temporal lag between action and thought. When carried out with technical expertise and psychological sophistication, they offer the potential for a much closer-to-the-event accounting. 'Action' can be brought to a halt every few minutes, explored with participants, and then re-engaged with provided appropriate reinduction is carried out. (We will discuss re-inductions below; see Yardley, 1987.) Under certain conditions the gap can almost be obliterated by eliciting the in-flow articulation and exposition of experiences. Above all role play can facilitate the exploration of *durée*. Apart from approximating very closely mundane temporality, the individual's own sense of time can be explored by exteriorizing its 'feltness', amplifying or diminishing the chronological sequence of time, and allowing an exploration, in-flow or *post hoc*, of the meaning and significance of the event/process within the individual experience of time. Time and space can here be infinitely expanded and their relationship potentially infinitely varied. The latter is in complete contradistinction to mundane time–space relationships or indeed to a scripted role play or piece of theatre, where thought object-products are given, prior to action and thought in the time-less zone of the written, but produced and bounded within an almost precisely predictable time period, following a prescribed usually linear chronology.

Paradoxically another interesting and significant feature of role play – which has probably been an unarticulated part of arguments favouring the action-basedness of role play – is the technique's harnessing of 'real' time as distinct from the elicitation of imaginary time in 'passive' role plays. As already implicit in the above arguments, thought needs no synchronization to mundane space–time objects and object relationships, whereas 'real' action must be integrated into 'real' space and time mundane object relationships. Hence one aspect – and a very epistemologically powerful aspect – is the possibility of the placing of participants into a more closely approximate real space time nexus, which brings its own different set of demands upon individuals and demands some level of 'realistic' orientation to these dimensions. Introspection and imagination both discard this time–space condition (experimentalist and introspectionist alike discard it by context stripping and spatialization of variables). There is a powerful parallel to be discovered in the realm of spatial relationships. Thinking of a room is not the same as negotiating the space in the room when there. Thought will probably not conceive of the slippery banana skin when planning the great entrance to impress one's lover. Objects implode with their own reality when they are actual. (And between total imagination and total concretization, secondary 'as-ifs' offer themselves as symbolic representatives somewhere on a negotiable continuum of internal demand projecting outwards and the implosion inwards of external objects.)

Objects of knowledge and experience rise in a time–space nexus but the 'fact' of their existence in this nexus, and the fact that we know objects *through* the time–space nexus, still leaves us with the question of how we might know objects that exist within this nexus.

Summary

Below an attempt is made to summarize the major steps that inductors should consider, extracted from the more complex discussions about induction themes above. All the above themes have been supported by, or generated from, participants' accounts of their experiences of role play. It is evident from the above that for the most part these themes are entirely consistent with the three overriding induction principles of Personalization, Particularization and Presencing, but they also often add a new dimension for consideration for role play inductions. Careful attention to the above themes, together with consideration of the earlier conceptual and methodological issues elaborated in Chapters 4, 5 and 6, should provide role play inductors with a very thorough grounding in the benefits and pitfalls of induction procedures. **Where methodological rigour is necessary or where the quality of a role play is important, there are no short cuts through the need for such thoroughness.**

Overview of practice guidelines

To summarize, the following steps are necessary to achieve sound role play practice.

1. The inductor must first fully understand the significance and ramifications of his or her epistemological framework in order to understand the constraints and freedoms within which role play operates.

2. The role play user must have a working understanding and conceptualization of role play processes.

3. The role play user must understand that any domain separated out which involves research, teaching or psychotherapy shares a primary level of 'as-ifness', which provides a certain but not absolute degree of protection from consequence.

4. The role play user must understand that any domain of interest is artificially separated from the flow, and the boundaries and demarcations of this domain will emerge initially from the a priori assumptions of the instigator, but then may be:
   (a) held and maintained authoritatively without negotiation; or
   (b) may be negotiated and transmuted (or not) with participants.

5. The role play user must recognize that co-operation and co-determination of boundaries etc. is likely to increase ecological validity and mundane realism, but makes the whole enterprise more complex and less 'controllable' by the inductor.

6. The role play user must understand that the coherence and unity of the task within these boundaries/episodes is dependent upon the manner in which meanings are constructed and ascribed. Hence, a role play which involves greater participation on the part of participants will increase diversity and reduce simple coherence, but again provide greater ecological validity.

7. The role play user must recognize that the treatment of individual participants will be principally determined by the epistemological stance of the inductor, and this will have repercussions for the actions that follow within the role play. Inductors should stand back from the content of the role play episode and should consider the manner in which they 'treat' the participants by virtue of the manner of their induction. Otherwise such strategies, unreflected upon, will tend to be absorbed within the meaning of the role play episodes themselves. Hence, perceived secrecy within inductions will become part of the role play enactments.

8. The role play user must understand that any framing and focusing, whether through the primary 'as-if' set up or secondary 'as-ifs' of the role play itself, reveal meaning and intention. Meaning emerges from what is not conveyed as much as from that which is explicitly constructed or elicited. Hence, what is made present or absent through default or deliberate strategy should be considered in terms of its significance for an adequate 'reading' of the role play episode.

9. The role play user must recognize that attention must be given to the individual's needs in a role play. Even where the inductor is to control and determine all key information, the inductor must seek to address the information requirements of role players so that they know what they are supposed to be aware of as interactants. Due consideration must be given, for example, to the extent to which participants understand the same stock of social knowledge as that which the inductor assumes to be common, and to the degree of familiarity with a supposedly common 'local' environment.

10. The role play user must understand that attention has to be given to the determination of action as situation based or individually based and consider the impact of such attribution on any ensuing action or experience on the part of the participants.

All the above overwhelmingly expose the centrality of the determining of 'meaning' – the question of who is authorized to construct meaning and to attribute meaning, and whether or not there are transactions that need to take place, either to get participants 'into line' by giving them clearer instructions about how to read meaning, or to share the determining of meaning and significance with them. Further to this are the following ten points (11–20).

11. Inductors must decide to what extent role plays will be Personalized for participants. Personalizing attention to seemingly inconsequential detail at even a minor level will undoubtedly facilitate role players, giving them comfort and security in an imaginary scenario. The greater the level of Personalization, the greater the ecological validity for individual participants, but also the greater the need to negotiate between different individuals to find a role play episode all can find workable (if it is intended that the episode shall have equal validity for all). In contrast, in a psychodrama psychotherapy session, for example, intense Personalization for one individual alone may not require negotiation of details, etc. with other participants; these 'other' participants will be explicitly made aware within a specific psychodrama that they are there predominantly to 'serve' the protagonist's experience of reality.

12. Inductors should realize that Personalization can also produce problems for participants especially with respect to over-exposure of self-behaviours, and over-transparency of thought, feeling and intention. Moreover, requiring a more personalized integration with a 'problem' character, perhaps one morally rejected, can give a participant a quite disagreeable and sometimes painful experience.

13. Particularization is key to all induction and although it is possible to overprescribe or elicit detail, in most cases inductors starve participants of information, leaving them adrift in featureless psychological landscapes without any sense of how to navigate their way through.

Inductors must examine what it is that is needed to be known for a role play to work. (Related points follow.)

14. The concept of Predictability, the need to make decisions about what is intended to be predictable or not within a role play, is important. It is acknowledged that this is a particularly difficult area epistemologically.

15. Presencing is intimately bound up with Particularization and Personalization and is, in a sense, so superficially simple that it is in danger of being ignored as too obvious. Yet it is a powerful means of attaching a participant – assisting an actor to believe in an imaginary universe and ensuring a degree of comfort that seems simply to arise from the inductor co-constructing this 'reality' with the participant.

16. Inductors must also consider the structural compatability of the 'as-if' universe they construct by means of the manner of their induction processes, with the structure of their target 'realities'. It is no use giving one participant the ascendancy in a role play because of the manner in which he or she was inducted if the expected ascendancy within the role play situation is supposed to lie elsewhere.

17. Differences in states of knowledge need constant attention and reflection. A role play is dynamic, and what is evident at the commencement of a role play may be drastically changed throughout its course – perhaps demanding measures for re-induction.

18. Inductors must be alive to actors' own worlds. Each person brings different abilities and different states of knowledge and experience to role plays. Furthermore, some individuals will have powers of empathy and expressive range, others will not.

19. Time is a dimension that is important in role plays, not only because it can be 'manipulated' within role plays as an experiential phenomenon, but also because its 'real' passage may have a profound impact upon both the role play and the role play experience.

20. Finally, the inductors must have clear strategies and procedures for returning role players to the mundane world and for closing off their 'visit' to, and exploration of, the role play world in which they have been engaged.

10

Afterword: Concluding Remarks

The major purpose of this book has been to present a theoretical and conceptual framework for role play that leads to the formulation of precise technical guidelines for role play inductions.

We commenced by considering, against an epistemological background, the range of domains in which role play is used, and the extant definitions of role play and their adequacy. Types of role play technique were also critically reviewed in some detail across several domains – notably those of social and clinical psychology research, and therapy and clinical assessment. These were elaborated in detail.

The most important principle that has, hopefully, been conveyed is that, although key induction techniques have been put forward and identified, these are essentially processes that have their grounding and justification within the context of total, comprehensive and integrated sound methodological approaches. Each stage of a role play construction and enactment can mirror, complement or distort every other preceding or successive stage. A role play inductor must look to the totality of the experience set in motion, as well as attending scrupulously to every induction detail, whether explicit or taken for granted. Such consideration brings us again and again, full circle to the earlier stated impossibility of the total decontextualization and isolation of role play technique from the epistemological systems within which its existence and function occur, and upon which role play techniques are dependent.

Evidently, as we have seen, a good deal of the use of role play has been for the purpose of conventional replication experiments and for functional simulation of social interactions. Clearly, role play can continue to be used legitimately in traditional research settings, and, if users improve their techniques and understandings of the structure of a role play, it is the contention here that such use is desirable and will improve the validity of the constructed research environment. However, given the epistemological position taken in this text, the substantial critiques of psychological experimentation (especially in the area of social psychology), and the recent conceptual and methodological advances in social and clinical psychology, where now should role play best be exploited?

Although we have been careful not to argue that role play 'belongs' to more radical methodologies than to conventional ones, it is the case that role play techniques may particularly suit more liberal and challenging methodologies, since they are likely to require a more flexible set of tools than either experimentation or objectivistic observation offer. Above all, role plays offer a *generative mechanism* for producing social interaction and verbal interaction, focused around individuals – having enormous flexibility with respect to the generation of action and the facilitation of account gathering.

Role play is, hence, very well suited to many of the emerging alternative approaches which we considered in Chapter 2, where quality qualitative data are needed, and, where it is important that the generating techniques underpinning the action are in themselves open to detailed scrutiny. At the heart of alternative methodology are the good practice principles covered in Chapter 2:

1. *The recognition that the social world is more complex and subtle than that constructed by researchers or didactic therapists*
2. *The recognition of the need to place the person as agent at its heart and to recognize as valid the subjective experience of the participant/ individual/subject of investigation*
3. *The recognition of the layered and multiperspectival nature of meaning*
4. *The recognition that action is embedded in contexts*
5. *The recognition of the co-constructed nature of the world*
6. *The recognition of the subtlety and complexity of the social world*
7. *The recognition of the limits of objectivism*

Although a note of caution has often been sounded throughout this text arguing for scrupulous attention to detail and form, role play does offer, none the less, a creative playground for action and ideas given its fluidity of form. With this in mind, we conclude by referring to the challenge offered in the radical writings of Feyeraband, 1975. Feyeraband advocated the 'breaking of time-honoured rules of research, the upsetting of the balance of power in scientific circles *by any means found*'. He argued trenchantly that the effect of scientific education and method is to stifle individuality and creativity, and that this is amply exemplified by the impoverished language (and method) used in scientific articles. Personal style, he argues, is suffocated, with ensuing barrenness of intellectual achievement. Feyeraband suggested that with respect to the then current stasis in methodology, action should precede ideas, and that there should be creative and anarchic assault on the bureaucratic minds of psychology. Much of his writing was prophetic and invocatory, and his call remained unanswered and unfulfilled. Yet the more recent radical developments in psychology that we have considered may be seen to have at last attempted to upset the power balance in favour of the subject. Role play techniques yet might well play their part here and help tumble the still mighty positivistic walls of Eriha (Jericho), while hopefully retaining and cultivating an overwhelming interest in their inhabitants.

Appendix 1: Other practical considerations in setting up a role play

A suitable environment

Almost any protected space will do, protected in the sense that it affords privacy. It must also have a degree of physical adaptability, for allowing different physical configurations of objects, but without so many fixtures and fittings that the space's identity is predetermined for particular functions and cannot adapt to others. If some inductions are to be carried out away from other participants then another roomspace is immensely useful. Accessibility of easily movable pieces of relatively featureless furniture is useful – functional furniture is more easily imagined to be comfortable furniture than the other way around. Featureless smaller objects are also useful to represent other objects, if you do not want to always have a full set of 'props' to hand. A piece of white chalk can be invaluable in providing temporary boundaries around a room, markers for doors and a variety of other objects. Writing 'washing machine' on a surface, for example, can be really helpful. The intention in a role play is not to reproduce a realistic identical environment to the target, but to provide clear symbolic markers of that environment. Video equipment can be usefully made available, provided it is relatively unobtrusive. Simple precautions – such as notices stating 'do not enter' – can be invaluable in protecting the space from unwanted intrusion. There is nothing like the hospital or university porter breezing into a room to perform some task to disrupt the most engaged role play and make participants feel quite insecure. Therapists should not really need to be told this.

The inductors

It is much easier to work in pairs than to take on the full responsibility for a role play on one's own. So much occurs within an induction procedure, and so much may arise within a role play, that it is very difficult for a sole inductor to be able to be fully aware of all that is necessary, in addition to keeping a strategic eye on the procedures. A clear distinction in roles is essential here. For example, within psychodrama the 'director' (principal inductor) focuses on the protagonist, on diagnostic issues, and on keeping the action going in a strategically useful manner, while the co-director looks

after the needs (induction and emotional needs) of the other participants
and helps out generally, as needed by the director. Clearly, the relationship
between inductors and participants will be grounded in the purpose of the
entire project. However, above all, the participants must be able to trust
the inductor and be able to rely upon clear instruction from the inductor.
The core skills of the inductor must be observational and empathetic
attunement, as no amount of 'directorial vision' will move actor Smith from
objective B to C if the director's vision takes no account of where the actor
actually is and what the actor needs.

Participants

How many and who? Again the purpose of the role play and whole
enterprise will largely determine the 'cast'. For group therapy, other clinical
criteria will determine membership. However, the usual rule that good
groups need a mixture of types of people and personalities is even more
salient in role plays, as individuals usually have limited 'acting skills'
(empathic and expressive resources); hence, if a range of behaviour is
required in a role play, there may be no one to provide these. Well trained
therapeutic aides, with some acting abilities and, above all, empathic
abilities, can be useful to provide a greater range of expressive resources.
Acting abilities are not paramount, as good inductions should overcome
many shortfalls. However, there is no doubt, some are more naturally
adept than others at understanding different types of people and expressing
a wide variety of behaviour. If at all possible there should be selection of
role players, again with a target of securing a wide variety of people with
differing experiences – unless, of course, the project requires high degrees of
similarity. Participants should be given a contract of sorts, so that they
know exactly what is expected of them in terms of confidentiality, time
limits, etc. Role plays can involve one person only, or very small groups as
well as large. The larger the group, the more there is to handle, and the
more difficult it becomes to strategically control, unless high levels of
scripting or stipulated scenarios are intended. There is a great advantage in
having a dedicated interested pool of participants who are concerned, not
only in the domain of research, but in the activity of role play as method.

Debriefing and ending

Ethically this is perhaps the most important part of role play. No inductor
should go into role play without first knowing how the debriefing and
ending will be brought about. All participants must first always explicitly
(through Presencing) be brought out of role (For example, 'You are no
longer Marjory Pitt you are now back to being yourself in time and place
present.'). This may sound ridiculously simple, but it is almost infallibly
successful in returning individuals to the mundane; if it is left out, they can

be left in an unclear state. It is also advisable to ask them as part of a debriefing to explain how they are left feeling and if there are any loose ends that emerge from their characters that they want to express. This again allows any unresolved issues to be aired and then put to one side. A procedural sequence for this should be something like the following:

1. We've come to the end of this role play, how are you feeling as your character? Any other thoughts or observations? (Address this to the participant while still 'in role'.)
2. You are no longer Marjory Pitt, you are yourself, back in the here and now. (Add further particularized detail to describe that specific here and now, if there is any difficulty in coming out of role.)
3. Do you have any residual feelings left as yourself, that you want to share with us?
4. Any other debriefing information and conversation as appropriate.

No role player should leave a session without such a clear ending and, indeed, there may be occasion within a role play where it is necessary or useful to bring someone out of role with as clear a debriefing as at the end.

Appendix 2: Worked examples of role plays in varying therapeutic contexts

Example of a role play within a behavioural/cognitive approach

The client

Mr T. is 48 years old, having recently retired from work on grounds of ill-health. He has a high level of trait anxiety and has over the past two years, preceding his retirement from work, been exposed to large and chronic amounts of situational stress, principally at work. Mr T. is unmarried and lives with his widowed elderly sister in the suburbs of a large conurbation. He has no close friends, has never had a girlfriend, and is socially anxious and retiring and rather unassertive.

The therapist has already made a therapeutic decision that such is the nature of the stress in relation to employment, and in relation to his major occupational skills, that the pursuit of re-employment at this time is inappropriate. It has been agreed with Mr T., however, that a more appropriate and immediately pressing goal is his social quality of life, and that his social anxiety, self-consciousness and lack of social skills are prime areas for consideration.

Before proceeding to an anxiety reduction or social re-education focus, within a role play format, an assessment of Mr T.'s 'normal' social behaviour is needed. Hence, we proceed with a need for a diagnostic role play.

Setting up a diagnostic role play

We must presume here that the behavioural/cognitive therapist has already undertaken a thorough assessment of the types of situations Mr T. finds stressful, together with an analysis of the antecedent conditions, and the behavioural and cognitive consequences of these, via conversation with Mr T. (A pre-existing advantage for role play within this behavioural–cognitive model of working is the degree of behavioural detail and specificity usually sought, and commonly gathered.) Using role play subsequently here to diagnose difficulties, provides an extra dimension to a diagnosis which is otherwise made only through 'cold' reporting of situations. Not only does the behaviour in question become available for external observation by the therapist, but the client himself is likely to reproduce behaviours that he has overlooked in his verbal reports, or that he so takes for granted that he does not distinguish these behaviours sufficiently to be able to identify them separately.

Selection of role play episode

With respect to role play diagnostic procedures, the therapist should then take responsibility for the selection of one of the above target situations, or of several of these from which Mr T. might make a choice himself. That selection first should be governed overall by the customary therapeutic decisions about the level of situational stress which the client is both able to tolerate and benefit from.

Second, that selection should also now be made with respect to the practicability of setting up a role play of it. Usefully guiding this latter choice will be various technical factors. For example, the therapist needs to consider his or her likely familiarity with the targeted situations, in order that not too much of the onus of description of the scene is on the client, particularly at an early stage. This latter strategy is not to be viewed as opposing the overall need for Personalization of role plays for participant-clients, but as a necessary balance to be achieved between holding and supporting the client therapeutically, and expecting too much autonomy too soon. Here the issues of 'who controls what' are also ones that require broad therapeutic strategies. As the client becomes more accustomed to role play procedures and the therapy, greater unfamiliarity for the therapist can be introduced. Other related factors needing consideration are the availability of other 'actors' and their likely familiarity with such a social context.

Let us now assume such decisions have been made. The situation to be role played is that of staying for a coffee following a church service – a situation that Mr T. normally avoids, if he can, but would prefer to participate in.

Introducing Mr T. to a diagnostic role play

Warming-up and transitional stages Moves towards setting up a role play should be organic yet also distinctive. Mr T. should make it clear that a role play activity is to be undertaken. However, the transition from talk to induction to action, potentially fraught, should be conversational and comfortable. Asking the client to describe in detail the church parlour where the coffee morning is to take place is a useful first and seemingly indirect step. In the first instance, this should take place via Particularization *before* Presencing, until the client is comfortable with the idea of role playing generally, and has less anxiety about the whole endeavour. Presencing, although necessary to **engage** the participant may be too threatening if introduced too quickly, without more indirect conversational warm up.

The inductor should first determine the physical characteristics of the spatial context and **with** the client begin to 'mark out' the imaginary space,

using either the conditional or the actual (presenced) language form
advisedly but with the definite strategy of progressing from the former to
the latter (under special circumstances this order may be reversed, where a
distancing from experience is being sought). A resistant, anxious or
suspicious client is more comfortable, in the first instance, with conditional
forms of description, for example: 'This would be the counter and over here
the windows, which look out over the green', and so on. Description should
then move to other persons present and inwards to the focus of the
interactional problem, which has been broadly identified with the client
prior to this. Even at this stage, the therapist must decide on the level of
detail that they want to elicit from Mr T., with respect to the width of
diagnosis or observation that they wish to make. Having culled sufficient
information so that the therapist has as clear an idea of the situation as the
client presenting it, the inductor must then move on to Presencing this (via
Particularized, and in this case Personalized, information). This is achieved,
by firmly moving into the assertive, actual form of grammatical expression,
preferably in a shared 'voice': 'We are now going to go into the church
parlour . . . here is the door, let's go through it . . .'. The 'accuracy' of the
information should be rechecked frequently with the client as it proceeds.

The inductor should proceed to mark out affirmatively the actuality of
this territory, in detail, and also similarly to mark out those persons who
are within the 'territory'. Mr T. should be given a very clear picture of the
point of departure of the role play, of when he is expected to take on
the 'action', and at least a rough estimate of the amount of time available
and a clear idea of who will stop the role play – the inductor or the client
himself.

So far we have only dealt with inducting the physical and general characteristics of the situation. There are, of course, other actors to be inducted.
Again, as we are dealing with the diagnosis of problems extracted from the
client's mundane and, in this case, problematic existence, it is important
that the client describes 'the other' in ways that are phenomenologically
valid for him. The latter may well prove insufficient to the task to be
undertaken by the other actor. If for present purposes we assume an adept
'actor', perhaps a therapeutic auxiliary pre-selected as an adept actor, it
may well be that the actor is able to generate action sufficiently creatively
and appropriately to be able to fill the inevitable informational gaps.
However, if this is not the case, the therapist must elicit from the client
sufficient *bridging* information to enable the 'other actor' to have sufficient
grasp of the role to enable him or her to provide a valid enactment for the
client – the validity of which also needs to be checked with the client.

On the whole, however, provided the situation is sufficiently presenced
and personalized that the client feels comfortable with minor departures
from expected behaviour on the part of 'the other', such departures will not
have too great a significance. In addition, provided that other situations are
also sampled for diagnosis, so that a good sampling of client behaviour is
elicited under a range of situations and circumstances, in order that the

client feels – and the therapist observes – that much of the differential repertoire in the area of problem is exhaustively demonstrated.

Role play for behaviour rehearsal for Mr T

Having analysed the diagnostic role play, as both observer and with the client, the therapist must then decide what direction to take – in particular, what aspect of anxiety reduction or social skills training to focus upon first. For example, if the therapist decides that Mr T.'s eye contact is entirely inappropriate, the question is how to proceed.

Within a social skills training, traditionally the therapist will design relatively decontextualized, didactically based, exercises for the client and then proceed to a standard social situation which may or may not be drawn from Mr T.'s own life. Clearly from the perspective taken here, the more ecologically valid the role plays of social situations, the more chance of real learning and generalization. Inevitably the focus must then become individualized since the medium of change is the client in the situation, not the situation or system, although the client may be induced as an agent of change to be a shaper of change by actively changing a problematic situation or system, albeit via behavioural or cognitive change undertaken by the client.

The control of the role play situation now should switch quite clearly between the therapist and the client. For although the therapist is likely to want to shape specific target changes in the individual client, and indeed should reassure the client that 'all is under control', it is only the client in the final analysis who can generate behaviour or alternative cognitions and who is able to be the 'expert' on ecological validity. If the 'teaching' task demands frequent moves in and out of the role play context, then, the therapist must ensure adequate re-engagement and modify re-induction procedures accordingly.

Overview of induction concerns here

Particularization   Much greater rigour is necessary here as compared to the diagnostic role play, particularly where the therapist constructs a situation in relation to a teaching point. Here, in order to facilitate and draw out new learning, the therapist may need actively to modify the role play environment, and give the client and other player sufficient particularized detail, relevant to the theoretical frame and focus, in order for them to be comfortably engaged. However, here as elsewhere the therapist must be sensitive to the personal implications of any stipulated Particularization, and not assume the client – or, indeed, the other actor – will read the information in an identical way to the therapist.

Personalization   This remains important insofar as it is compatible with the therapist's goals. But, above all, the client must own the physical space, and indeed the psychological and social space, to foster engagement, so that the situation has real generalizability for the client.

Presencing This remains an important function, perhaps even more important when the client has to enter a world that is in significant ways constructed by the therapist and not by himself.

Psychotherapeutic approaches and role play

Role play techniques, particularly already as expressed in psychodrama, lend themselves to psychodynamic formulations and interventions, principally because techniques can so easily be adopted that facilitate projective material and also allow both progressive and regressive explorations of individual subjective meaning systems. For example, one can ask participants to 'act out' a dream or a fantasy in order to create a 'concrete' representation of such, which then allows subjective exploration of this material. This evidently necessitates the client's experience being allowed to predominate in the selection of material, and in the focus of analysis and intervention. Even the physical setting up of a role play, with the client simply describing the space, immediately potentiates the role play setting itself as a projective domain in which 'objects' and their juxtaposition are already potentially resonant with meaning. These meanings can be subjected to scrutiny. Alternatively these objects can be viewed as a dynamically salient framework in which, and from which, deeply psychological action can occur.

Clearly the purpose of role play within such a context is much more orientated to 'classic' psychotherapeutic goals, that is, experiential learning, catharsis, regression, transference, insight, working through, and the understanding of individual, family and group dynamics. Using role play, rather than merely 'discursive' methods as in more conventional psychotherapies, clearly heightens certain kinds of experience and potentiates others. There are also certain hazards such as 'acting-out' which necessitate careful control strategies by the inductor (see below) but which, in general, are excluded by careful attention to Particularization. It is not the intention here to provide a full justificatory account, rather to focus upon some particular aspects of role play technique that are of significance for psychodynamically oriented therapies.

Clearly, the concretization of otherwise verbal experience in a role play, adds a dimension of enormous experiential value for psychotherapy clients. Not only is there the potential for increased ecological validity, but the malleability of space and time can enable participants to immerse themselves in the otherwise reality-incongruent characteristics of the intrapsychic world of fantasy and dream.

These advantages in themselves are of some significance, but there are subtler aspects. For example, moving clearly in and out of roles within a role play, by virtue of the therapist's clear framing and boundary establishment, can help to control therapeutic processes such as 'regression in the service of the ego'. The client can learn a sense of mastery and control, moving with help from more primitive to more integrated states of psychic functioning. It can also help to affirm or strengthen ego boundaries (or self and other boundaries) by frequent but clear movement from one role to another (whether an internal or external role).

Ego-defences can be strengthened or maintained as safe havens, by the therapist joining with the defence system and by legitimizing it as part of a role. Or, defences can be gently or indeed robustly challenged from the position of another role, or by introducing challenge within the role, rather than more directly and threateningly from the therapist. For example, if Mark has a paranoid stance towards those who 'may' hurt him, a role and complementary role may be created which legitimizes this psychological stance; or a counter role may be created which challenges this stance; or, the therapist may 'join' with the paranoid role, with the client, so that two 'actors' enact the one same role but introduce an aspect to the role that gently begins to challenge this position, from 'within'. Where, as is often the case, clients are too enmeshed in their own reality, stepping back from the enacted role by observation of another actor enacting the same role or by exchanging roles with another, can help distance a client and open up new perspectives. Using role play allows movement between distance-experience modes, to deep and even primitive, experience-close modes. The level of depth achieved will relate directly to the extent that the therapist uses affective and fantasy laden material versus more 'objective' behavioural or cognitive material.

Group therapists will be especially aware of the transference issues between clients, and the ways in which these might impact upon the choice of role partners; and the extent to which this may need controlling by the therapist. Whereas some of the implications of 'real' relationships between participants, and indeed issues concerning individuals' abilities to identify with 'characters' have been identified (see Chapter 9), these become both more complex and profound when viewed within a psychodynamic framework. For example, if Susan chooses Mike to be her 'abusing father' because there is a transference relationship here which reflects important aspects of the abusing father, certain considerations follow. First, this may help Susan 're-experience' important psychological events that may then be dealt with within a therapeutic context. However, there are clearly dangers – for Mike as well as for Susan, and for the 'real' relationship between them. For Mike, this may evoke a past damaging experience for him, or may 'fix' him, in a relationship to Susan that is dominated by inappropriate psychopathological characteristics.

If a role play is powerful for a target protagonist, it is also powerful for other role play interactants. How will a therapist handle this? What role play structuring becomes important and what therapeutic messages must be given? And indeed, what of the audience – the other non-role-playing clients? Do we make the epistemological mistake of assuming that no active involvement means no involvement? As clinicians well know, it is sometimes the child who watches and is not 'actively' abused but who has no 'legitimate' voice, who becomes most damaged.

It is not the intention to try and convey an entire perspective here, or to pre-empt the wide range of clinical and therapeutic skills that experienced practitioners will already possess. But it the intention to alert users to thinking through these issues in relation to role play use, and to be particularly sensitive to interactions between the distinctive characteristics of role play and known therapeutic phenomena. Evidently, different theoretical persuasions will yield different such phenomena, which again are not capable of treatment within this text. For present purposes, all that must be stated is that therapists must identify their own orientation-driven concerns, their own clinical-empirical experience, and consider these in relation to the common induction issues identified in the earlier chapters.

An example of a clinical case using role play within a broadly psychodynamic framework

Mrs R. is 34 and presents with anxiety and depression since the birth of her second child, her first daughter. Her depression is sufficiently severe that the care of her children has mostly been taken on by her younger sister and her mother. The latter is now estranged from both Mrs R.'s father and stepfather. Although Mrs R. has always been anxious, she has not, on her own report, until now experienced serious depression and she has never consulted for any mental health problem. She has from time to time, since her marriage, presented herself at her GP's surgery with occasional physical disorders, somewhat psychosomatic in presentation. As a child she was rarely seen by her GP.

Mrs R. is initially a very evasive and limited informant, clearly distressed but vague about reasons for her present difficulties. She at first reports an uneventful, happy childhood, and that she was well cared for. After some considerable time, Mrs R. indicates that there is a history of sexual abuse and that since the birth of her daughter this formerly well suppressed material has come to the fore for her. Mrs R. has a good relationship with her husband, although this is deteriorating, due to her increasing suspiciousness and rejection of all men.

We consider primarily the setting up of group therapy, although some elements of a role play might well be taken into an individual therapy context. We have to make some pre-emptive assumptions about Mrs R. for the sake of the exercise here. One of these assumptions is that, generally, Mrs R. is genuinely asking for psychotherapeutic help and is suitable for such.

Is role play indicated?

Caution is the major issue here. Why use role play when much may be achieved through less 'active' techniques? Cases such as these, with high levels of eventful and potentially sensational trauma, need particular caution. There may be a temptation to dramatize therapy events, in the 'degraded' sense of the word. 'Theatricalizing' experience, without very good reason, is dysfunctional as far as the individual is concerned, insofar as it removes the real power of experience away from the centre of the self to a false and performing self. Care is needed in using role play techniques to minimize such a potential danger.

If the client is already in a group setting, where the main medium is role play or psychodrama, then the caution emphasized here must be applied to the question of which events are to be role played. Even in a group using role play as the prime medium, more time should be spent on discussion than role play activity *per se*. Role play is not a therapy technique in itself, it is merely a medium for therapeutic process and activity. Even within the relatively formalized therapeutic activity of psychodrama, customarily the actual 'acting out' only takes up part of the therapy time. Much attention is given to ordinary therapeutic talk and interaction, particularly in 'de-roling' and sharing.

Role play is easily understood to be a highly stimulating medium, which may 'loosen up' feelings, thoughts and actions through the 'projective' use of roles, but it must also be constructed so as to have **containment** powers with respect to therapy. This means particular attention must be paid to clear boundary maintenance, both for individual roles and situations, to the extent that the boundaries may be quite artificial in terms of mundane reality, but offer relative safety in their definitiveness.

Clearly, role play is more safely used in less emotionally charged situations such as social skills training, and is also potentially less powerful here. Precisely because of its power to engage and stimulate affect and fantasy, to make events vivid and experience-near, much more caution is needed in relation to role play within a psychotherapeutic context than a behavioural or cognitive therapy one.

Possible valid clinical reasons for using role play here, as a psychotherapeutic medium of choice

First, Mrs R. is completely unable to communicate with her husband or family about her difficulties, but desperately wants to be able to do so. Talking about these difficulties seems experience-remote and difficult for her adequately to describe verbally.

Role play can be used to allow her to practise communicating with her family, in situations that are deliberately constructed so as to produce those affect states and psychological relationship conditions in which she anticipates she would have to do the communicating. These provide, on the one hand, 'objective' and 'subjective'

*assessment of these attempts. Role play also allows a potential deepening under-
standing, in playing or observing their roles, of her husband and family members, so
as to de-centre from her overwhelmingly if understandable position.*

Second, Mrs R. is plagued by nightmares and hallucinatory-type experiences focusing on the abusing father. Talking about them in any detail is
experienced as traumatic, but she feels a pressing need to do so.

*Mrs R. needs to be able to control her fantasy world by creating, with her therapist,
a transitional externalized world of bad objects that she can move in and out of at
will with her therapist's help. The degree of contact with a fantasy figure can be
systematically increased until the figure can be confronted as a reality based person,
or externalization of an internal bad object. Developing the fantasy other into a full
person via personalization may, hopefully, also allow a less split and polarized
experience of the problematic persons or internalized objects.*

Third, although Mrs R. is able to talk about the traumatic experiences, and
despite a considerable length of therapy contact, she is quite unable to risk
any direct experience of these traumatic events and persons, but feels and
believes that she must do this to move on.

*As in the points above, role play can allow Mrs R., by gradual degrees, to
approximate the trauma she experienced, provided that a very careful attunement is
made in relation to her mental state and therapeutic tolerance. This must never,
however, be undertaken unless the client wants to therapeutically re-experience this
event, and unless the clinician is confident that it is appropriate and containable.*

Fourth, Mrs R. is quite unable to see the abusing father as anything but a
monster over whom she has no control and who, despite being dead, is free
to attack her at any time he chooses. This particular fear has generalized
out to a fear of an uncontrollable world, one in which she and her new
daughter are particularly at risk.

*Therapeutically challenging the above fear may be facilitated by encouraging her to
view this same world through another's perception, by taking on the role of a person
who she knows feels much safer than she does, or upon whom she can depend.
Using the movement in and out of roles, can help to control the process of
transmuting internalizations (see, Kohut, 1971 and 1977) to help construct stronger
self-cohesiveness and firmness in the face of perceived danger to the self, whether
internal or external.*

Looking generally, interactionally and actively at the world that she sees
and experiences through roles may help her to discriminate the symbolic
power of objects-for-her from their more likely meaning status. This may
be particularly important with respect to her daughter, and it may be useful
for her daughter to be role played, to try and help her differentiate the
psychological state and needs of her daughter from her own state, and to
disentangle the over-identification with the daughter with respect to victim
status. (This would be likely to involve a subjective playing of the daughter
as contrasted with an 'objective' playing.) Also helpful is the mere active
breaking up of the overwhelming world of enmeshed objects into smaller,
less enmeshed objects, so that measured amounts of trauma can be taken
on, and making the desensitization process more manageable.

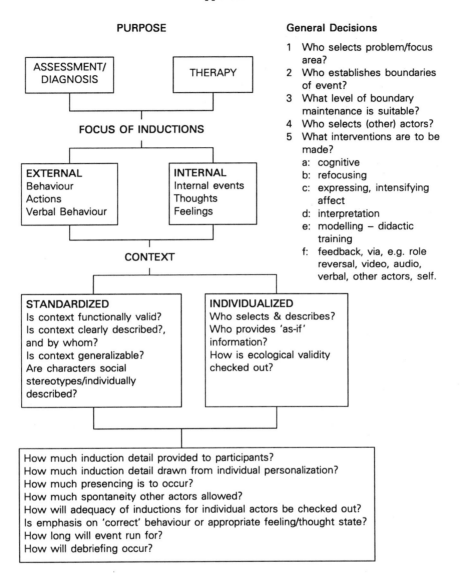

PURPOSE

General Decisions

1 Who selects problem/focus area?
2 Who establishes boundaries of event?
3 What level of boundary maintenance is suitable?
4 Who selects (other) actors?
5 What interventions are to be made?
  a: cognitive
  b: refocusing
  c: expressing, intensifying affect
  d: interpretation
  e: modelling – didactic training
  f: feedback, via, e.g. role reversal, video, audio, verbal, other actors, self.

ASSESSMENT/ DIAGNOSIS   THERAPY

FOCUS OF INDUCTIONS

EXTERNAL
Behaviour
Actions
Verbal Behaviour

INTERNAL
Internal events
Thoughts
Feelings

CONTEXT

STANDARDIZED
Is context functionally valid?
Is context clearly described?, and by whom?
Is context generalizable?
Are characters social stereotypes/individually described?

INDIVIDUALIZED
Who selects & describes?
Who provides 'as-if' information?
How is ecological validity checked out?

How much induction detail provided to participants?
How much induction detail drawn from individual personalization?
How much presencing is to occur?
How much spontaneity other actors allowed?
How will adequacy of inductions for individual actors be checked out?
Is emphasis on 'correct' behaviour or appropriate feeling/thought state?
How long will event run for?
How will debriefing occur?

Figure A.1   *An example of a decision-making strategy for setting up a role play*

Note, no therapeutic goal of catharsis has been mentioned here. Catharsis for its own sake is therapeutically indulgent and dangerous. It is only if such heightened re-experience is highly likely to promote a different outcome; for example, in being able to share pain positively with a trusted caretaking 'other' – the therapist – that it can be a legitimate goal. There are rarely justifications for cathartic reliving of an event, certainly not precipitously and dramatically, without an enormous amount of preparatory work, within a context of extreme safety. Using role play for catharsis as a major goal is usually irresponsible.

Whatever the eventual goals, the first decision is not here *where* to start a role play, but *whether* to start with this particular client. Indeed, even prior to this there are other group dynamic issues to consider. Someone has to decide on who will get the major therapeutic attention of the group that day. Unlike conventional group psychotherapy – where this decision is likely to be the product of the group dynamic, with some guidance from the therapist – role play or psychodrama demands a more active decision on the part of the therapist, who, by virtue of using a highly interventionist technique, is much more active in the therapy and, thus, must take more responsibility for the choice of 'protagonist' and focus. There are many relevant issues here for the whole group. There is a potential threat to a group, as well as to an individual, at any particular stage in its development, if interactional role play occurs that is too demanding for the group in relation to its current strength and cohesiveness.

Appendix 3: Empirical research on the principal induction technique

General introduction

Despite the massive use of role play and the voluminous literature discussing role play, as has been already discussed, there has been almost no attempt, *empirically, systematically and directly*, to investigate technique. Moreover, where this has occurred (see also Chapter 5) the manipulations are highly limited. (See Galassi and Galassi (1976) who varied the stimulus presentation (taped prompt or live prompt) and the demand response format (single versus multiple response); Ammerman and Hersen (1986) who manipulated the expectations of subjects in relation to confederate behaviour; and Eisler, Hersen, Miller and Blanchard (1975) who manipulated role plays with respect to the confederate's gender and familiarity.)

Other technical manipulations have arisen more indirectly from the numerous validity studies (see, for example, Gorecki et al., 1981; Higgins, Frisch and Smith, 1983; Chapter 4, this text.) Here, researchers are principally concerned with technical aspects of role play only in so far as these throw light on validity in terms of experimental-criterion studies. There has been almost no concern with subjects' experience of role play; ecological validity is not considered. Nevertheless, there has been a growing – albeit still limited – concern with reproducing subjects' typical behaviour (see de Armas and Brigham, 1986; Bellack et al., 1990b; McNamara and Blumer, 1982; McReynolds et al., 1981). Moreover, even where technical manipulations are related to 'typical' subject behaviour they remain unrelated to any explicit conceptual framework which recognizes role play as a truly distinct technique or set of procedures. Hence, as has already been argued throughout this book, no technical developments of any magnitude or range are achieved or facilitated.

Here, the results of three separate but interrelated experimental pieces of research are briefly reported (full report available: Yardley, 1984b and 1987), which directly test out the three principal induction techniques of Personalization, Particularization and Presencing. Furthermore, a series of qualitative workshops is briefly summarized, although much of the significant material has already been integrated into Chapter 9. In the experimental studies, the three key induction techniques of Personalization Particularization and Presencing were systematically and directly manipulated to examine the impact upon, primarily, participants' experience of reality and 'involvement/engagement', but also the impact upon observers and the content of role plays. The results of these empirical studies, which are summarized below, clearly demonstrated the increasing efficaciousness of these three induction processes in relation to their increased utilization, both in relation to quantitative and qualitative measures. Also important, the facilitation of participants' detailed feedback of their experiences of induction procedures provided qualitative evidence which required the further refinement of induction concepts, and stimulated the consideration of additional induction features. This qualitative material is also integrated in Chapter 9.

The experiments

In a set of three separate experiments, which involved differential manipulation of the three different induction techniques of Personalization, Particularization and Presencing, the following emerged as statistically significant (Yardley, 1984b). Overall, it was found to be the case that, for participants, enhancing the specific induction processes of Personalization, Particularization and Presencing led to an increase in actor involvement and in the experience of the role play as real; although, as discussed in Chapter 9 ('Control as a structural issue', p. 126) and further on in this appendix, this is differentially a stronger or weaker effect in relation to precise structural aspects of the role plays. Hence, in two (of the three) role experiments undertaken, in which a dyad role played either a father–adolescent interaction or an inmate–prison officer interaction, there was a very strong and significant effect upon one actor in each dyad, in line with predictions about actor involvement and experience of reality. The effect on the other actor was less strong but, nevertheless, an overall clear trend in precisely the same direction of change was described. Detailed qualitative data also strongly testified to the strength of the induction procedures.

The positional difference between actors, reported above, appeared to relate entirely and interestingly to normative power and control issues, in turn related to knowledge-status, and structure and control issues as above. The effect of the increase of the three induction processes was unambiguously powerful in all three experiments. The first experiment was somewhat distinct from the second and third in that it involved only single non-interacting actors (elsewhere misleadingly termed 'passive' role plays, see Chapter 3) and, hence, there were no interactive effects arising from differential knowledge, and control positions, between actors – see discussion under 'Control', Chapter 9 and below.

The first experiment involved 33 individual participants being required to situate themselves, on three different occasions, in an imaginary context, following three different induction conditions of differing degrees of Personalization, Particularization and Presencing (in an act of what is termed 'passive' imagination elsewhere in the literature which has an identical structure to 'guided fantasy'). Subjects were then required to respond verbally, at some length, to highly specific and probing open-ended prompt questions, while within the role play, and subsequently on completion of the role play, 'from outside'. The results of this experiment indicated a powerful positive linear relationship between increasing the three induction processes of Particularization, Personalization and Presencing, and the level of experienced reality, involvement and engagement in a role play. So subjects in a fully inducted 'passive' role play found they were most highly involved and engaged (statistically significant at a high level) in the most highly inducted condition and were also in complementary manner least aware of the experimenter/role play inductor in this condition.

The second experiment involved role plays based on a situation believed to be common to most adolescents – that of an adolescent returning home considerably later than expected, on a weekday night, with the father awaiting the son's arrival. One of two actors, in each of 14 experimental dyads, took on the role of the son and the other took on the role of the father. *In the minimal induction condition* both actors were given a very simple four-line description of the scenario; *in the enhanced condition*, the 'actor-son' was asked to provide particularized and personalized information, on which to base the 'father' role and in which to embed the scenario. (Although the fullest induction condition here demanded only a modest degree of personal exposure, and by no means represented an entirely ideal and full induction, from a technical perspective.) The latter enhanced induction proved sufficiently powerful to significantly increase the experience of involvement, reality and engagement, as compared with the minimal induction levels of Personalization, Particularization and Presencing, although interestingly only for the actor-son: actor-fathers did not discriminate between conditions. This experiment had also involved increasing the level of Particularization, Personalization and Presencing *differentially between actors*, allowing further comparisons to be made between induction conditions; so that for one actor – the actor-father – an induction was fully particularized and presenced, but not personalized, whereas for the other actor of the pair – the actor-son – the induction was fully particularized, presenced **and** personalized. Again, there is no doubt about the differential significant positive effect of the fuller induction for the actor of the pair who received the personalized induction as compared to the 'other', who only received a particularized and presenced induction. The seeming indiscrimination of actor-fathers between conditions appeared to be explained by the repeated assertions of actor-fathers that they had insufficient information in both conditions (see below, 'Structural compatability').

The third and final experiment involved actors in dyads who took part in a 'prisoner–prison officer' scenario, unfamiliar to both actors of each pair, role playing two separate induction conditions: one of which involved minimal Particularization and Presencing, and the other a much higher level of Particularization and Presencing. Again, for one actor – the 'officer' – increasing the induction processes of Particularization, Personalization and Presencing produced a linear positive effect upon experienced involvement and reality, whereas the effect was much less marked for the 'inmate' actor. Scrutiny of the qualitative accounts and careful analysis of the structural conditions of the role play situation explain these results (see below, Control), which again seem to relate to the question of who needs to be in control in the 'situation'. With the exception of the theme of 'control', and 'observer/actor differences', the qualitative participant accounts from these experiments are integrated into Chapter 9.

Contents of the scripts generated

Following on from the above, but this time viewed entirely from external 'observational' perspectives, it is useful to consider in more detail the actual contents of these role played episodes. On the basis of detailed analysis of all the scripts generated in all the experimental conditions, and in relation to all the scripts generated in the workshops (all of which were also transcribed), there are found to be distinct differences in the styles of the interaction between actors entirely dependent upon the level of inductions. Without any exception, minimal induction role plays generate exclusively stereotyped and 'demand characterized' themes, which involve high levels of confrontation, high degrees of polarization, highly stereotyped and limited conversations, extreme comic acting and a dominance of one role over another with respect to conversational initiative-taking.

There are, furthermore, and without any doubt or evidence of contradiction, consistent and striking differences with respect to the distinctiveness and heterogeneity of the various role plays in the enhanced induction situations, over and above the minimal induction situations, providing a rich diversity of interactions as compared with the less strongly inducted interactions, which consistently produce shallowness and stereotypicality. Participants tended to play for laughs either when furnished with little information, or when not positively facilitated into 'producing' detailed or personalized role plays. This strong movement towards exteriorizing their own role plays towards an 'observer' perspective is mirrored in actor–observer differences discussed below.

Structural compatability between mundane reality and role plays

Arising from the qualitative accounts are themes which clearly implicate the necessity of some structural explanation (see also Chapter 9). Clearly structural differences differentially affected roles over and above the induction requirements of Particularization, Personalization and Presencing. Based on this piece of research alone, the extent and power of structure upon role plays appears to be considerable. For example, in the adolescent–father role plays referred to above, across both minimal and enhanced inductions, 'fathers' uniformly complained of lack of information, however, 'sons' seldom complained in either condition – although clearly in the 'minimal' induction situation 'sons' were as bereft of information as the 'fathers'. Equally, in the 'inmate–officer' role play, 'officers' in the 'power' position complained of lack of information across conditions, whereas 'inmates' did not.

What seems to happen here and elsewhere is that, where either the 'power' of the situation or the 'need for response' lies, then it is the individual in that place who 'needs' the information and who has the 'responsibility' of acting upon it. Hence, 'sons', in the minimal induction role play (who all sought to minimize the effects of an encounter universally interpreted as being with a potentially angry father, and who indeed sought to 'escape' the situation), took on a relatively passive role which called upon little in the way of resources. In contradistinction, the 'fathers' (interestingly, the almost exclusive focus of external observers' concern), needed information with which to be active and 'in control'.

For, if the father–son role play situation is normatively most clearly defined, as one in which the 'father' may be expected to take the initiative – because the 'father' stayed up to signify his alarm at the 'son's' late homecoming – then the control of the situation and the initiative must be seen as his. The 'son' may merely respond to the 'father's' initiative. Moreover, the 'son' is free to 'create' any story that he likes about his lateness, within the bounds of the constructed skeleton plot, indeed 'creative' justificatory accounts are almost a 'demand' of the normative situation.

Lack of information itself is not such a problem, therefore, for an individual in a 'role' that is essentially that of 'respondent' rather than 'initiator'. But, for an actor whose 'role' demands that he or she take the initiative, lack of information is highly disruptive, and is experienced as such by the actor. Where the 'respondent' actor is furnished with detailed information or has elicited detailed personalized information and the 'other' actor is deprived of information, this paradoxical state of affairs is even more incongrous and inappropriate structurally.

The above illustrates *the complexity of the relationship between action, knowledge and control,* (see also Chapters 5,6,8 and 9) which impact upon, and indeed derive from, both the structural realities of the role play and the structural features of the 'as-if' framing. Moreover, in an 'as-if' situation there are extra problems of knowing which state of knowledge belongs to which frame, that is the 'as-if' frame itself or the induction frame external to the 'as-if' frame. (This potential ambiguity is also alluded to by Ginsberg, 1979.)

Control as a structural issue

One person role plays

Of all the role play experiments here described, based on considerable experience and use of role play technique, the most powerful effect of the three induction processes of Particularization, Personalization and Presencing arises in relation to single participants. Such individuals are involved in an individual imaginative task, not required to interact with another person in a role play, although they are required to make externally available responses. In such a setting, the effects of Personalization appear to be untrammelled by the limitations imposed, for instance, by another actor's acting abilities. The latter may diminish the credibility of an imaginative situation. Most importantly, the problematic issue of who controls the information becomes irrelevant, except in relation to information stipulated by an experimenter or role play facilitator, because the control of the imaginative internal act lies above all with the 'subject'. Such a focus upon individuals is more typical of psychodrama than other role play techniques where the particular intention will be to provide a projective exposition for the 'protagonist'.

Two or more person role plays

In two or more person interactions, the control issues become more problematic. It would seem that in situations where the 'character' would mundanely control the situation relative to another, then the actor playing that character **ought** to have greater control of the induction information for there to be *structural consistency*. However, the question of who mundanely controls an interaction, and/or information pertinent to that interaction, is an extremely complex one. Moreover, uncertainty is always a part of interactions, with the exception of highly formalized and ritualized interactions. It is rare, for one actor to have an entirely predictable dominant control of information.

The above is clearly confusing for induction purposes. *Actors will not always, if ever, be able to decide whether inadequacies, of experienced information and control, belong to the induction procedures or to the situation or character being 'simulated'.* Personalizing the situation for one actor, but not another, introduces a particularly one-sided form of control, atypical of most of the mundane interactions which role play users need to examine.

In, for example, the father–son experiment, it was possible to make some direct comparison between the processes of Personalization and Particularization. Whereas actor-sons, who had a personalized induction, were clearly and overwhelmingly more 'involved' in the enhanced condition than in either of the other conditions, the actor-fathers did not distinguish as clearly between the minimal (low Particularization, low Presencing) versus the enhanced induction (high Particularization, high Presencing). Here again the factor of 'control' emerges. Severe limitations were placed on ecological validity by the actor-fathers' lack of informational control *vis-à-vis* the actor-sons. The latter owned, and controlled, the relevant information necessary for the enactment. Mundanely, the fathers would be expected to have control. This lack of control seems to have seriously impeded actor-fathers' sense of spontaneity and efficacy, and led to a certain disinterest in their role.

In the inmate–officer experimental role plays, neither actor had personalized information, so that for induction purposes, the actors were in an equivalent position in terms of control of information. Here again, the same control principles emerge, in that the actor-officers, who had a more particularized and presenced induction, experienced the 'as-if' situation as more real and were more involved. However, this was not true for the actor-inmates. This is consistent with the father–son experiment, where situational and induction control factors appear to have interacted. Again, in the prison situation, one would mundanely expect the officers to be in control. The induction did not favour either set of actors in terms of control, and although this did not therefore strengthen the structural position of the actor-officers, neither did it undermine their position (unlike the actor-fathers). The relative lack of interest of the actor-inmates seems consistent with the passivity and powerlessness of their situation. Neither group received personalized inductions, and this may have had even greater negative impact on the 'inmates', given that the 'as-if' problem with which they were presented involved a situation that was supposed to be highly personal and salient for the 'inmate'. The qualitative accounts provided did in fact highlight *the lack of sufficient information*. Of related interest is the extent to which both participants and external judges were much more interested.

Of course, much of the control of the role play lies with the inductor, particularly where, in addition to setting up the induction parameters, further induction material is introduced during the course of the role play.

Accounting interest in different induction conditions and actor–observer differences

Accounts were not only gathered directly from the participants; those judges who were asked to rate the role plays for realism and involvement were also asked to provide qualitative accounts of their observations of the role plays. Comparisons between actor and observer accounts are informative.

Of some significance is the seeming difference in interest of judges in attending to the differentially inducted role plays. Far fewer accounts were produced by actors with respect to the 'minimal' condition role plays, as compared to the more fully inducted role plays. Yet, **external** judges appeared to be more interested in both sets of role play experiments in the minimal condition, and, moreover, were certainly more interested in the conventionally more powerful 'fathers' and 'prison officers' rather than 'sons' and 'inmates'.

In addition, and of relevance to the actor–observer debate, almost all of the qualitative themes related not to performance aspects of the role play, as requested – that is, to whether or not the 'actor' achieved a good understanding and/or portrayal of their 'character' – but to normative and prescriptive evaluations of the actions engaged in by the actors, for example 'fathers' as 'out-of-touch', 'authoritarian', 'responsible', 'interested', 'too lenient', 'too unemotional', etc.; 'officers' as 'too caring', 'too emotional', etc.

Even more interesting was that judges appeared to demand polarized behaviours as criteria of 'reality', so that external judges seemed more likely to see the 'fathers' as too unconcerned and lacking authority, and the 'officers' as 'too caring' and as 'too lenient', in the enhanced condition; whereas they were more likely to see the 'fathers' and 'officers' as unreasonable and authoritarian in the minimal condition – *and yet more realistic*. Exactly the same patterns occurred with respect to 'sons' and 'inmates' – the more reasonable their behaviour, the less were they viewed as realistic, which is in contrast to the views of the participants.

The above accentuates the potential distortions arising from an emphasis upon 'the external observer' when constructing and inducting a role play procedure. Such an emphasis is certain, given all the evidence of the above, to create stereotyped and mundanely unrealistic simulations that disregard the central part of the 'social actor/agent'.

Qualitative workshops

These involved a systematic programme of three-hour weekly workshops over a period of six months. They also involved a core group of 12 participants, with some variation in numbers over time. The workshops were designed to progress through various levels of induction provision and styles, working co-operatively with participants to gather highly detailed feedback on their reactions to differing induction procedures. These participant observations were systematically transcribed and analysed, as well as the full transcripts from all the proceedings. All the major themes so gathered, together with the observations and analyses made by the author are integrated into Chapter 9 and illustrated by vignettes drawn from those workshops.

References

Abe, K., Akagi, M., Nishikawa, K. and Yoshoika, S. (1988) 'The modified Kimmel-Azrin method of nocturnal enuresis in childhood', *Japanese Journal of Behavior Therapy*, 13 (2): 1–8.

Abrams, D. B., Binkhoff, J., Zwick, W. and Liepman, M. (1991) 'Alcohol abusers' and social drinkers' responses to alcohol-relevant and general situations', *Journal of Studies on Alcohol*, 52 (5): 409–14.

Adams-Webber, J. and Rodney, Y. (1983) 'Relational aspects of temporary changes in construing self and others', *Canadian Journal of Behavioural Science*, 15 (1): 52–9.

Alexander, C. N. and Scriven, G. D. (1977) 'Role playing – an essential component of experimentation', *Personality and Social Psychology Bulletin*, 3: 455–66.

Alverson, H. and Rosenberg, S. (1990) 'Discourse analysis of schizophrenic speech: A critique and proposal', *Applied Psycholinguistics*, 11 (2): 167–84.

Ammerman, R. and Hersen, M. (1986) 'Effects of scene manipulation on role-play test behaviour', *Journal of Psychology and Behavioural Assessment*, 8 (1): 55–67.

Armstrong, J. (1982) 'Strategies for implementing change: An experimental approach, *Group Organisation Studies*, 7 (4): 457–75.

Aronson, J. and Carlsmith, E. (1968) 'Experimentation in social psychology', in G. Lindzey and J. Aronson (eds), *Handbook of Social Psychology*, Vol. 4, Reading, MA: Addison Wesley.

Atkinson, J. and Heritage, J. (1984) *Structures of Social Action: Studies in Conversational Analysis*, Cambridge: Cambridge University Press.

Axline, V. (1971) *Dibs in Search of Self*, Harmondsworth: Pelican.

Badenoch, A., Fisher, J., Hafner, R. and Swift, H. (1984) 'Predicting the outcome of spouse-aided therapy for persisting psychiatric disorders', *American Journal of Family Therapy*, 12 (1): 59–71.

Bagarozzi, D. A. and Anderson, S. (1982) 'The evolution of family mythological systems; considerations for meaning, clinical assessments and treatment', *Journal of Psychoanalytic Anthropology*, 5 (1): 71–90.

Bakan, D. (1967) *On Methodology*, San Francisco, CA: Jossey Bass.

Baluk, U. and O'Neill, P. (1980) 'Health professionals perceptions of the psychological consequences of abortion', *American Journal of Community Psychology*, 8 (1): 67–75.

Baron, R. M. (1977) 'Role playing and experimental research', *Personality and Social Psychology Bulletin*, 3: 505–13.

Bellack, A. S., Hersen, M. and Lamparski, D. (1979a) 'Role play tests for assessing social skills: Are they valid? Are they Useful?' *Journal of Consulting and Clinical Psychology*, 47 (2): 335–42.

Bellack, A. S., Hersen, M. and Turner, S. (1979b) 'Relationship of role play and knowledge of appropriate behaviour for assertion in the natural environment', *Journal of Consulting and Clinical Psychology*, 47 (4): 670–8.

Bellack, A., Turner, S., Hersen, M. and Luber, F. (1984) 'An examination of social skills training for chronic schizophrenic patients', *Hospital and Community Psychiatry*, 35 (10): 1023–8.

Bellack A. S., Morrison, R. L., Mueser, K. T. and Wade, J. (1989) 'Social competance in schizoaffective disorder, bipolar disorder, and negative and non negative schyiphrenia', *Schizophrenia Research*, 2 (4–5): 391–401.

Bellack, A. S., Morrison, R. L., Wixted, J. T. and Mueser, K. T. (1990a) 'An analysis of social competence in schizophrenia, *British Journal of Psychiatry*, 156: 809–18.

Bellack, A., Morrison, R., Mueser, K. and Wade, J. (1990b) 'Role play for assessing the social competence of psychiatric patients', *Psychological Assessment*, 2 (3): 248–55.

Bem, D. J. (1967) 'Self-perception: An alternative interpretation of cognitive dissonance phenomena', *Psychological Review*, 74 (3): 183–200.

Bem, D. J. (1968) 'The epistemological status of interpersonal simulations', *Journal of Experimental Social Psychology*, 4: 270–4.

Benne, K. P. and Sheats, P. (1948) 'Functional roles of group members', *Journal of Social Issues*, 4: 41–50.

Benson, D., McMahon, C. and Sinnreich, R. (1972) 'The art of scenario design', *Simulation and Games*, 3 (4): 439–63.

Bergmann, J. (1990) 'On the local sensitivity of conversation', I. Markova and K. Foppa (eds), *The Dynamics of Dialogue*, Harvester: Hemel Hempstead.

Berne, E. (1961) *Transactional Analysis In Psychotherapy*, New York, NY: Grove Press.

Berne, E. (1968) *Games People Play*, Harmondsworth: Penguin.

Biddle, B. J. and Thomas, E. J. (1966) *Role Theory*, London: Wiley.

Bilaniuk, M. (1988) 'Using sociometry and role play to prepare housewives to re-enter the work force'. *Journal of Group Psychotherapy, Psychodrama and Sociometry*, 1 (2): 82–3.

Blanchet, A., Cocci, P., Doukhi, F. and Nathan, T. (1991) 'Interactions therapeutic-patient dans une therapie ethno-psychoanalytic', *Psychologie Francaise*, 36 (4): 323–30.

Blumberg, E. J., Chadwick, M. W., Fogarty, L. and Speth, T. W. (1991) 'The touch discrimination component of sexual abuse prevention training with unanticipated negative consequences', *Journal of Interpersonal Violence*, 6 (1): 12–28.

Blumberg, S. and Hokanson, J. (1983) 'The effects of another person's response style on interpersonal behaviour in depression', *Journal of Abnormal Psychology*, 92 (2): 196–209.

Bordewick, M. and Bornstein, P. (1980) 'Examination of multiple cognitive response dimensions among differentially assertive individuals', *Behaviour Therapy*, 11: 440–8.

Borgatta, E. P. (1955) 'The analysis of social interaction: actual, role playing and projective', *Journal of Abnormal and Social Psychology*, 51: 394–403.

Borgatta, E. P. and Bales, R. F. (1951) 'Task and accumulation of experience as factors in the interaction of small groups', *Sociometry*, 16: 329–52.

Bouchard, M. A. and Guerette, L. (1991) 'Psychotherapy as a hermeneutical experience', *Psychotherapy*, 28 (3): 385–94.

Bourque, P. and Ladouceur, R. (1979) 'Self-report and behavioural measures in the assessment of assertive behaviour', *Behaviour Therapy and Experimental Psychiatry*, 10: 287–92.

Bowers, K. S. (1973) 'Situationism in psychology: an analysis and a critique', *Psychological Review*, 80 (5): 307–36.

Bowles, G. and Duelli Klein, R. (1983) *The Theories of Women's Studies*, London: Routledge and Kegan Paul.

Brecht, B. (1964) *Brecht on Theatre*, London: Methuen.

British Psychological Society (1995) *Proceedings of Social Psychology Section Annual Conference* (20–22 Sept 1994), 3 (1)

Brodbeck, H. (1995) 'The psychoanalyst as participant and observer in the psychoanalytic process'. *Psychoanalysis and Contemporary Thought*, 18 (4): 531–58.

Bromley, D. B. (1986) *The Case-Study Method in Psychology and Retailed Disciplines*, Chicester: Wiley.

Bromley, D. B. (1991) 'Academic contributions to psychological counselling: 2 Discourse Analyses and the formulation of case-reports, *Counselling Psychology Quarterly*, 4 (1): 75–89.

Bronfenbrenner, P. (1977) 'Towards an experimental ecology of human development', *American Psychologist*, July: 513–31.

Brook, P. (1972) *The Empty Space*, Harmondsworth: Pelican.

Brown, S. (1968) 'Scenarios in systems analysis', in E. S. Quado and W. I. Boucher (eds), *Systems Analysis and Policy Planning: Applications in Defence*, New York: Elsevier.

Butler, S. F. and Strupp, H. H. (1986) 'Specific and non specific factors in psychotherapy: a problematic paradigm for psychotherapy research', *Psychotherapy*, 23: 30–40.

Burke, K. (1969) *A Grammar of Motives*, Berkeley, CA: University of California Press.

Cantril, H. (ed.) (1960) *The Morning Notes of Adelbert Ames Jr*, New Jersey: Rutgers U.P.

Chalmers, J. B. and Townsend, M. A. (1990) 'The effects of training on socially maladjusted girls', *Child Development*, 61 (1): 178–90.

Chiauzzi, E. J., Heimberg, R. G., Becker, E. and Gansler, D. (1985) 'Personalized versus standard role plays in the assessment of depressed patients' social skill', *Journal of Psychopathology and Behavioural Assessment*, 7 (2): 121–33.

Cooper, J. (1976) 'Deception and role playing: On telling the good guys from the bad guys', *American Psychologist*, 31 (8): 605–10.

Corder, B. F., Hairzlip, T. and De Boerp (1990) 'A pilot study of a structured, time-limited therapy group for sexually abused pre-adolescent children', *Child Abuse and Neglect*, 14 (2): 243–51.

Corsini, R. J. (1966) *Role Playing in Psychotherapy: A Manual*, Chicago, IL: Aldine.

Courtney, R. (1972) *Play, Drama and Thought*, London: Cassell.

Coutu, W. (1951) 'Role playing vs role taking: An appeal for clarification', *American Sociological Review*, 16: 180–7.

Cross, D. G. and Gaffney, L. R. (1984) ' "Bad therapy" as a training technique, an empirical analysis', *Australian Journal of Family Therapy*, 5 (1): 45–51.

Cunningham, C. (1985) 'Training and education, approaches for parents of children with special needs', Special Issue, *British Journal of Medical Psychology*, 58 (3): 285–305.

Dahrendorf, R. (1968) *Essays in the Theory of Society*, London: Routledge and Kegan Paul.

Darroch, R. K. and Steiner, I. D. (1970) 'Role playing: an alternative to laboratory research', *Journal of Personal and Social Psychology*, 14 (1): 302–11.

de Armas, A. and Brigham, T. (1986) 'Moderated role play validity: Do some subjects role play more naturally than others', *Behavioral Assessment* 8 (4): 341–47.

de Leon, P. (1975) 'Scenario design: an overview', *Simulation and Games*, 6: 39–60.

De Waele, J. P. and Harré, R. (1979) 'Autobiography as a psychological method', in G. P. Ginsberg (ed.), *Emerging Strategies*, New York: Wiley.

De Weerd, H. (1974) 'A contextual approach to scenario construction', *Simulation and Games*, 5 (4): 403–14.

Demarest, D. S., Hooke, S. J. F. and Erickson M. T. (1984) 'Preoperative intervention for the reduction of anxiety in paediatric surgery patients', *Children's Health Care*, 12 (4): 179–83.

Denzin, N. K. (1989) *Interpretative Biography*, Newbury Park, CA: Sage.

Denzin, N. K. (1987a) *The Alcoholic Self*, Newbury Park, CA: Sage.

Denzin, N. K. (1987b) 'A phenomenology of the emotionally divided self', in K. Yardley and T. Honess (eds), *Self and Identity: Psychological Perspectives*, Chichester: Wiley.

Denzin, N. K. and Lincoln, Y. S. (1994) *Handbook of Qualitative Research*, Thousand Oaks, CA: Sage.

Dewey, J. (1969) 'The theatrical analogy reconsidered', *The American Sociologist*, 4: 309.

Duelli Klein, R. (1983) 'How to do what we want to do: Thoughts about feminist methodology', in G. Bowles and R. Duelli Klein (eds), *Theories of Women's Studies*, London: Routledge and Kegan Paul.

Eders, F. and Smit, G. (1992) 'Effectiveness of a skills training programme for residential child care workers', *Children and Youth Services Review*, 14 (6): 541–52.

Edwards, D. and Potter, J. (1992) *Discursive Psychology*, London: Sage.

Ehrlich, J. and Sipes, A. L. (1985) 'Group treatment of communication skills for head trauma patients', *Cognitive Rehabilitation*, 3 (1): 32–7.

Eisler, R., Hersen, M., Miller, P. and Blanchard, E. B. (1975) 'Situational determinants of assertive behaviour', *Journal of Consulting and Clinical Psychology*, 43 (3): 330–40.

Elliott, R. (1983a) 'Fitting process research to the practising psychotherapist', *Psychotherapy Theory Research and Practice*, 20 (1): 47–55.

Elliott, R. (1983b) ' "That in your hands": A comprehensive process analysis of a significant event in psychotherapy', *Psychiatry*, 46: 113–29.

Elliott, R. (1984) 'Comprehensive process analysis (CPA): describing change pathways in significant therapy events', Unpub paper University of Toledo, USA.

Erins, C. (1992) 'Toward integrating feminist psychotherapy and feminist philosophy', *Professional Psychology, Research and Practice*, 23 (6): 453–66.

Essig, T. S. and Russell, R. L. (1990) 'Analyzing subjectivity in therapeutic discourse: Rogers, Perls, Ellis and Goria revisited', *Psychotherapy*, 27 (2): 271–81.

Fajardo, B. (1993) 'Conditions for the relevance of infant research to clinical psychoanalysis', *International Journal of Psychoanalysis*, 74 (5): 975–91.

Feyeraband, P. (1975) *Against Method: An Outline of an Anarchistic Theory of Knowledge*, London: Verso.

Fielder, D. and Beach, L. R. (1978) 'On the decision to be assertive', *Journal of Consulting and Clinical Psychology*, 46 (3): 537–46.

Fiske, D. W. (1978) *Strategies for Personality Research*, San Francisco, CA: Jossey Bass.

Flavell, J. (1968) *The Development of Role Taking and Communication Skills in Children*, New York: Wiley.

Forward, J. Canter, R. and Kirsch, N. (1976) 'Role Enactment and deception methodologies', *American Psychologist*, 31: 594–604.

Foxx, R. M. and Faw, G. D. (1992) 'An eight year old follow up of three social skills training studies', *Mental Retardation*, 30 (1): 63–6.

Freedman, J. L. (1969) 'Role playing, psychology by consensus', *Journal of Personality and Social Psychology*, 13 (2): 107–14.

Frederickson, N. and Simms, J. (1990) 'Teaching social skills to children: Towards an integrated approach', *Educational and Child Psychology*, 7 (1): 5–17.

Fulmer, R. H. (1983) 'Teaching the family life cycle: a guide for a workshop using simulated games', *American Journal of Family Therapy*, 11 (4): 55–63.

Gabriel, J. (1982) 'Using role play as a training and supervisory role', *Child Welfare*, 61 (6): 383–7.

Galassi, M. and Galassi, O. (1976) 'An investigation into the validity of role play as a procedure for counsellor skill assessment', *British Journal of Guidance and Counselling*, 17 (2): 155–65.

Gallagher, M. S. and Hargie, O. D. (1989) 'The effects of role playing variation on the assessment of assertive behaviour, *Behaviour Therapy*, 7 (2): 343–47.

Gammon, E. and Sheldon, R. (1991) 'The coping skills training programme for parents of children with developmental disabilities: an experimental evaluation', *Research on Social Work Practice*, 1 (3): 244–56.

Gask, L., Goldberg, D., Porter, R. and Creed, F. (1989) 'The treatment of somatization: evaluation of a teaching package with general practice trainees', *Journal of Psychosomatic Research*, 33 (6): 697–703.

Geller, D. M. (1978) 'Involvement in role playing simulations: a demonstration with studies on obedience'. *Journal of Personality and Social Psychology*, 36 (3): 719–35.

Gergen, K. J. (1973) 'Social Psychology as History', *Journal of Personality and Social Psychology*, 26: 309–20.

Gergen, K. J. (1978) 'Experimentation in social psychology, *European Journal of Social Psychology*, 8: 507–27.

Gillett, G. (1987) 'Constructs, structures and meanings', *Inquiry*, 30: 101–12.

Gillett, G. (1995) 'The philosophical foundations of qualitative psychology', *The Psychologist*, 8 (3): 111–14.

Ginsberg, G. P. (1979) 'The effective use of role-playing in psychological research', in G. P Ginsberg (ed.), *Emerging Strategies in Social Psychology*, New York: Wiley.

Glenn, A., Gregg, D. and Tipple, B. et al. (1982) 'Using role play activities to teach problem solving', *Simulation and Games*, 13 (2): 199–209.

Glueckhauf, R. L. and Quittner, A. L. (1992) 'Assertiveness training for disabled adults in wheelchairs: self-report, role-play and activity pattern outcome', *Journal of Consulting and Clinical Psychology*, 10 (3): 419–25.

Goffman, E. (1959) *Asylums*, Garden City, NY: Doubleday.

Goffman, E. (1961) *The Presentation of Self in Every Day Life*, Garden City, NY: Doubleday.

Goldfried, M. (1980) 'Towards the delineation of therapeutic change principles', *American Psychology*, 35 (11): 991–9.

Goldfried, M. (1991) 'Research issues in psychotherapy integration', *Journal of Psychotherapy Integration*, 1 (1): 5–25.

Goldfried, M. and Padawar, W. (1982) 'Current status and future directions in psychotherapy', in M. Goldfried (ed.), *Converging Themes in Psychotherapy: Trends in Psychodynamics, Humanistic and Behavioural Practice*, New York, NY: Springer Publication.

Goldstein, A (1973) *Structured Learning Therapy*, London: Acadamic Press.

Gorecki, P., Dickson, A. L., Andersen, H. N. and Jones, G. G. (1981) 'Relationship between contrived in-vivo and role play assertive behaviour', *Journal of Clinical Psychology*, 37 (1): 104–7.

Graham, J., Rohrback, W., Flay, B. and Anderson Johnson, D. (1989) 'Convergent and discriminant validity for assessment of skills in resisting role play alcohol offer', *Behavioural Assessment*, 11: 353–79.

Greenberg, I. (1974) *Psychodrama, Theory and Therapy*, London: Souvenir Press.

Greenberg, L. S. (1967) 'Role playing: an alternative to deception', *Journal of Personality and Social Psychology*, 7 (2): 152–7.

Greenberg, L. S. (1986) 'Change process research. Special Issue: Psychotherapy Research', *Journal of Consulting and Clinical Psychology*, 54 (1): 4–9.

Greenberg, L. S. and Rice, L. N. (1981) 'The specific effects of a gestalt intervention', *Psychotherapy, Theory, Research and Practice*, 18: 31–7.

Greenblat, C. S., Kutz, S., Gagnon, J. H. and Shannon, D. (1989) 'An innovative program of counselling family members and friends of seropositive haemophliacs', *Aids Care*, 1 (1): 67–75.

Grotowski, J. (1975) *Towards a Poor Theatre*, London: Methuen.

Hamilton, V. L. (1976) 'Role playing and deception: a re-examination of the controversy?', *Journal for the Theory of Social Behaviour*, 6 (2): 233–50.

Haney, C., Banks, C. and Zimbardo, P. (1973) 'Interpersonal dynamics in a simulated prison', *International Journal of Criminology and Penology*, 1: 69–97.

Harbeck, C., Peterson, L. and Starr, L. (1992) 'Previously abused child victims' response to a sexual abuse prevention programme: a matter of measures', *Behavior Therapy*, 23 (3): 375–87.

Harré, R. and Secord, P. F. (1972) *The Explanation of Social Behaviour*, Oxford: Blackwell.

Heading, B. (1982) 'The man and the mask', in J. A. Jackson (ed.) *Role*. Cambridge: Cambridge University Press.

Heatherington, L. (1989) 'Toward more meaningful clinical research: taking context into account in coding psychotherapy interaction', *Psychotherapy, Theory, Research, Practice and Training*, 26 (4): 436–47.

Hedberg, N. L. and Stoel-Gammon, C. (1986) 'Narrative analysis: clinical procedures', *Topics in Language Disorders*, 7 (1): 58–69.

Hendrick, C. (1977) 'Role taking, role playing and the laboratory experiment', *Personal and Social Psychology Bulletin*, 3, 467–78.

Henriques, J., Hollway, W., Urwin, C., Venn, C. and Walkerdine, V. (eds) (1984) *Changing the Subject: Psychology, Social Regulation and Subjectivity*, London: Methuen.

Henwood, K. and Pidgeon, N. (1992) 'Qualitive research and Psychological Theorising', *British Journal of Psychology*, 83: 97–111.

Henwood, K. and Pidgeon, N. (1995) 'Remaking the link: qualitive research and feminist standpoint theory', *Feminism and Psychology*, 5: 7–30.

Heritage, J. (1984) *Garfinkel and Ethnomethodology*, Oxford: Blackwell.

Hersen, M., Bellack, A. and Himmelhoch, J. (1980) 'Treatment of unipolar depression with social skills training', *Behaviour Modification*, 4 (4): 547–56.

Higgins, R. L., Alonso, R. R. and Pendleton, M. G. (1979) 'The validity of role play assessments', *Behavior Therapy*, 10: 655–62.

172   *Role Play*

Higgins, R. L., Frisch, M. B. and Smith, D. (1983) 'A comparison of role played and natural responses to identical circumstances', *Behaviour Therapy*, 14: 158–69.

Holland, R. (1977) *Self and Social Context*, London: Macmillan.

Holmes, P. (1988) 'Don't tell us–show us: the use of role play in the teaching of psychoanalytic theory', *Journal of Adolescence Teaching*, 11 (1): 65–71.

Holmes, P. and Karp, M. (1991) *Psychodrama: Inspiration and Technique*, New York: Routledge.

Hollway, W. (1989) *Subjectivity and Method in Psychology*, London: Sage.

Holmes, D. and Bennett, D. (1974) 'Experiments to answer questions raised by the use of deception in psychological research', *Journal of Personality and Social Psychology*, 29 (3): 358–67.

Honess, T. M. and Edwards, A. (1987) 'Qualitative case study research with adolescents', in T. M. Honess and K. M. Yardley (eds), *Self and Identity: Perspectives Across the Lifespan*, London: Routledge and Kegan, Paul.

Honess, T. M and Yardley, K. M. (eds) (1987) *Self and Identity: Perspectives Across the Lifespan*, London: Routledge and Kegan Paul.

Horowitz, M. (1979) *States of Mind: Analysis of Change in Psychotherapy*, New York: Plenum.

Horowitz, M. (1982) 'Strategic dilemmas and the socialization of psychotherapy research', *British Journal of Clinical Psychology*, 21 (2): 119–27.

Horowitz, I. and Rothschild, B. (1970) 'Conformity, as a function of deception and role playing', *Journal of Personality and Social Psychology*, 14 (3): 224–6.

Hovrath, P. (1984) 'Demand characteristics and differential process in psychotherapeutic change', *Journal of Consulting and Clinical Psychology*, 52 (4): 616–24.

Huddleston, R. (1989) 'Drama with elderly people', *British Journal of Occupational Therapy*, 52 (8): 298–300.

Illich, I. (1973) *Tools for Conviviality*, London: Calder & Boyars.

Iser, W. (1980) 'Interaction between text and reader', in S. Suleiman and I. Crossman (eds), *The Reader in the Text*, Princeton, N. J: Princeton University Press. pp. 106–20.

Jackson, J. A. (ed.) (1982) *Role*, Cambridge: Cambridge University Press.

Jackson, H., Minas, I., Burgess, P. and Joshua, S. (1989) 'Negative symptoms and social skills performance in schizophrenia', *Schizophrenia Research*, 2 (6): 457–63.

Janis, I. and King, B. (1954) 'The influence of role-playing on opinion change', *Journal of Abnormal Psychology*, 46: 11–18.

Jessee, E. and L'Abale, L. (1981) 'Enrichment role-playing as a step in the training of family therapists', *Journal of Marital and Family Therapy*, 7 (4): 507–14.

Johnson, D. (1980a) 'Cognitive organisation in paranoid and non-paranoid schizophrenia: a study of self-other representations in improvisational role playing and on the Rorschach', *Dissertation Abstracts International*, 41 (5): 1919–13.

Johnson, D. (1980b) 'Fluid and rigid boundaries of paranoid and non-paranoid schizophrenia on a role playing task', *Journal of Personality Assessment*, 44 (5): 523–31.

Jones, E. E. and Nisbett, R. E. (1972) 'The actor and the observer: divergent perceptions of the causes of behaviour', in E. E. Jones and R. E. Nisbet (eds), *Attribution: Perceiving the Causes of Behavior*, Morristown, N.J: General Learning Press.

Jordan, J. (1985) 'Drugs on the street: a group therapy game for drug abusers', *Small Group Behaviour*, 16 (1): 105–9.

Jupp, J. J. and Griffiths, M. D. (1990) 'Self concept change in shy, socially isolated adolescents following social skills training emphasising role plays', *Australian Psychologist*, 25 (2): 165–77.

Kaakinen, J. (1992) 'Living with silence', *Gerontology*, 32: 258–64.

Kaaya, S., Goldberg, D. and Gask, L. (1992) 'Management of somatic presentations of psychiatric illness in general medical settings', *Medical Education*, 26 (2): 138–44.

Kadden, R. M., Litt, M. D., Conney, N. L. and Busher, D. A. (1992) 'Relationships between role-play measures of coping skills and alcoholism treatment outcome', *Addictive Behaviours*, 17 (5): 425–37.

Kanfer, F. (1990) 'The scientist–practitioner connection: a bridge in need of constant attention', *Professional Psychology Research and Practice*, 21 (4): 264–70.

Kanfer, F. H. and Phillips, J. S. (1969) 'A survery of current behavior therapies and a proposal for classification', in C. M Franks (ed.), *Behavior Therapy Appraisal and Status*, New York, NY: McGraw-Hill.

Keane, T., Black, J., Collins, F. and Vinson, M. (1982) 'A skill training programme for teaching the behaviour interview', *Behavioural Assessment*, 4: 53–62.

Kelly, G. (1955a) *The Psychology of Personal Constructs*, vol. 1, New York, NY: Norton.

Kelly, G. (1955b) *The Psychology of Personal Contructs*, vol. 2, New York, NY: Norton.

Kelly, J. A. and Christoff, K. A. (1985) 'Job interview training', *Psychiatric Aspects of Mental Retardation Reviews*, 4 (2): 5–8.

Kern, J. (1982) 'The comparative external and concurrent validity of role plays for assessing heterosocial performance', *Behaviour Therapy*, 13: 666–80.

Kern, J., Killer, C. and Eggers, J. (1983) 'Enhancing the validity of role play tests: a comparison of role play methodologies', *Behaviour Therapy*, 14 (4): 482–92.

Kiesler, D. (1981) 'Some myths of psychotherapy research and the search for a paradigm', *Journal of Consulting and Clinical Psychology*, 42 (2): 212–15.

Klein, K. (1982) 'Disconfirmed expectancies and imagined distress in a role play of a visit to the dentist', *Motivation and Emotions*, 6 (2): 181–92.

Klingman, A. (1983) 'Simulation and simulation games as a strategy for death education', *Death Education*, 7: 339–52.

Klosinski, G. (1991) 'Questions of guidance and supervision at the beginning of psychotherapy in children and adolescents', *Psychotherapy and Psychosomatics*, 53 (1–4): 80–5.

Knapp, P. A. and Deluty, R. H. (1989) 'Relative effectiveness of two behavioural parent training programs', *Journal of Clinical Child Psychology*, 18 (4): 314–22.

Koch, S. (1964/1959) *Psychology: A Study of a Science*, vol. 3, New York, NY: McGraw-Hill.

Kohut, H. (1971) *The Analysis of the Self*, New York, NY: International Universities Press.

Kohut, H. (1977) *The Restoration of the Self*, New York, NY: International Universities Press.

Kolko, D. S., Luar, L. L. and Sturnick, D. (1990) 'Inpatient social cognitive skills training groups with conduct disordered and attention deficit disordered children', *Journal of Child Psychology and Psychiatry and Allied Disciplines*, 31 (5): 737–48.

Kopel, S. A. and Arkowitz, H. S. (1974) 'Role playing as a source of self-observation and behaviour change', *Journal of Personality and Social Psychology*, 29 (5): 677–86.

Krueger D. L. and Smith P. (1982) 'Decision-making patterns of couples: a sequential analysis', *Behavior of Communication*, 32 (3): 121–34.

Kuhn, T. S. (1962) *The Structure of Scientific Revolution*, Chicago, IL: Chicago University Press.

Lauffer, A. (1973) *Journal of Simulation & Games*, 4.

Lazurus, A. (1966) 'The results of behaviour therapy in 126 cases of severe neurosis', *Behaviour Research and Therapy*, 1: 67–79.

Levine, M. (1974) 'Scientific method and the adversary model: some preliminary thoughts', *American Psychologist*, 29: 661–77.

Levinson, D. J. (1959) 'Role, personality and social structures in organizational selling', *Journal of Abnormal and Social Psychology*, 58: 170–80.

Levinson, R. L. and Herman, J. (1991) The use of role playing as a technique in the psychotherapy of children', *Psychotherapy*, 28 (4): 660–66.

Lewis, B. (1995) 'Psychotherapeutic discourse analysis', *American Journal of Psychotherapy*, 49 (3): 371–84.

Lewis, A. and Antaki, C. (1986) *Mental Mirrors: Metacognition in Social Knowledge and Communication*, London: Sage.

Lincoln, Y. and Guba, E. (1985) *Naturalistic Inquiry*, Beverley Hills, CA: Sage.

Linton, R. (1936) *The Study of Man*, New York, NY: Appleton. Century Croft

Lyons, M., Bradley, O. and White, J. (1984) 'Videotaping and abnormal psychology: dramatised clinical interviews', *Teaching of Psychology*, 11 (1): 41–2.

Mahrer, A. R., Paterson, W. E., Theriault, A. T., Toessler, C. and Quenneville, A. (1986)

'How and why to use a large number of clinically sophisticated judges in psychotherapy research', *Voices: The Art and Science of Psychotherapy*, 22, 57–66.

Mair, J. M. M. (1970) 'Experimenting with individuals', *British Journal of Medical Psychology*, 43: 245–56.

Mann, J. H. and Mann, C. H. (1956) 'Experimental evaluation of role playing', *Psychological Bulletin*, 53 (3): 227–34.

Mann, J. H. (1959) 'The effect of role playing experience on role playing ability', *Sociometry*, 22: 64–74.

Mansfield, F. (1991) 'Supervised role play in the teaching of the process of consultation', *Medical Education*, 25 (6): 485–90.

Manstead, A. S. R. (1979) 'A role playing replication of Schacter and Singers 1962 study of the cognitive and physiological determinants of emotional state', *Motivation and Emotion*, 13: 251–264.

Markova, I. and Foppa, K. (eds) (1990) *The Dynamics of Dialogue*, Hemel Hempstead: Harvester.

Marmar, C. (1990) 'Psychotherapy process research: Progress, dilemmas, and future directions', *Journal of Consulting and Clinical Psychology*, 58 (3): 265–72.

Marmor, J. (1968) *Modern Psychoanalysis*, New York, NY: Basic Books Inc.

Marmor, J. (1973) 'The future of psychoanalytic therapy', *American Journal of Psychiatry*, 1 (30): 197–202.

Marr, D. and Fairchild, T. (1993) 'A problem solving strategy and self esteem in recovering chemically dependant women', *Alcoholism Treatment Quarterly*, 10 (1–2): 171–86.

McCall, G. T. and Simmons, J. L. (1966) *Identities and Interactions*, New York, NY: Free Press.

McCall, G. T. and Simmons, J. L. (1982) *Social Psychology: A Sociological Approach*, New York, NY: Free Press.

McFall, R. M. and Lillesand, D. B. (1971) 'Behaviour rehearsal with modelling and coaching on assertion training', *Journal of Abnormal Psychology*, 77: 313–23.

McFall, R. M. and Marston, A. R. (1970) 'An experimental investigation of behaviour rehearsal in assertive training', *Journal of Abnormal Psychology*, 76: 295–303.

McGuire, W. J. (1973) 'The yin and yang of progress in social psychology', *Journal of Personality and Social Psychology*, 26 (4): 46–56.

McIntyre, T., Balfour, J. D. and McIntyre, S. (1983) 'Assertion training: the effectiveness of a comprehensive cognitive behavioural treatment package with professional nurses', *Behavioural Research and Therapy*, 22 (3): 311–18.

McNamara, J. and Blumer, C. (1982) 'Role playing to assess the social competence', *Behaviour Modification*, 6: 519–49.

McReynolds, P., Devoge, S., Osborne, S., Pither, B. and Nordin, K. (1981) 'A role playing test for the assessment of interpersonal styles', *Journal of Clinical Psychology*, 37 (2): 359–62.

Mead, G. H. (1934) *Mind, Self and Society*, Chicago, IL: University of Chicago Press.

Menzel, H. (1978) 'Meaning who needs it?', in M. Brenner, P. Marsh and M. Brenner (eds) *The Social Context of Method*, London: Croom Helm.

Merton, R. K. (1968) *Role Sets: Social Theory and Social Structure*, New York, NY: Free Press.

Messinger, S. L., Simpson, H. and Towe, R. D. (1962) 'Life as theater: some notes on dramaturgical approach to social reality', *Sociometry*, 2 (5): 98–110.

Milgram, S. (1963) 'Behavioural study of obedience', *Journal of Abnormal and Social Psychology*, 67: 371–8.

Miller, A. E. (1972) 'Role playing: an alternative to deception? A review of the evidence', *American Psychologist*, 27 (7): 623–36.

Mischler, E. G. (1979) 'Meaning in Context: is there any other kind?', *Harvard Educational Review*, 49 (1): 1–19.

Mitrofan, I. and Mitrofan, N. (1989) 'Global and specific dysfunctions in adopting and performing conjugal roles', *Revista De Psicologie*, 35 (2): 129–40.

Mixon, D. (1971) 'Behaviour Analysis: treating subjects as actors rather than organisms', *Journal for the Theory of Social Behaviour*, 1 (1): 19–31.

Mixon, D. (1972) 'Instead of Deception', *Journal for the Theory of Social Behaviour*, 2: 145–77.

Mixon, D. (1977) 'Temporary false beliefs', *Personality and Social Psychology Bulletin*, 3: 479–88.

Mixon, D. (1979) 'A note on role playing', *British Journal of Social and Clinical Psychology*, 8: 395–6.

Monti, P., Abrams, D., Brinkoff, J. and Zwick, W. (1990), 'Communication skills training, communication skills training with family and cognitive behavioural mood management training for alcoholics', *Journal of Studies on Alcohol*, 51 (3): 263–70.

Moon, J. and Eisler, R. (1975) 'Anger control: an experimental comparison of three behavioural treatments', *Behaviour Therapy*, 14: 493–505.

Moore, K. (1984) 'Training social workers to work with the terminally ill', *Health and Social Work*, 268–73.

Moreno, J. L. (1946 [1972]) *Psychodrama*, vol. 1, New York, NY: Beacon House.

Moreno, J. L. (1953) *Who Shall Survive?*, New York, NY: Beacon House.

Moreno, J. L. (1959) *Psychodrama*, vol. 2, New York, NY: Beacon House.

Moreno, J. L. (1969) *Psychodrama*, vol. 3 New York, NY: Beacon House.

Moreno, Z. (1969) 'Psychodramatic rules, techniques and adjunctive methods', *Group Psychotherapy*, 22, 213–19.

Morrow-Bradley, C. and Elliott, R. (1986) 'Utilization of psychotherapy research by practising psychotherapists', *American Psychologist*, 41 (2): 188–97.

Movahedi, S. (1977) 'Role playing: an alternative to what?', *Personality and Social Psychology Bulletin*, 3: 489–97.

Muccigrosso, L. (1994) 'Sexual abuse prevention strategies and programs for persons with developmental disabilities', *Sexuality and Disability*, 9 (3): 261–71.

Much, N. C. (1992) 'The analysis of discourse as a methodology for a semiotic psychology', *American Behavioral Scientist*, 36: 52–72.

Mueser, K. T., Bellack, A. S., Douglas, M. S. and Morrison, R. L. (1991) 'A prevalence and stability of social skills, deficits of schizophrenia', *Schizophrenia Research*, 5 (2): 167–76.

Mueser, K. T., Bellack, A. S., Morrison R. L. and Wixted, J. T. (1990) 'Social competence in schizophrenia: premorbid adjustment, social skill and domains of functioning', *Journal of Psychiatric Research*, 24 (1): 51–63.

Musiol, M. (1992) 'De l'incoherence du discours au desordre de la pensee chez la schizophrenie', *Psychologie Francaise*, 37: 221–33.

Neimeyer, R. A. (1993) 'An appraisal of constructivist psychotherapies', *Journal of Consulting and Clinical Psychology*, 61 (2): 221–34.

Nezu, C., Nezu, A. and Arean, P. (1991) 'Assertiveness and problem solving training for mildly mentally retarded persons with dual diagnosis', *Research in Developmental Disabilities*, 12, (4): 371–86.

Nicholson, P. (1991) 'Developing a feminist approach to depression following childbirth', in S. Wilkinson (ed.), *Feminist Social Psychology: Developing Theory and Practice*, Milton Keynes: Open University Press.

Nye, C. H. (1994) 'Narrative interaction and the development of client autonomy in clinical practice', *Clinical Social Work Journal*, 22 (1): 43–57.

O'Donohue, W. and Elliott, A. (1991) 'A model for the clinical assessment of the sexually abused child', *Behavioural Assessment*, 13 (4): 325–39.

O'Leary, C., Willis, F. and Tomich, E. (1987) 'Conformity under deceptive and non-deceptive techniques', *The Sociological Quarterly*, 11: 87–93.

Olsen, T. and Christiansen, G. (1966) *The Grindstone Experiment: Thirty One Hours*, Toronto: Canadian Friends Service Committee.

Omer, H. and London, P. (1988) 'Metamorphosis in psychotherapy: end of the systems era', *Psychotherapy*, 25 (2): 171–80.

Oppelaar, L., Bleys, F. C. and Gerritsma, J. (1983) 'Use of simulation techniques in an intermediate course linking up preclinical and clinical studies', *Medical Teacher*, 5 (3): 96–103.

Orne, M. T. (1959) 'On the social psychology of the psychological experiment', *American Psychologist*, 17: 776–83.

Osiejuk, E. (1993) 'Discourse functions and hemispheric asymmetry', *First International Congress of the Polish Neuroscience Society: A Congress in the Decade of the Brain*, Warsaw, Poland: U. Warszawaki, Wydzial Psychologiie Warsaw.

Perles, F. S., Hefferline, R. F. and Goodman, P. (1973) *Gestalt Therapy: Excitement and Growth in the Human Personality*, Harmondsworth: Penguin.

Piaget, J. (1926) *The Language and Thought of the Child*, New York, NY: Harcourt, Brace and Co.

Pilgrim, D. (1984) 'Some implications for psychology of formulating all illness as deviancy', *British Journal of Medical Psychology*, 57: 227–33.

Plummer, K. (1993) *Documents of Life*, London: Allen and Unwin.

Plummer, K. (1995) 'Life story research', J. Smith, R. Harré and L. Van Langenhove (eds), *Rethinking Methods in Psychology*, London: Sage.

Polanyi, M. (1966) *The Tacit Dimension*, London: Routledge & Kegan Paul.

Potter, J. and Wetherell, M. (1987) *Discourse and Social Psychology: Beyond Attitudes and Behaviour*, London: Sage.

Potter, J. and Wetherell, M. (1995) 'Analyzing discourses', in J. Smith, R. Harré and L. Van Langenhove (eds), *Rethinking Methods in Psychology*, Ch 8. Vol 2

Rakos, R., Mayers, M. and Schroeder H. (1982) 'Validity of role playing and self-predictioning of assertive behaviour', *Psychosocial Reports*, 50: 435–444.

Rasing, E. (1993) 'Effects of a multifaceted training procedure on the social behaviours of hearing impaired children with severe language disabilities', *Journal of Applied Behavior Analysis*, 26 (3): 405–6.

Reason, P. and Heron, J. (1988) *Human Inquiry in Action*, London: Sage.

Reason, P. and Heron, J. (1995) 'Co-operative Inquiry', in Smith et al. (eds), *Rethinking Methods in Psychology*, London: Sage.

Reynolds, B. (1981) 'Dating skills in the group treatment of erectile dysfunction for men without partners', *Journal of Sex and Marital Therapy*, 7 (3): 184–94.

Rheinhart, L. (1972) *The Diceman*, St Albans: Panther.

Rhodewalt, F. and Agustsdottir, S. (1986) 'Effects of self presentation on the phenonenal self', *Journal of Personality and Social Psychology*, 50 (1): 47–55.

Rice, M. T. and Josefowitz, N. (1983) 'Assertion popularity and social behaviour in maximum security psychiatric patients', *Corrective and Social Psychiatry*, 29 (4): 97–104.

Rickert, V., Sottolano, D., Parrish, J. and Riley, A. (1989) 'Training parents to become better behaviour managers: The need for a competency based approach', *Behaviour Modification*, 12 (4): 475–96.

Riessman, C. K. (1990) 'Strategic uses of narrative in the presentation of self and illness: a research note', *Social Science and Medicine*, 30 (11): 1195–1200.

Rohrback, L. A., Graham, J. W., Hansen, W. B., Flay, B., Anderson Johnson, C. (1987) 'Evaluation of resistance skills training using multi-trait, multimethod role play skill assessment', *Health Education Research*, 2 (4): 401–07.

Roman, M. and Porter, K. (1978) 'Combining experiential and didactic aspects in a new group therapy training approach', *International Group Psychotherapy*, 28 (3): 371–87.

Romanyshyn, R. (1978) 'Psychology and the Attitudes of Science', in R. S. Valle and M. Kings (eds), *Existential Phenomenological Alternatives for Psychology*, New York, NY. Oxford University Press. pp. 18–47.

Romanyshyn, R. (1982) *Psychological Life From Science to Metaphor*, Milton Keynes: Open University Press.

Romanshyn, R. (1987) 'Mirror as metaphor of psychological life', in K. Yardley and T. Honess (eds), *Self and Identity: Psychological Perspectives*, Chichester: Wiley.

Rommetveit, R. (1979) *On Message Structure*, London: Wiley.

Rosenthal, R. (1966) *Experimental Effects in Behavioural Research*, New York, NY: Appleton Century Crofts.

Rosenthal, R. and Rosnow, R. L. (eds) (1969) *Artifact in Behavioural Research*, London: Academic Press.

Rosnow, R. (1990) 'Teaching research ethics through role play and discussion', *Teaching of Psychology*, 17 (3): 179–81.

Rothbaum, B. (1992) 'The behavioural treatment of trichotillomania', *Behavioural Psychotherapy*, 20 (1): 85–90.

Rychlak, J. F. (1977) *The Psychology of Rigorous Humanism*, London: John Wiley.

Salto, C., Guarch, J., Cirici, R. and Obiols, J. (1990) 'Importancia de al intervention psicosocial en el curso de la esquizofrenia', *Revista de psiquiatria de la facultad de medicina de Barcelona*, 17 (6): 282–90.

Sarbin, T. R. (1954) 'Role theory', in G. Lindzey (ed.), *Handbook of Social Psychology*, vol. 1, Cambridge, MA: Addison-Wesley.

Sarup, G. (1981) 'Role playing issue importance and attitude change', *Social Behaviour and Personality*, 9 (2): 191–202.

Schachter, S. and Singer, J. E. (1962) 'Cognitive, social and physiological determinants of emotional state', *Psychological Review*, 69: 379–99.

Schaffer, W. and Hasegawa, C. (1984) 'Use of empathy algorithm with a role playing client', *Journal of Clinical Psychology*, 40 (1): 57–64.

Schramski, T. G. and Harvey, D. R. (1983) 'The impact of psychodrama and role playing in the correctional environment', *International Journal of Offender Therapy and Comparative Criminology*, 27 (3): 243–54.

Schultz, A. (1968) 'On multiple realities', in C. Gordon and K. J. Gergen (eds), *The Self in Social Interaction*, NY: Wiley 71, 2,4; 73, 2,4; Collected papers (2) Hague: M. Nijhoff

Schutz, A. (1971) *Collected Papers*, Vol. 2, Hague: M. Nijhoff.

Schutz, A. (1973) *Collected Papers*, Vol. 1, Hague: M. Nijhoff.

Schwartz, R. M. and Gottman, J. M. (1976) 'Toward a task analysis of assertive behaviour', *Journal of Consulting and Clinical Psychology*, 44, 910–20.

Shapiro, D. (1995) 'Finding out how psychotherapies help people change', *Psychotherapy Research*, 5 (1): 1–21.

Sheikh, A., Mason, D. and Taylor, A. (1993) 'An expressive group with the elderly', *British Journal of Psychotherapy*, 10 (1): 77–82.

Sherif, K. (1977) 'Crisis in social psychology: some remarks towards breaking through the crisis', *Personality and Social Psychology Bulletin*, 3, 368–82.

Shoham, S and Salomon, V. (1990) 'Interrelating research processes of process research', *Journal of Consulting and Clinical Psychology*, 58 (3): 295–303.

Shotter, J. (1994) *Conversational Realities: Constructing Life Through Language*, London: Sage.

Sievert, A., Cuvo, A. J. and Davis, P. K. (1988) 'Training of self-advocacy skill to adults with mild handicaps', *Journal of Applied Behaviour Analysis*, 21 (2): 299–309.

Simionato, R. (1991) 'The link between empirical research, epistemic values, and psychological practice', *Australian Psychologist*, 26 (2): 123–27.

Simons, C. and Piliavin, J. (1972) 'Effect of deception on reactions to a victim', *Journal of Personality and Social Psychology*, 21(1): 56–60.

Słoma, J. (1983) 'Psychological experiment as experimental theater', *Polish Psychological Bulletin*, 14: 159–69.

Sluckin, A., Weller, A. and Highton, J. (1989) 'Recovering from trauma: gestalt therapy with an abused child', *Maladjustments and Therapeutic Education*, 7 (3): 147–57.

Smith, J. A., Harré, R. and Van Langenhove, L. (eds) (1995) 'Idiography and the Case Study', *Rethinking Methods in Psychology*, London: Sage.

Smith, J. A. (1995) 'Semi structured interviewing and qualitative analysis', in J. A. Smith, R. Harré and L. Van Lagenhove (eds), *Rethinking Methods in Psychology*, London: Sage.

Smith, J. A. (1990) 'Transforming identities: a repertory grid case-study of the transition to motherhood', *British Journal of Psychology*, 63: 239–53.

Smith, J. A. (1994) 'Reconstructing selves: an analysis of discrepancy between woman's contemporaneous and retrospective accounts of the transition to motherhood', *British Journal of Psychology*, 85: 371–92.

Smith, J. L. (1975) 'A games analysis for attitude change: use of role enactment situations for model development', *Journal for the Theory of Social Behaviour*, 5: 63–79.

Smith. M. C. and Hasnip, J. H. (1991) 'The lessons of deafness: deafness awareness communication skills training with medical students', *Medical Education*, 25 (4): 319–21.

Smith, T. W. (1983) 'Change in irrational beliefs and the outcome of rational emotive psychotherapy', *Journal of Consulting and Clinical Psychology*, 51(1): 156–7.

Stanislavski, C. (1948a) *An Actor Prepares*, New York: Theatre Art Books.

Stanislavski, C. (1948b) *Building a Character*, New York: Theatre Art Books.

Stanislavski, C. (1968) *Creating a Role*, London: Mentor.

Stanton, H. and Litwak, E. (1955) 'Toward the development of a short form test of interpersonal competence', *American Sociological Review*, 20: 688–74.

Sterling, M. and Bugental, B. (1993) 'The meld experience in psychotherapy supervision', *Journal of Humanistic Psychology*, 33 (2): 38–48.

Stolorow, R., Brandchaft, B. and Atwood, G. (1987) *Psychoanalytic Treatment: An Intersubjective Approach*, Hillsdale, NJ: The Analytic Press.

Stricker, G. (1967) 'A pre-experimental enquiry concerning cognitive determinants of emotional state', *Journal of General Psychology*, 76: 73–9.

Strickland, L. H., Barefoot, J. C. and Hochenstein, P. (1976) 'Monitoring behaviour in surveillance and trust paradigm', *Representative Research in Social Psychology*, 7: 51–7.

Strupp, H. (1978) 'Psychotherapy research and practice: an overview, in S. Garfield and A. Bergin (eds), *Handbook of Psychotherapy and Behaviour Change*, Chichester: Wiley.

Stryker, S. (1987) 'Identity theory: developments in extensions', in K. Yardley and T. Honess (eds), *Self and Identity: Psychosocial Perspectives*, Chichester: Wiley.

Sturm, I. E. (1971) 'Implications of role-playing methodology for clinical procedure', *Behaviour Therapy*, 2: 88–96.

Swartz, S. (1994) 'Issues in the analysis of psychotic speech', *Journal of Psycholinguistic Research*. 23 (1): 29–44.

Swink, D., Siegel, J. and Spodak, B. (1984) 'Saint Elizabeth's Hospital Action training lab for Police'. *Journal of Group Psychotherapy, Psychodrama and Sociometry*, 37 (3): 94–103.

Thines, G. (1977) *Phenomenology and the Science of Behaviour*, London: George, Allen & Unwin.

Thorngate, W. (1976) 'Possible limits in a science of social behaviour', in C. H. Strickland, F. E. Aboud and K. J. Gergen (eds), *Social Psychology in Transition*, New York, NY: Plenum Press. pp. 121–39.

Thorley, G. and Yule, W. (1982) 'A role play test of parent-child interaction', *Behavioural Psychotherapy*, 10 (2): 146–61.

Toulmin, S. (1977) 'Self knowledge and knowledge of the self', in T. Mischell (ed.), *The Self: Psychological and Philosophical Issues*, Oxford: Blackwell.

Trower, P., Bryant, B. and Argyle, M. (1977) *Social Skills and Mental Health*, London: Methuen.

Turner, R. H. (1968) 'The self-conception in social interaction', in C. Gordon and K. Gergen (eds), *The Self in Social Interaction*, Vol. 1, New York, NY: Wiley.

Turner, R. H. (1987) 'Articulating self and social structure', in K. Yardley and T. Honess (eds), *Self and Identity: Psychosocial Perspectives*, Chichester: Wiley.

Valenti-Hein, D., Yarnold, P. and Mueser, K. (1994) 'Evaluation of the dating skills programme for improving heterosocial interactions in people with mental retardation', *Behavior Modification*, 18 (1): 32–46.

Vandendriessche, G. (1991) 'Psychoanalysis and hermeneutics', *Psychologica Belgica*, 31 (1): 67–105.

Van Langenhove, L. (1995) 'Idiography and the case study', in J. Smith, R. Harré and L. Van Langenhove (eds), *Rethinking Methods in Psychology*, London: Sage.

Wachtel, P. L. (1977) *Psychoanalysis and Behavior Therapy*, New York, NY: Basic Books.

Waite, L. M. (1993) 'Drama therapy in small groups with the developmentally disabled', *Social Work With Groups*, 16 (4): 95–108.

Wamboldt, F., Wamboldt, M. and Gurman, S. (1985) 'Marital and family research: the meaning for the clinician', *Family Therapy Collection*, 15, 10–26.

Wassenaar, D. R. (1987) 'Researching family therapy' *South African Journal of Psychology*, 17 (1): 25–29.

Way, B. (1967) *Development Through Drama*, London: Longman.

Wehrenberg, S. B. (1986) 'Simulations: capturing the experience of the real thing', *Personal Journal*, 65 (4): 101–105.

Weist, M., Vanatta, K., Wayland, K. and Jackson, C. (1993) 'Social skills training for abused girls: interpersonal skills training for sexually abused girls', *Behavior Change*, 10 (4): 244–252.

Wessberg, H. W., Mariotto, M. J., Conger, A. J., Farrell, A. D. and Conger, J. C. (1979) 'Ecological validity of role plays for assessing heterosocial anxiety and skill of male college students', *Journal of Consulting and Clinical Psychology*, 47: 525–35.

Widdicombe, S. and Wooffitt, R. (1995) 'Social selves in (inter) action: Realising conceptual shifts through empirical research', *Proceedings of the British Psychological Society*, 3 (1): 60.

Williams, C. (1981) 'Assessment of social behavior: behavioral role play compared with S1 scale of MMPI', *Behavior Therapy*, 12: 578–84.

Williams, A. (1989) *The Passionate Technique*, New York, NY: Routledge.

Willis, N. H. and Willis, Y. A. (1970) 'Role playing versus deception: an experimental comparison', *Journal of Personality and Social Psychology*, 16, 472–77.

Wilson, T., Momb, D., Hunt, R. D. and Heiber, M. A. (1982) 'Reparenting young schizophrenic people', *Int. Child Welfare Review*, 55: 31–8.

Wirrshing, W. C., Marder, S. R., Eckman, T. A. and Liberman, R. P. (1992) 'Acquisition and retention of skills training methods in chronic schizophrenia in outpatients', *Psychopharmacology Bulletin*, 28 (3) 241–45.

Wolf, V. B. (1993) 'Group therapy of young latency age sexually abused girls', *Journal of Child and Adolescent Group Therapy*, 3 (1): 25–39.

Wolpe, J. (1969) *The Practice of Behavior Therapy*, New York, NY: Pergamon Press.

Woolgar, S. (1988) *Science: The Very Idea*, London: Tavistock.

Yardley, K. M. (1979) 'A critique of social skills training', *British Journal of Medical Psychology*, 53: 55–62.

Yardley, K. M. (1982a) 'On distinguishing role plays from conventional methodologies', *Journal for the Theory of Social Behaviour*, 12 (2): 125–39.

Yardley, K. M. (1982b) 'On engaging actors in as if experiments', *Journal for the Theory of Social Behaviour*, 12: 291–304.

Yardley, K. M. (1984a) 'A critique of role play teminology in social psychology experimentation', *British Journal of Social Psychology*, 23: 113–20.

Yardley, K. M. (1984b) *The Individual and Contexts: A Generative Approach Towards the Understanding of Role Play Methodology'*, Doctoral Thesis, University of Wales.

Yardley, K. M. (1987) ' "What do you mean? Who am I?" Exploring the implications of a self-concept measurement with subjects' in K. Yardley and T. Honess (eds), *Self and Identity: Psychosocial Perspectives*, Chichester: Wiley.

Yardley, K. M. (1990) 'Psychology process and research: missing persons and missing values', *Counselling Psychology Quarterly*, 3 (1): 43–55.

Yardley, K. M. (1995) 'Role play', in J. Smith (ed.), *Rethinking Methods in Psychology*, London: Sage.

Zilboorg, G. and Henry, G. W. (1941) *A History of Medical Psychology*, New York, NY: Norton.

Zimbardo, P. G. (1974) 'On the ethics of intervention in human psychological research with special reference to the Standford Prison Experiment', *Cognitions*, 2 (2): 243–56.

Zimmerman, J. L. and Dickerson, V.C. (1993) 'Separating couples from restraining patterns and the relationship discourse that supports them', *Journal of Marital and Family Therapy*, 19 (4): 403–13.

Index